HARD
PRES$ED

Other books by Glenys Roberts

Metropolitan Myths
Bardot – A Personal Biography
Treasure!

HARD PRES$ED

GLENYS ROBERTS

QUARTET BOOKS
London New York

First published by Quartet Books Limited 1989
A member of the Namara Group
27/29 Goodge Street, London W1P 1FD

Copyright © by Glenys Roberts 1989

British Library Cataloguing in Publication Data

Roberts, Glenys
    Hard pressed.
    I. Title
    823'.914 [f]

    ISBN 0-7043-2630-2

Typeset by AKM Associates Ltd, Southall, Middx
Printed and bound in Great Britain by
The Camelot Press PLC, Southampton

For S. B. M.

The newspapers in this book are imaginary. The characters and organizations are fictitious. Only the spirit which led to the demise of the old Fleet Street has been faithfully recorded as a bewildering part of all our histories.

'A person should have the thing he loves. It should be given to him to take care of so that they both may prosper.'

Harry Coote (1888–1970)
Chairman of Coote Newspapers

1

Stop Press

The managing editor lay back in his three-piece suit, his hand-made shoes on his office desk. It was 10.30 in the morning, and all things considered he was surviving rather well. It was not raining and he had arrived early enough to bag his favourite spot by the door in the company car park. There were just two hours to get through before lunch.

At this time of the morning Hamish Grant was accustomed to taking a break. After all, he had already been up since seven. The pace was punishing, and so it had been ever since the new boys took over. It had been nothing but balance sheets ever since they arrived, and he, as managing editor of the Evening Newspaper, was supposed to balance them. Marketing surveys, consumer guides, readership breakdowns – hell's bells, free speech was dictated these days by men in shiny suits with potted palms in their offices. Accountants with graph paper got out of bed at 5 a.m. to jog all the way into town from the stockbroker suburbs and be in the office at first light to count up all the column inches of advertising in the Evening Newspaper in time for the morning editorial conference.

Conference was at breakfast time by any civilized standards. Conference, where editorial reaction to the daily news was decided, got under way before a chap had time even to make a choice between the boiled eggs and the kippers.

Grant flicked through all the morning newspapers which were spread out over his desk. Murder, mayhem, tits and other protuberances. He sighed. Things had not been at all like that in the good old days of Fleet Street, the 'real' days, as he liked to call them.

Under the 'real' regime he had meandered across from his town flat some time before lunch and tossed a few ideas in the way of the old editor (who was a sportsman and a gentleman) if he happened to meet him on his way to the back bench. He would exchange some gossip with the faggot who ran the Diary, lob his trilby at the hatstand just inside his office door, call his wife in the country to tell her he had arrived safely and buzz the circulation manager only to find the chap had gone off to dinner.

This gave Grant the leisure he needed to telephone the bookmaker where he kept an account, and to hasten the end of the morning with a quick nip behind the coat stand *pour le morale*. It was the rich fabric of idleness, the daily caress of gossip that prompted ideas which filled newspapers. Everyone knew it. And ideas flowed with whisky.

Grant searched behind the stand now, in the cupboard by his briefcase where the stuff always used to be. But the cupboard was empty, of course. Lord Gold had come down from the fifth floor that first morning he arrived, poking in everyone's drawers, opening cupboard doors and intoning threats about going to hell on firewater as if he belonged to Alcoholics Anonymous. Whenever Gold found a bottle, he confiscated it and poured the contents out on to the street below. It beggared belief. How the devil did these fellows think you could run a dry newspaper? Such a thing was unheard of.

The unheard-of thing had come true, the nightmare had become a reality. For six months now not a drop had been allowed on the premises, ever since Sir Aubrey Coote amalgamated his remaining newspaper interests with the business empire of the damned puritanical peer.

It had been August Bank Holiday when, overnight, Lord Gold took a half-share in Coote Newspapers. It had taken everyone by surprise because no one who was anyone was in the office at all. Some of them were in their cottages in the Dordogne, others were spending a last weekend in their time-shares near Marbella. Hamish Grant had just opened up a bottle of Château Plonk for lunch in his crumbling cottage on the Draycott estate just outside Little Nelling down the motorway. A chap had to rein in his horns, maybe, but no way would he ever exchange his little piece of old England for a breeze-block box on some filthy foreign stretch of sand. Let the fabric of British society change, Grant's world would remain the same, he was determined of it.

That society was changing Grant was in no doubt, and Emmanuel Gold, the new proprietor, well, half-proprietor of the Evening Newspaper, was a symbol of the change. Gold had not even been born in the country, he did not speak the Queen's tongue properly. Gold was a self-made man all the way from his nylon toupée to his machine-washable socks. He had a transport company, cigarettes, rag-trade interests, a small airline, but apart from personally reading the small-print in his contracts, he had never expressed any fondness for the printed word.

The wonder was, thought Grant, that such a person knew enough about newspapers even to entertain the idea that he could make a living from them. It was generally agreed, at least in the Street itself, that newspapers obeyed a different set of rules from any other business. Gold would find that out, Grant thought. He was cursed with the compulsion of every little upstart to be a manipulator of public opinion, and to do it in the area of the written word, as if to prove they had missed nothing by missing out on a formal education. The written word was a ticket to eternity and every Tom, Dick and Emmanuel, as in Gold, wanted to get on board the salvation train these days.

Grant was aroused by a sound like a fly trapped under a drinking glass, which was exactly what he felt like. It was the new editor, Tony Cheever, making use of the internal buzzer. 'How about this for a first edition headline?' Cheever asked. Vulgar headline, thought Grant, vulgar chap. Gold's protégé. 'Very eye-catching,' he told the new editor warmly.

Ten thirty-two by the office clock. It was a shaming state of affairs if you could not tickle your inspiration with a toot or two from time to time just as it used to be in the old days. Alcohol released the muses. Everyone knew that, except Gold, who walked round with a Japanese calculator in one hand and a copy of the Old Testament in the other. Gold had been married to the same woman all his life, he lunched on his wife's sandwiches in the boardroom, and some people even said he had halted the Saturday paper, not for economic reasons, but to please the Chief Rabbi.

The problem was more than a dearth of alcohol. The strange fact of the matter was that Sir Aubrey Coote had only sold half his interest in the Evening Newspaper to Lord Gold. The result was that the organization had two proprietors. Its identity had been riven in two, all issues totally fudged, since the lugubrious Gold took up residence on the fifth floor. It was a farce. Emmanuel Gold and Aubrey Coote could not have been more different, one from the other. Gold was congenitally morbid, sitting in his whitewashed office always with a tedious lecture at the ready about his ancestors in Armenia and all that he owed to their concept of hard work and duty, not to mention suffering and the sanctity of the family. 'This is a family noosepaper,' he would say. 'Femily noosepaper' was how he pronounced it, and it was a phrase always on his lips. He did the same to every other 'a' in the language. ' "Wenker"? What is this "wenker"? We will not have "wenker" in a femily noosepaper.'

Aubrey, dear Aubrey, who had sold Gold half his patrimony, was quite another matter. Aubrey was a lingering remnant of the class system that had defined the country for so long, the last scion of the Coote dynasty, which, along with the rest of the ruling class, had opted out of the leadership role. Well, not quite the last of the Coote line as it happened, but he might as well have been.

Grant groped in the cupboard in case he might have missed something lurking there after all. But Gold had disposed of it all all right. It had trickled down the gutters of the Street into the sewers below and on into the underground River Fleet. Some of the young lads from the Diary, who were still fast on their feet, had got wind of the smell and run downstairs and stood with their mouths open under the managing editor's office window to catch the whisky before it completely ran away.

It was Gold's last gift to them. 'A femily noosepaper is run on nothing stronger than tea,' he said, a point of view which many of the chaps thought reflected in the editorial policy. It was weak and conciliatory, like the last strains from the little perforations of a multi-purpose canteen tea-bag. 'The femily is the lode-star of our lives,' Gold would continue. 'This noosepaper will be one big heppy femily.' He kept a tryptich of pictures of his own family in a leather wallet on his partner's desk: Claudia with her degree in medicine, Victor the accountant of the femily, Emmenuel junior the lawyer, a whole limited company of over-achievers. A femily noosepaper was a dreg, thought Grant.

Many times in the next few weeks he would think back to these reflections and wonder if he himself had somehow not invoked, through lese-majesty, the events which were about to follow. It was not as if he was not fond of his own family. A gentleman was, as long as they stayed in the country where they belonged. Besides, Grant had a lot to thank his own family for, including the best job a man could ever have: a couple of short stints on the telephone sandwiched round lunch at the Savoy Grill was what it had amounted to to keep free speech alive in the good old days.

The telephone rang now. It was Tibbet, the circulation manager, who, true to form, was just about to go off to dinner. Strange for him to pick up the phone to make a call himself, however. He always used to wait until he was called. None of the lads below stairs ever liked to initiate work.

'The lads are off,' Tibbet announced now.

'Off where?' asked Grant. He glanced at his grandfather's watch. It still did its job as well as any modern timepiece, only needing a new strap from time to time.

'Off home, that's where,' said Tibbet.

'Not until 5.30, they are not,' replied Grant. 'Not until the last edition's on the streets.'

'I've got news for you, Mr Grant,' replied Tibbet unfazed. 'They've been and gone already. Walked right off the job.'

'Hell's bells!' said Grant.

'I beg your pardon?' said Tibbet.

It was a measure of the senior man's distress that he had momentarily forgotten that the working classes did not respect management if they understood what it was saying. He rephrased his anxiety more politely.

'What is your problem?' he asked, and he looked again at his watch. It still pointed to exactly the same time as when last he looked. Not much time to solve the Tibbet problem, whatever it was, before he was expected in the local wine bar, El Vino, to discuss a horse.

'It's your problem, actually,' said Tibbet, quick as a flash. 'Only, one of your girls got out of hand. Taking liberties with one of my drivers. They won't stand for it, you know.'

'What the hell do you mean?' asked Grant, who did not like emergencies. With one hand he groped in his cupboard while he balanced the telephone in the other. He was jerked back by the new regulation shorter trip-proof lead, and anyway he found nothing. 'Which girl? Who do you mean?' he asked.

Tibbet sounded very self-satisfied. 'Sonia Fraser, that's who I mean,' he said.

Grant started in his chair despite his phlegmatic constitution. Anything to do with Sonia Fraser was potential dynamite. Hell's bells, they could even put him out to grass over this. In his mind's eye he pictured the young lady in question. Sonia was a sassy little number who had recently been taken under the wing of the features editor, Frank Morley. Sonia had ambition, you could say that for her, and so did Frank, but their two ambitions were not one and the same. Sonia wanted to make a success of herself while Frank wanted to make her. He was always sending her off on jobs for which she did not have the experience and squeezing her byline* in the paper whatever rubbish she wrote. Morley obviously thought the deal was that when the lineage came up right so would Sonia Fraser.

Poor fool, sighed Grant, his hand cupped over the telephone. She was far too canny to give her favours to Frank Morley. She was one of those women with involuntary class, which was as it should be, considering her background. All the same, there had been some disturbing rumours about her behaviour. First you gave women the vote, next thing you knew they were dropping their knickers for all comers. Grant didn't like working women because

---

* For those unfamiliar with the quaint terminology of newspapers and the print, there is a glossary to be found on pp. 285–6.

you could never tell what they were going to do next.

'You there, guv?' asked Tibbet. 'Did I say something?'

'So what on earth did little Miss Fraser do?' asked Grant. He hoped he sounded authoritative.

'Ho, ho, little Miss Fraser, that's a good one, that is,' laughed Tibbet. 'There's nothing little about our Miss Fraser. She is on the large side, is little Miss Fraser, at least in parts. A well-developed girl, shall we say, Mr Grant?'

'And what did The Honourable Miss Fraser do?' asked Grant, spelling it out coldly now to command a little respect. The world really was becoming an intolerable place. All education seemed to do for these chaps was give them the liberty to speak back at you.

'She jumped on the van, that's what she did.' Tibbet ignored the warning. 'Practically blackmailed the young driver. Threatened him that if he didn't co-operate he could drive his van all the way to the Job Centre.'

Grant put his head in his hands. The idea was ridiculous: Jock Fraser's young daughter threatening any one of the vanmen who prided themselves on their brawn and their biceps and drove round in sleeveless T-shirts in mid-winter to show them.

'It was in Fulham yesterday afternoon,' Tibbet continued. 'After lunch – a long one for little Miss Fraser, as you put it, at least from the look of things. Mike Green had just finished with his Late Extras, and bless my soul if she didn't thumb a lift.' He paused to allow this information to sink in. When there was no reaction from the other end he continued, 'My Mike Green was forced to stop his van for your Miss Fraser, Mr Grant.'

Grant sighed. He was beginning to get the gist of the thing. It was the usual old demarcation dispute, dressed up this time, as luck would have it, in a mini-skirt.

'Presumably Mike Green is over the age of consent,' he sighed again.

'Mike Green was not asked for his permission, Mr Grant,' continued Tibbet. 'Miss Fraser was practically lying down in the street. What else could my lad do but stop? Things did not end there, Mr Grant. Your Miss Fraser put my Mike Green in an impossible position. There were only two things he could do in the circumstances. Run her over or find out what she was doing in the gutter. What he found out was that she wanted to board his van. My Mike Green had no alternative but to allow your Miss Fraser to ride on said vehicle back to the office. Use of the vans by unauthorized personnel is against regulations, Mr Grant.'

'I see,' said Grant icily. In his mind he ran a rule over the size of the problem. It was about a size ten, but for the chest. Sonia was blonde and slender but, as Tibbet had so delicately intimated, she had the largest tits in the business. He pictured her. It wasn't really that her bosom was all that monstrously large, it was just that Sonia Fraser allowed it to be admired. She encouraged it. In a profession where women usually wore shapeless ethnic outfits buttoned up to the chin and dank fringes over their eyes, Sonia Fraser threw back her hair, flashed her blue eyes, cinched her waist and bared her cleavage. He had to admit it was a recipe for success even without all the rest she had going for her. She had the shamelessness of all her family. You had only to look at the mother. For a second a disturbing little memory gripped Grant. If Sonia Fraser had been lying down in the street, most people would have stopped for her.

'You there?' inquired Tibbet again.

'Was Miss Fraser all right?' asked Grant.

'Never better, as it turned out,' said Tibbet suggestively.

'So what's Mike Green's problem, then?'

'It isn't his problem,' said Tibbet reasonably enough. 'It's the rest of them as has a problem. They don't like it, see. The lads are sticklers for propriety, you know that. Your reporters are not allowed to ride on their vans. Your reporters don't have no union cards. No cards, no rides. Result, no papers. They're not delivering the papers until they have an explanation.'

'You should not have let them go, Tibbet,' intoned Grant. 'Now, you get them back to work in time to deliver this afternoon's editions and we will say no more about the matter.'

'I am sorry to say I can't do that, Mr Grant,' said Tibbet. 'It is not only management that is sensitive to the infringement of their position. In the modern egalitarian world, everyone's rights are protected by the Employment Acts, reinforced, moreover, by customs and practices which go back ever since the print was invented. Sonia Fraser has overstepped the mark and we are entitled to a concrete retraction of the position she maliciously adopted by indiscriminate use of inappropriate body language.'

Hamish Grant thought he understood what Tibbet meant with this regurgitation of the jargon of indoctrination which was the last stand-by of the polytechnic classes. All Tibbet wanted was an apology. He wanted the respect the twentieth century said was due to him.

With all the pessimism in the world, Grant could not really see this little problem delaying by too much his discussion of Rum Baba's form with the boys at El Vino. Sonia Fraser would see the sense of tendering her regrets to the van drivers for their inconvenience in the same light-hearted fashion she must have made her original request to them. He picked up the internal phone and rang Sonia Fraser's extension.

2

Standfirst

'Jesus, Sonia,' said Arthur Mitchell. 'Jesus, do that again.' They were lying on the unmade queen-size bed in his bachelor apartment in a converted warehouse in fashionable dockland overlooking the River Thames. With one ear Arthur was listening to the morning radio, which was a habit of his in any situation. Arthur was editor of Britain's oldest Sunday Newspaper, had been for ten years, and as such he could never bear to be without the news.

'Haven't you got to go to work?' asked Sonia.

'I can't go to work until you do that,' said Arthur.

'Till I do what?' Sonia asked flirtatiously.

'You know what to do,' he said. 'You know what it is I like.'

'Tell me what it is you like, Arthur,' she persisted. 'Describe it to me, Arthur,' but still he wouldn't put it in words.

'What will you give me if I do what you like?' asked Sonia.

'I'll buy you dinner tonight,' said Mitchell. 'That's what I'll do.'

'That's boring. You always buy me dinner.' Sonia yawned and fished for her tights on the floor, showing him an arse so like a doughy little bun he imagined himself branding it with a sizzling cross.

'What do you want, then, Sonia?' he said instead.

'You know what I want,' she said.

Now it was Arthur's turn to reach for his socks. 'Listen, darling, you know I can't do what you want,' he said.

'Well, neither can I do what you want then,' she said and put one foot in the leg of the tights.

'That's not fair, Sonia.' Mitchell lay back on the black sheets.

10

He had thought satanic black appropriate to a bachelor apartment. He pulled her back on top of him. Then he pushed his thighs towards her mouth. (He was fifty last birthday so he was a lazy lover.) 'If you don't do it I shall come all over conference,' he said.

'You're the editor, you can do what you like.' Sonia stood up, pulled the black tights up as far as her white buttocks and left them there so that her crotch was naked and just about on a level with his face. 'As far as I could see from last week's paper, a little creative emission would not come amiss for a change,' she said.

Arthur couldn't take a woman's insult seriously when he was distracted by her pubic hair. She had the palest little wisps and curls. They grew rather sparse, so he could see the flesh beneath. The whole delicious vision still hovered on a level with his mouth.

'No matter what you do I can't give you that job,' he said with determination.

'I don't see why not,' said Sonia, trying with one foot to find a shoe under the bed. As her foot moved so did the pubic hair. It was such a bewildering thing, that apron of hair, exciting his curiosity even when he did not want it to. It was like an invitation on a mantelpiece. Nature was such an arch-showman, he thought.

'People like my stuff,' she said. Arthur said nothing. 'Frank Morley is convinced I have a great future,' she went on. 'He thinks I have editorial qualities. You wouldn't want it said that they have more judgement on that little paper which you despise than the great Arthur Mitchell, who is a legend in his own lifetime, who practically invented typefaces and has written three books about them, now would you?'

He pulled her towards him again. Sonia really pouted most engagingly. He forced her to kneel down and put her head in his lap. He stroked her hair for a minute like the paternal figure she made him feel. She made him sound as old as Caxton, for Christ's sake. 'You're going to be sensational, Sonia,' he said patronizingly. 'But whatever Morley tells you is for his own good, not yours. You mustn't run before you can walk or you might blow it and not get another chance.'

'Blow it? You blow it, Arthur,' she said, shaking herself free, standing up again and shoving that pale hair in his face again. 'Go on, what are you waiting for? Give yourself a treat. Give me a treat for a change, for Chrissake. Didn't anyone ever tell you that's the way to keep a woman in line?'

Arthur winced. As he got older he was puzzled by the vulgarity of the young. If you could not make them feel guilty you had no power over them. Sex used to make them feel guilty, but no longer. He made a mental note to tell this observation to his woman's editor so that she could commission a piece for her pages. An absence of guilt was changing all the rules.

Meanwhile he took Sonia's hand in his. Despite his furious senses he was a serious man. 'Stick with me, baby,' said Arthur Mitchell. He thought he had heard young people saying that to each other. 'When the time's right I won't let you down, I promise.' There were just fifteen minutes till he had to leave the place. 'Experience is worth a lot of talent in this business, Sonia,' he said. 'Especially at this time, with newspapers struggling to survive right, left and centre. I don't intend my paper to be the one that gives up the ghost. I haven't fought all this time to come all this way and to leave empty-handed. This paper has a long history behind it and I am not going to be the one that writes the end to it.'

'You don't have to pull the history lesson on me of all people,' she said. She was taking the longest time getting dressed.

'It's like a relay race and I'm the one with the torch in my hand now,' Arthur continued, warming to his theme. 'The newspaper's voice is my voice. It is my duty to bring it out loud and clear and surge right ahead of the competition so I can hand it on to the next man with space to spare, room to manoeuvre.

'I know it looks easy at times. I know it looks like a simple matter of stirring and muck-raking and mentioning a bunch of pompous people with handles to their names and padding the whole thing out with a few pictures of pandas and the Princess of Wales. But there's another sort of politics beyond the obvious, and then there's the law, Bleidenstein takes care of that, of course,' he paused for breath, 'not to mention the law that things are always ten times more difficult than they look, and my job is to be a discreet go-between between all the factions, the public, the staff, the management, the unions, none of it easy in times of recession, *and* to keep a little truth alive.'

It was a long speech for a man in bed, and Sonia yawned sarcastically. 'So that's what you're worried about,' she said. 'You're worried about your job.'

'What do you mean?' For a moment Arthur was afraid she meant something more sinister than her spoiled-little-girl chat. Had she heard something around on the Street? Her connections were such that she easily might have done. The Street existed on gossip, and for it, and an editor's job was the most fragile there was. Was he, the great Arthur Mitchell, in any danger? When he thought what he would do if he lost his influence, it made him physically ill.

'You're afraid people won't respect you,' she said. She had found both shoes now and she turned round and bent down to put them on, thrusting her little white buttocks into his face, buttocks which were just a fraction overweight, he noticed, not for the first time. 'You're afraid that if you offer me a job they'll say you only gave it me because you are fucking me,' she said triumphantly.

'Ssh,' said Arthur violently. Although that was indeed what he had been doing for six months now, although it was what he fully intended to do again if he could only get one in before they left the bachelor flat this morning, he did not like it put that way. It wasn't because he was aware of any particular finer feelings towards Sonia. He was aware only of the shiny little cushioned strip of slightly parted blue-pink skin between the thighs with its wisps of wet hair which she was was presenting to his face as she bent down to find the rest of her wardrobe.

Arthur just didn't like such things put into words, that was all. Words made things true, as he knew from his job. Once a thing was down in black and white it became part of accepted wisdom, even if it wasn't strictly gospel when it started out. People's ages, their feelings, their follies. He shuddered. These thoughts were far too philosophical for the occasion. What he really felt like doing was hitting her right across her white arse, which was no more than she deserved, and before she recovered from the blow,

plunging a part of himself between those blue-pink strips of skin.
He gasped at the uncivilized thought. She turned around.

'You don't like the word "fucking",' she taunted. She was
saved by the chimes of Big Ben on the radio.

'It's not that.' He got out of bed. Now he really did have to go
to work. 'I don't like you to use it,' he said. 'If your father ...' he
stopped himself just in time. 'If my daughter talked like that ...'
Again he stopped in mid-sentence. There he was, sounding old
again. Christ, he *was* old. His daughter was almost the same age
as Sonia.

'Well, I'm not your bloody daughter,' she said. 'And you're
very far from being my father, so I'll talk how the hell I like.'

'Not about us, you won't.' He tried to sound romantic so she
would calm down. Romance was what women liked.

'It's all right,' she said sourly. 'I haven't told anyone, if that's
what you're worried about. I'm good at keeping secrets.'

Arthur was suddenly very relieved. A picture of Nora formed in
his mind. He didn't love his wife, he was almost sure of it, but life
was more complicated than that.

'Let's take a rain-check, darling,' he said to Sonia. 'Get
dressed.' He kissed Sonia quickly and disappeared into the
bathroom. Just as he was about to close the door the telephone
rang. Sonia moved to answer it.

'No!' he cried. 'No one has this number.' Arthur Mitchell shot
across the room, summoning the most energy he had managed
since winning the hundred yards aged eleven at his Birmingham
grammar school. He took the receiver from Sonia's hand and lay
back on the bed with it in an effort to sound completely relaxed.

'Arthur, are you there?'

'Nora,' he said. Sonia lay down beside him.

'Will you be home tonight?' Nora's voice was so plaintive it
made him feel sadistic. 'Only I want to go shopping this morning
so I can be back for Laurie's half-day.'

Arthur couldn't bring himself to say anything.

'It's Thursday,' Nora added as if that explained it all.
Everything she ever said was either an explanation or an apology.

'Yes, of course,' said Arthur.

14

'I don't know why you need to rent that flat in town.'

'We put the paper to bed late.'

Sonia gagged on the black sheets.

'You will be back tonight?' asked Nora.

'No, I mean yes. Perhaps. I know he has a half-day on Thursday.' From his toes to his crotch and back again an irresistible sensation was beginning to engulf Arthur. He found it exciting to think he had to keep his head clear of it.

'How do you think I feel stuck out here in this house alone when you have to work all hours God made?' Nora was saying. 'All you ever cared about is your job. I bet you're working even when I am speaking to you now.'

Even as Nora was speaking to him, Sonia's mouth was in the very place it had refused to be earlier and with her hands she was caressing Arthur's thighs. But the thing that really drove him crazy was the way she had straddled him while she caressed him and the shiny blue-pink skin between her buttocks was only inches from his face.

'It isn't even as if I have any real friends here,' Nora was saying. 'I left everyone behind in Birmingham.' The whining explanation made it easier for Arthur. 'It was so nice in the old days when the children were young. Didn't you think so, Arthur, we were happy then?' The third weapon in her armoury was the rhetorical question. It was the way she made it all all right for herself.

'Goddamit, Sonia,' he put his hand over the receiver.

'Say something, Arthur, why don't you say something? Are you angry with me?' But he could scarcely hear Nora's voice. It had gone far, far away. He had gone far away. It happened all at once, taking him by surprise, a sensation full of exquisite marital guilt which made his teeth chatter helplessly.

'Jesus Christ!' he wailed.

'Arthur, what's the matter?' Nora was worried. 'Are you sick?'

'Jesus Christ,' he said sharply into the receiver this time. 'For Christ's sake stop nagging and feeling sorry for yourself.'

'You *must* come home tonight,' said Nora in a very small voice.

'I will,' he said in an equally small one.

However did he get to be so goddam old? However did he get to be a family man? Arthur showered without a word to Sonia. He was late for work. He pushed her out of the front door ahead of him, vowing there was no future for him with her around. The vows, however, were made silently. The door opened into a puddle of mud. The apartment block was still being built. Several workmen in hard hats whistled when they saw Sonia, who neatly side-stepped the mud and sent it splashing over Arthur's trousers with the edge of her stilettos. She was mad at him.

'So much for breakfast, darling. What time's dinner?' she asked turning round and putting her tongue inside his mouth. He could taste the sex on it still.

'I'm late, I'll let you know, Sonia,' he said.

'Oh well,' she sighed wiping her lips conspicuously with the back of her hand, 'I should be thankful for small mercies, I suppose. I was beginning to think your Bodoni was bolder than your libido, Arthur.'

It was a beautiful morning and she skipped into it.

'You unutterable bitch!' he said.

'Yes, sir!'

3

Galley

Tibbet's words were not strictly true. The lads at the Evening
Newspaper had not gone off home already although they had
indeed gone off the job. They were actually holding a meeting
down in the van bay. Charlie Crumm, Mike Green's foreman,
understood the problem completely. He had understood it the
moment he saw a bit of crumpet climb down from Mike's van
and disappear up the back stairs.

'What's that?' he had demanded.

'That's Sonia Fraser, that's what that is,' said Green, puffing
out his barrel-chest like a pigeon in the snow. 'That one gets her
name in the paper and her picture too. Last night she wrote about
her favourite TV hero. She's got the same hero as my mum.'

'I don't care who your mum's bloody hero is,' yelled Crumm,
who had been in the army. 'I do care what you are carrying Sonia
Fraser for! What *are* you carrying her for?'

'What am I carrying her for?' asked Mike Green. 'What do you
mean, what am I carrying her for? Wouldn't you carry her?' He
flexed his biceps and pumped his fists. 'I mean, who wouldn't
carry her? Nudge, nudge, wink, wink, if you know what I mean?'

'Well, that's exactly the point, isn't it?' said Crumm, sticking
his thumbs in his trouser pockets. 'Why are you carrying her and
not me? Why aren't all the lads carrying her? Why can't we all
have a bit of the action? If you carry her, mate, they'll all be at it.
They'll be carrying girls everywhere they go and then where will
we be? There'll be no bloody room for the newspapers.'

'Come off it, Charlie,' said Mike Green. 'There's no need to go
over the bloody top. It's not gonna happen every day. It was just
one of those things. It was a coincidence, that's what it was. She

17

couldn't get a taxi. I just happened along. Look, it's like this. She's in Fulham, so am I. We are both going back to the Street, so where's the harm in it? It makes sense, doesn't it?'

Charlie Crumm could look very ferocious with his arms akimbo. He put them akimbo now. 'What is it that you are here to carry, Michael?' he said, spitting out every word and trying to retain his teeth. 'Describe it to Mr Crumm, there's a good lad. Is it about five feet six inches tall with a pair of nice bare tits hanging out of its nice little white blouse and a pair of nice little slim little legs going all the way up to its lovely little armpits? Does it have fuzzy blonde hair and big blue eyes and little white hands and big cherry-red lips? Is that what you are here to carry, Michael Green?'

'No, Mr Crumm.'

'Does it measure about twelve by fifteen inches in measurement? Is it black and white and read all over, joke, get it, and about thirty-six pages in all – not more, because we do not get paid for heavy work, not less, because it simply would not be worth our while getting out of bed for?'

'That's it, Mr Crumm.'

'Good lad,' said Crumm sarcastically. 'And what's it called, that which you are supposed to carry?'

Mike Green looked confounded.

'It's called a noosepaper. N – O – O – S – E . . .?' There was a note of query in his voice. He had been foolish to try to spell it out, but he had to go on now. 'Paper,' he concluded briskly. 'And what else are you supposed to carry, Michael Green?'

'Nothing, Mr Crumm.'

'Oh yes you are, lad. What about the billboards? Aren't you supposed to carry billboards? Yes, you are. And what about returns? You are supposed to carry returns. Plus sales declarations. Are you supposed to carry sales declarations?'

'Yes, Mr Crumm.'

'And are you supposed to carry editorial staff?'

'No, Mr Crumm.'

'Let me get this quite straight so as we both understand it,' said Crumm. 'You, Michael Green, van driver of the Evening

Newspaper, are not supposed to carry aboard your vehicle the editorial staff thereof, of the Evening Newspaper, that is. Right?'

'Right,' said Michael Green.

'Well, that's that then, isn't it, lad?' said Crumm, nodding with an overwhelming sense of satisfaction. 'Point proved. If the editorial staff can't find a taxi on their way home, that's their hard cheese, isn't it? If they can't find their way back to the office to do their expense accounts of an afternoon, what's that to do with you? That Miss Fraser is using you, Michael. She is using you for her own convenience to save her time and her money, that's what she is doing. Mark my words. You probably thought she was after your baby-brown eyes, didn't you, lad? You probably thought she was after your great hairy chest? Or did you think she was after those centre-forward's thighs?

'You are an arsehole, Michael Green. What are you? An arsehole, that's what you are. And why are you an arsehole?' Crumm's thumbs found their way to his trouser belt this time and his fingers hung over it like so many bananas. 'I'll tell you for why. Look at it Crumm's way. If she doesn't take a taxi but she charges for a taxi, why, she is in pocket, isn't she, Michael? And if she doesn't take a taxi and she charges for a taxi because you are carrying her on your van, what are you, Michael?'

Green looked at his feet.

'Did you say something? Am I hard of hearing? What are you? Speak up, lad.'

'I dunno, Charlie,' said Michael Green.

'You're a wally, that's what you are, Michael, and what else are you?'

Green shrugged.

'You are an exploited wally,' said Crumm. 'You, my lad, have been exploited. But never you mind, exploitation is what we have unions for. So we are never exploited by the people upstairs. My family fought hard for that right not to be exploited, and you are letting my family down, Michael. You are letting me personally down. And if you want to get on in this job, you must not let the likes of me down. This is a communal exercise which can only succeed if we all observe the strictest demarcation lines. Your contract is to carry papers and your job is not to exceed your contract or else, mark my words, we will all be made redundant. Is that clear?'

'I just thought . . .'

'Your job is not to think, Michael Green, or else you can get a job upstairs.'

'Yes, Mr Crumm.'

'Do you want a job upstairs?'

'No, Mr Crumm.'

'Are you satisfied with the job you have got?'

'Yes, Mr Crumm.'

'Not on the evidence I have,' said Crumm spitefully. He prided himself on the surprise tactics which he instinctively used whenever a conversation seemed to be winding down to its natural end.

'Oh, get along with you, Charlie, I mean, what do you mean, Mr Crumm?'

A note of panic had entered Mike Green's voice as soon as he heard the threat in his foreman's words. It made Charlie extremely pleased to hear the note of panic because it meant he had everything under control. Moreover, a fertile new possibility had struck him along with this evidence of his powers of manipulation.

'I mean do you want to keep your job, that's what I mean. I mean this is a time of unemployment, Michael. If you are not happy here I can easily arrange for you to join Maggie's millions if you like. Then you can spend all day picking up blondes in the street. Then you'll have all bloody day to bloody think.'

'Of course I want to keep my job, Mr Crumm,' said Mike Green. 'My dad had this job, just like yours. And my grandpa. My family has always worked on the Evening Newspaper. My dad was invalided off and then it was my turn. I'm the earner in the family now. He'll damn near kill me.'

Crumm smiled with satisfaction. His envy had turned into irritation, his irritation into a plan which had firmed up nicely now Michael Green could be guaranteed to do what he wanted.

'I'll see what I can do, lad,' he patted Green on his tattooed biceps in a kindly sort of a way. 'I'll put it to the lads, lad, I'll see what I can do.'

4

The Change

Arthur Mitchell's life was about to change in a way he could not put down to Sonia Fraser. The fact was he had had it pretty easy up till now. Though there were problems as an editor of his Sunday Newspaper, apart from the ones he had described in bed, when it came down to it, unlike the editor of an evening newspaper or a daily, he had only one paper to put out a week.

It was what left him time to write his pamphlets and develop his reputation as one of the great theorists of the Street. His Sunday ran itself. It was an institution. There was always somebody to put it out because it was notoriously overstaffed. Men who had been in the same job for fifteen or twenty years were unsackable even though they might not pull their weight.

They were unsackable because of prohibitive redundancies which had been negotiated in better days, and moreover, though none of these hard-bitten newsgatherers liked to admit to such woolly thinking, they were unsackable for humanitarian reasons.

A third of the editorial staff never wrote anything at all. One half of the editorial staff had not had their names in the paper for the last ten years. Consequently they spent most of the time in the pub, drunk out of their minds. This they were apt to call consumer-testing the new vintages. Or else indulging in long lunches with writing acquaintances whose ambition it was to appear in the paper one day so long as there was not too much work involved. This they called auditioning new talent. It was either that or taking the shortest route into the Thames off Blackfriars Bridge.

Without this dead weight, the Sunday Paper might have cut a brisker figure, but Mitchell, who was devoted to it as an

22

institution, saw that it would be difficult to explain away the lemming-like behaviour *en masse* of people who had once had the same dreams as himself. Moreover, if the career of any old-timer could be cut short in this callous way, how soon would it be before the finger of time pointed at future old-timers, namely, at Mitchell, too?

As a social upstart, insecurity was Mitchell's worst problem, and the worst of it was that whatever he tried there was no way of laying the insecurity to rest. The more he worried about it, the more insecure he became, and there was no one with whom to discuss any of this. It was another of the problems of having an ignorant wife and a young, callous and well-connected mistress. So he wrangled with himself about how to increase efficiency and save money. He wanted the Street to prosper in the electronic age, even if all the indications were that the public wanted blander fare than the newspaper he was used to editing. He wanted a virile alternative to snapping on a little black button and watching any old depravity on the box for twenty-four hours on the trot.

The irony was that not even his proprietor, whose problem it was at the end of the line, could be persuaded to discuss this eventuality or make contingency plans for an electronic future. Mitchell had tried to warn him that changes were on the horizon. At first it was just a vague feeling of uneasiness, but it had become much more than that since Lord Gold bought into the Evening Newspaper down the Street, shattering a happy arrangement with the Coote family that had lasted for three generations. This move proved that change was afoot and coming closer all the while. Even so, Arthur could not make his own proprietor at the Sunday Paper share his concern. The man was senile, confined to a wheelchair if not totally supine most of the time. Whenever the paper needed money, a nurse would awaken him and guide his freckled hand across the bottom of a cheque. Then the old man would flop back, apparently comatose under his tartan rug.

His son was naturally as worried about this sort of behaviour as was Arthur Mitchell, though for quite different reasons. But even he could not get his father to give any thought to a future the old man himself was never going to see. The heir thought this irresponsible and had made several attempts to have the old man certified as incapable before he frittered away everyone's livelihood. All attempts were to no avail, for the proprietor always surprised his doctors on these occasions by sitting bolt upright in full and vigorous command of his faculties.

As soon as the authorities had departed, he would then scream at his son with all the vigour of a man many years his junior. 'It's mine, the paper's mine,' he would scream. 'And if you or anyone else tries to consign me to an early grave, I will see that you do not get one penny of my considerable fortune when I die. And that includes all the oil.' He would next get on to his lawyer and dictate an alternative will in which his millions would go to the cats' home. He liked cats much better than human beings, and was surrounded by unneutered Persians, who were allowed to make a toilet of any living room if that was what they liked.

As Arthur Mitchell was about to leave his editorial conference on that momentous day, he took a telephone call informing him that the old proprietor had died at last. The alternative will had never been signed. The considerable newspaper empire, with its star British properties, Mitchell's Sunday and its highly acclaimed sister Daily, was safe from the cat-litter tray. Without even waiting to bury the old man, his son had immediately sold all his newspaper interests to Frederick Fisher.

Arthur Mitchell waited now in the discretion of the panelled dining room of the Connaught Hotel in Mayfair for Frederick Fisher to arrive. Everyone had heard of Frederick Fisher. No one liked what they had heard. His reputation had crossed the Atlantic long before he did. He was self-made. He was Texan. That was it in a nutshell. Of him it was said that, like many Americans, he prided himself that his strength lay in his myopia: Fisher's focal point was said to be about four inches in front of his nose.

Mitchell was looking for a man in a ten-gallon hat and wearing a boot-lace tie. But the man who joined him at the table was dressed in a dark blue English pin-stripe suit. His outfit was completed by an obvious Jermyn Street striped shirt and red-spotted silk tie. He wore his blond hair long to his collar and

looked at the world over tortoiseshell half-moon spectacles. He
looked like a businessman from the City. Yet he talked with an
American accent, and what he said was straight from the hip.

This is what he said: 'I'm Frederick Fisher. You can call me F.J.
You know me and I know you, Mitchell. We both have a
reputation in newspapers. But you don't own them. I do. I own a
great many of them. I am not a newcomer to the business.
Newspapers is all I've ever done with my life. I know how to
make ends meet with newspapers. I even know how to make
money and to give value for it. I love newspapers. I want us to
work together.' He waved the waiter away from his side of the
table. 'You eat if you want, Mitchell,' he said. 'I never do.'

Then he continued his original train of thought with barely a
pause. 'You have made a pretty fine Sunday read and I
congratulate you on it, but the Daily in this organization is a pile
of shit. It's old-fashioned, it's pedantic, it's boring. It has
absolutely no appeal to women, which is a pity, because the
majority of women are just looking for something to read
because,' he grinned, 'let's face it, women have nothing better
to do.'

Mitchell looked for a moment as if he was about to protest, but
Frederick Fisher held up his hand. For that of a big man, it was
strangely small and finely made.

'You have a big following, Mitchell, and we can cash in on
that,' he continued. 'Here's what I want you to do. I want you to
take over both papers, the Daily and the Sunday. I want you to
revamp the Daily, bring it in line with your Sunday. I want you to
fight the unions with me, put an end to the overstaffing which has
been draining this business in this country for so long, and bring in
the new technology. We'll merge the papers immediately and
have the first seven-day-a-week quality newspaper put out by the
same staff before Murdoch can do it over at *The Times*.

'I want a quality newspaper, but I want a modern one. I want it
to be about real people, not jerk-off theorists. I want it to be done
my way. It has to be done my way or I'll close the newspapers and
sell off the assets. I won't sell the titles. I'll keep them and I'll bide
my time. I am not interested in someone else making a success out

of my failure. I'm a winner. I always have been a winner. I've had a charmed life. I work on the theory that I always will have a charmed life. What do you say, Mitchell?'

Arthur began to open his mouth to say something, but Frederick Fisher continued without waiting for an answer. 'There's no way out. If I go, the papers go,' he said. 'And even if your government decided that the newspapers had to be saved as one of the great British institutions it wouldn't be able to find anyone else to buy them. I've listened to all the alternatives. There are none.

'Do you know, Mitchell, there's only two people with balls in this whole world-wide newspaper business? I know, because I'm one of them and I'm the one with the biggest balls. Maybe there's someone else in the Far East who wants to slug it out with me. Maybe. We'll see. I'm on to the yellow fellows after this one. Newspapers are about to become a global affair. With the new technology we can beam anything by satellite anywhere in the world. I am looking into simultaneous translation machines. Everyone on the same information standard – have you any idea what that means, Mitchell? That'll be your greatest force for peace since Hiroshima.

'We can beam our information into the goddam ether if that's what we want. We can sell newspapers to Martians. The sky's the limit. I sent one edition up in the Shuttle from Cape Kennedy, Mitchell. Did you know that? Did that piece of news ever reach you over here? I had a little capsule of news from American presses released into outer space for those little green buggers to pick up on, if they exist. I haven't heard from them yet, but when I do I'll have the greatest scoop of the century. They can call me direct. Martians are the only people in the world – guess you can't say that – hell, no one else in the universe has my private number. It's unlisted. I call in. No one calls me.'

Arthur was aware his mouth was wide open and a forkful of salmon coulabiasse had somehow stopped in mid-air before reaching it. He shut it abruptly. Fisher was still speaking.

'Meanwhile I've done my English homework. I've heard all about in-house co-operatives in Gray's Inn Road, I've heard about writers' papers and I have just one word to say about that, bullshit. No one wants to read an undergraduate sheet put out by a lot of ageing hippies who can't stand the facts of life.

'Newspapers may need caring writers, Mitchell, but they also need caring proprietors. That's me. They need the abrasive rub between the two. That's the grit that makes things happen. I'm your sandpaper, Mitchell. I'm the sand in your oyster. I'm the irritation that'll make your life hell. I know a lot of things. I know the price of power. I know why desperate men kill each other. I was dragged up in a place where they did, often. Do you know about things like that, Mitchell? No, you don't, and you don't even know why I am telling you, do you? I am telling you because those are the things that teach you a whole lot about the human race. I know why things are the way they are. You know how you would like them to be. That's why we will make a great team, Mitchell.

'This is a last chance for your outdated island, Mitchell. I'm gonna give you freedom. I'm gonna give you the future. I'm gonna make it pay. Freedom of advertising equals freedom of speech, and on the printed page, too, which is the outlet of considered men if considered men have anything to say. Ain't that a dream? They said it couldn't be done, Mitchell. They said it was all about television now. I like television fine, but I like newspapers better. Newspapers are different because the very act of reading them is an individual stand. I'm an individual and I like the individual stand. That's why I like newspapers.

'You like newspapers, too. At least we'll have an interesting life, and that's what life's for, Mitchell. You won't find me a cynic whatever happens,' he paused, 'but I don't plan to be a poor man either.'

Mitchell had still not been able to get to his food and Fisher had not even ordered any. He was fidgeting in his chair. He seemed like a person lined up on the blocks waiting for some starting gun. Even the other diners had stopped eating. They were listening in to the conversation. At the door the waiters were lined up. They were listening to the conversation, too. No one moved except to ask his neighbour from time to time who on earth was the excitable blond man.

'Shake on it, Mitchell,' Fisher said. 'If you are half the man I think you are you won't need time to think about it.'

Arthur was bowled over. There was nothing he could say, no negotiation to be done without sounding exactly the sort of inconclusive being whom Frederick Fisher said he despised. He couldn't reason, he couldn't doubt, he couldn't call Bleidenstein who was his lawyer. He couldn't even enthuse without sounding naïve, or worse still sycophantic. He certainly couldn't talk about money when the man was offering idealism. Besides, he didn't want to talk about any of these things. He wanted the job. He liked the man. He liked Americans. He liked fresh blood and the future which was one of the reasons he liked Sonia Fraser, damn her.

'See you in your office at 6 p.m., Mitchell,' Fisher was saying. 'Have a brandy now, there's no hurry.' He stood up and danced out of the room.

It was only with a brief momentary shadow of foreboding that Arthur Mitchell realized Frederick Fisher had left him to pay the bill at the Connaught and that they did not take American Express.

5

First Edition

Hamish Grant could not find Sonia Fraser. She was not in the office. She was not in the nice little up-and-coming terrace house in Clapham which she called home. Frank Morley seemed to remember her saying something about being on to something good, but he couldn't remember where it was, what it was, or if and when she was coming back into the building. Morley himself was looking for her to write a piece by 4.30 which he had decided to call 'A Girl's Guide to the British Season'.

'What do you think about the title?' he asked. 'I'm rather pleased with it myself.'

Hamish Grant did not give two hoots for Morley's title. Vulgar fellow knew nothing about the Season. 'Very entertaining,' he said. Grant's problems were rather more pressing. Quite apart from his appointment to discuss the prospects of selling Rum Baba for stud, he could see himself getting blamed for the whole situation in which the Evening Paper now found itself.

It was Hamish who had introduced Sonia Fraser to Frank Morley, albeit at the request of Sir Aubrey Coote. Sir Aubrey had asked him to find out whether Sonia was employable as a favour to her mother whom he kept meeting on some beach in Jamaica. Aubrey said if Lady Fraser told him about her daughter Sonia one more time he thought he would have to take a machete to her in among the sugar cane. So Aubrey Coote asked Hamish Grant to do something about the girl, and Grant told Morley. Morley naturally took her on board. Now what to do? Grant would simply have to ask Aubrey. In the old days, when Aubrey's father Harry had been alive, that is what he would have done. He would have asked Harry. Correction, he and Harry would have conferred.

Now he rose reluctantly to his feet, took the lift to the fifth floor and sloped into the anteroom of Coote's office over the blue designer pile. A blonde secretary was sitting at the desk filing her nails. When she saw Grant coming she put the emery board into her top drawer and started typing. She had nails about an inch long and she hit the typewriter horizontally, admiring her fingers as she did so, as if she was still in the act of having a manicure.

'Sir Aubrey's away,' she said without looking up from the keyboard.

Hamish peered through the glass door into Coote's office. It was indeed more or less deserted. The only sign of life was a dartboard on the wall plastered with pictures of *Playboy* bunnies. Hell's bells, each bunny was skewered by darts through the crotch or the breast. A few had misfired and were hanging from the navel or the thigh. When Aubrey Coote got restless, he played darts with himself. There was a hand-written scoring table next to the dartboard: twenty points for each nipple; bull's eye for the clitoris. There was a dart on the January Playmate's thorax, and another on her vulva. Having hit the jackpot, Coote must have got bored and left.

'Where is he?' asked Grant.

'I dunno. Abroad,' said the girl without looking up. 'Anything that needs signing goes to Bleidenstein. Or Lord Gold.'

Grant took stock. He could not ask Sir Aubrey Coote what to do now because he did not know where Sir Aubrey Coote was. Neither did he have any means of finding out. Aubrey had always made it quite clear that his movements were his own business, and since Gold arrived things had got a whole lot worse. Aubrey Coote had taken the peer's presence as a licence to disappear completely. Now Grant would have to speak to Gold. But Gold did not speak to Grant. He spoke only to Cheever.

The abiding problem of the paper, even before the arrival of Lord Gold, was that Aubrey Coote's private life was a good deal more exciting to him than anything that could happen to him in his work. The newspaper was merely a discarded plaything to him, whereas it had been a lifeline to his father, Harry. Fleet Street still spoke in hushed tones of the old man, a figure in the mould of Beaverbrook himself who had been old Coote's rival for years. But Harry Coote knew by the time Aubrey was a teenager that great newspaper proprietors were born and not made, and that his son and heir was not one of them. Hamish Grant still remembered the days when Harry had begun to see the writing on the wall. The lad just had no flair for the print. He could barely read, he was no negotiator, and he hated getting his hands dirty.

Harry Coote, by contrast, had loved everything about the Inky Way, including the inconvenient fact that the black stuff came off on his fingers when he read his morning papers. Aubrey had his newspapers ironed by the butler to stop all that. But over the years he had come up with an even better method. It was never to read them, never even to touch them. They stayed unread on the hall table by the door. Father and son had had nothing at all in common.

Harry Coote particularly loved the wedding-cake building he had had erected in the Street to his own design, with the golden figure of himself on top where the bride and groom would have been. Aubrey had always been completely indifferent to it, even though he alone stood to inherit its every brick. Yet Harry had started him at an early enough age, taking him on a tour of the machine room, which Aubrey thought noisy, standing with him to watch the loading of the blank bales of paper, which Aubrey thought dangerous, and loitering with him on the editorial floor, which Aubrey thought boring.

Harry tried to ignore these inauspicious beginnings, but he was frankly puzzled. Aubrey was the only thing in life which puzzled him. Harry remembered the great surge of love he had felt for life when, as a boy of only five, he had first gone to his father's printing works and stood hand in hand with him to watch the huge bales of paper roll off the giant presses. There was no other destiny for him, he knew it, and by a curious and felicitous combination of talent and events he ended up owning the whole thing, paper and presses. To him this was not curious at all, only felicitous. A person should have the thing he loved. It should be given to him to take care of so that they both might flourish.

31

It had been towards the end of Queen Victoria's reign when Harry, a little boy in a flat cap, stood hand in hand with Calvin Coote before the great machines in his printing works in Staffordshire. The Cootes were not poor, but by no means could they ever have dreamed of owning two national newspapers and a London evening. Calvin was not an imaginative man, but he was as practical and hard-working as his name suggested. He did not care much for the contents of newspapers, he did not have time to read them, but he knew how to print them efficiently for other people.

He was also an ailing man with several mouths to feed, and when Benjamin Hardacre, the papers' owner, finally failed to settle his debts to Coote's press, Calvin saw no alternative but to take Hardacre to court. Hardacre did not part with a penny of his remaining money, but he did part with the newspapers. This solution, not totally satisfactory to the old man, was suggested to him by his son, who was now in his twenties. Harry, just back from the Great War, set to reviving the ailing publishing house in the spirit of the new generation, the one that had miraculously survived and would never again be able to look backwards.

Everything was to be different from now on: their attitudes to women, to politics, to work, to fashion and to newspapers. Harry introduced the pleasure principle to British readers. He jacked up the size of the type, took the stories across several columns. He made newspapers fun. But Harry's pleasure was pleasure through duty. He worked closely with the Hardacres' remaining two outlets, and by the mid-1930s he had added them to his empire, which stood tall in an anxious world. It was a fanatically patriotic empire, anti appeasement and the Abdication, pro the sort of paternal feudalism which he insisted had laid the foundation for Great Britain's greatness one thousand years before. He looked forward to founding a great family which would put into practice his social theories about continuing mutual responsibility.

After Calvin was dead, Harry found himself a rich industrialist's daughter for a wife. There was subsequently only one thing wrong with his publishing dynasty: Aubrey Coote, his only son. Aubrey quite simply despised the very things for which Harry had an easy knack. All through his life, Harry nurtured the one illusion that once he was gone his playboy son would shape up. But when Harry died of a heart attack shortly after Beaverbrook went, the great age of newspapers seemed to die everywhere. Aubrey exchanged horses and mistresses with equal enthusiasm and read the paper only when his own name appeared in the gossip columns, in which piece of egotism he was equally matched by his wife Felicity, an early Page Three girl usually known as Flicker.

Flicker and Aubrey had very quickly added to the line, Hamish remembered that all right. It had been quite a scandal at the time. The boy was called Michael, but no one had seen him for years. Briefly he found himself wondering what had happened to Michael Coote. Perhaps he was dead, for would any son and heir stand by and see his patrimony sold off bit by bit as conspicuously as Aubrey had been doing it?

At the memory of Harry, Grant was surprised to find tears in his eyes for the second time that day. He thanked providence that, as a senior executive with twenty years' service, he had his own little room off the open-plan editorial floor, which allowed him the privacy to reminisce. Before the new boys arrived, he had never worried about office furniture, but now the whole place was obsessed with such things. Who had a personal fridge – no booze in them, of course – and how big it was in relation to the editor's own model. Who had what car with how many doors. Who had an electric typewriter instead of the old Remington uprights which the writers on the editorial floor were still using to type their copy against deadline. Writers would put up with anything. It was a masochistic profession.

While the writers had crummy green lino to provoke the muses, who had carpet? Grant had carpet. Admittedly, it was a rather depressing hairy brown instead of the beige fitted job of business management and the blue of ownership. Grant had to admit he was not top-notch. There had been a time when he was young, idealistic, enthusiastic, when he had thought the sun shone the length and breadth of Fleet Street and had supposed his name would soon be on the billboards wherever he looked.

GRANT AND PHILBY
BEST FRIEND TO A SPY

GRANT WITH DAYAN
HOW WE WON THE SIX-DAY WAR

GRANT HOLDS THE SCALPEL
FOR HEART-SWAP BARNARD

What dreams he had had of filing against all the odds from fly-blown far-off places and pinning his herograms from the editor-in-chief on the walls of every brothel in the Third World. The paper had been one of the most controversial in Fleet Street, with a scorpion's sting and true scorn for those who recoiled from tough play. The old editor was no Fellow of All Souls, that would have been out of place in the Street, but he was a cerebral cocksman, a man who collected scalps and the grey matter beneath them and did his bit for the flesh, too, no doubt.

For Grant, newspapers had seemed to be such a perfect springboard. It had not been difficult for his father to get him a trial job on the gossip column straight from Harrow. (University, it had been generally agreed, would have been a waste of time for he was not a scholar.) But he was nineteen, good-looking, eager, well-connected and happily disposed to almost anything amusing. There were good reasons for Harry Coote to take notice of such an exceptional young man at the time, he had thought, but now he knew it had been Harry, not Hamish Grant, who was exceptional.

It did not matter who you were, if Harry Coote thought the good of the paper was at stake, you would hear from him. You might meet him anywhere – in the lift, in the corridor, in the machine room. Or you might simply find a note, congratulatory or extremely rude, on your office desk. Coote noticed every cog in the organization from secretary to editor. He talked to the cleaning lady and to the man at the front desk. It created a marvellous loyalty to the organization, and a cohesive atmosphere that had gone out of the window these days.

Though his employees might not always recognize Harry

Coote, he knew every one of his employees. He knew them by name. But it was for the young reporters that the proprietor had a particularly soft spot, and for them he often put his enormous private wealth at their disposal. If a young face entertained him, or a manner provoked, its owner would as often as not find an air ticket booked in his or her name for a weekend in the South of France.

They were not supposed to refuse, whatever their apprehensions told them would be the result of the outing. Coote had no use for anyone on the paper with less than an inquiring mind. Coote would introduce them to international figureheads, government ministers, stars, tax exiles and crooks on the run, and if the price of a superb dinner at the Villa Inglese in excellent company was a room *en suite* with his, those were the unwritten rules.

Coote was as likely to order a bottle of Cristal and talk through the night as to lust after his young staff. That he had a roving eye, Grant had no doubt, but the roving always came second to the paper. Young men and women were expected to service him through conversation and ideas as much as anything, and in the morning Coote, like a vampire, had taken their strength and appeared glowing at breakfast while they slept till lunch.

Grant was not sure on this chill morning whether his eyes were burning out of grief for the loss of Coote, who had had a good time, or for his own loss of hope. The appalling thing about life was how you became redundant without even realizing it, before you even got to grips with what was happening. Grant did not feel older and a sunny day still put a spring in his step. He did not even think he looked older, but he knew other people found him positively senile. People like the present editor of the paper, Tony Cheever, who had come up through quite a different school.

Grant hated the new editor. Cheever was hated by all the old regime, but he had been imposed on them by their saviour Lord Gold and that was that. This was not the sort of thing a human being could contemplate without a drink. Grant got up to grope in the cupboard once more. Still nothing. He did not like thinking without drinking, but he was forced to if he was going to get the paper back on the streets. Gold had agreed to bale Aubrey Coote out of a sticky corner with an injection of funds from his airline business only if he could control the key posts on the paper. This was how Tony Cheever became editor.

Cheever was an upstart, part of the continuing tendency to provincialize Fleet Street, a member of the God-forsaken Liverpool mafia which had somehow wangled themselves into editorial posts of influence in the capital with their tasteless ideas about the new socialism, their myopic vanity and their rotten tailors, always writing books about whither journalism and going on television as if they were pop-stars.

Cheever was terrific on television. It was because of his hair. The advertisers had noticed his trendy locks. Endless plugs for sanitary towels and miracle detergents indicated where the viewing public lay. Bored housewives could be persuaded to listen to certain late-night current-affairs programmes because, in their heart of hearts, they wanted to run their fingers through Tony Cheever's floppy black tresses. They didn't give a tampon for his ideas. It wasn't ideas that mattered on television, it was hair and teeth, reflected Grant, stroking his own sparsely equipped head and fiddling with his bridge. As long as you had too much of both and kept talking rubbish it was all right. Tony Cheever's teeth came into a room before anything else about him. 'Hell's bells, Simon,' Grant would say last thing at night to his son, who had inherited his mother's aristocratic incisors, 'don't you bother if you don't want to wear your braces, you can always be a TV star.'

Though thoughts of Tony Cheever usually reduced Grant to desperation, this time he realized he would have to swallow his pride and take his problem to the man in question. Cheever would probably go straight down to the van bay and sort everything out as one working-class lad to another. They all watched him on television and they all reckoned the box more than they did the newspapers they carried, which were heavy, old-fashioned and fit only for wrapping your skate and samosas in. Tony would slap them all on the back of their T-shirts and winge away in his Merseyside drawl. He sounded as if he had caught a permanent cold on the ferry. He would slip down there in his perma-press suit with the rip-off YSL tie signed on the front, and he would be a hero to them because they could see the initials on it. Cheever would go downstairs, put his arm round the chaps and say something about the great femily noosepaper pulling together. Hamish Grant decided to swallow his pride and alert his editor on the internal telephone to the situation.

'Who?' Cheever asked his secretary when she told him Grant was on the line. He hated the managing editor with his old-school pretensions. 'No, I can't take it now. Tell him I'm late for lunch. And after that I am going straight to the train station.'

6

Strap

Well before Tony Cheever set out for lunch, Frederick Fisher was already back in his new office on the tenth floor awaiting the arrival of Jeremy Pringle, who distinctly fancied himself as the most sophisticated editor Fleet Street had ever known. Pringle was editor of the Daily Newspaper, sister to Arthur's Sunday, both of which had just become part of the Fisher stable.

He was also furious. The extraordinary meeting called by this Confederate cowboy meant he would have to cancel his weekly lunch at his club with a member of the Cabinet. Over the years, Pringle had cultivated some very good connections as well as some very pleasant habits. Now, instead of being able to get to grips with history in his usual leisurely way over a grilled sole and a bottle of Pouilly Fumé, Pringle would have to muddle through alone on an empty stomach.

The summons came from Freddy Fisher's office immediately upon the news of the sale, and the time for the meeting was fixed there and then. Pringle's sense of protocol had been affronted by the swiftness of events, only revealed to the Board of Directors as the merest afterthought. Still, he thought, the foreign chap showed a decent enough strain in wasting no opportunity to seek his, Pringle's, own advice about the future of the Daily. But what exactly did Pringle think about the future of the paper? He decided to drop into his club anyway to try to get a line on the whole damned affair.

Once he was there, Pringle changed into a clean starched shirt, although he had put on a fresh one that very morning. Pringle was a traditionalist, exerting the sort of influence these vulgar New World parvenus, with all their money, could never buy. As he dressed with care he thought about the coming meeting. At worst he saw the intrusion into his routine as an opportunity to give this Southern hick the once-over and report his findings to the other members of the Board, who would then, if necessary, invoke the help of the Monopolies Commission or any other official body whereby the Establishment could oust the intruder. Pringle, like Fisher, had done his homework and knew that the new proprietor had multiple video interests back in the States and had been sniffing around a couple of satellites in England to boot.

He attached his woollen socks to his suspenders and fancied his chances of organizing some other financial structure for the paper in the very likely event that the American was not a suitable proprietor. Just because some little whipper-snapper had inherited an oil fortune, for that was what he presumed must be the case with Fisher, it did not mean he could do what he liked with it. An English newspaper was not the same as an American hole in the ground. It was a piece of history. It was public property. More importantly, in the case of this particular newspaper, which also happened to be Britain's Oldest Newspaper, it was Pringle's property and Pringle's history because their names had been inextricably intertwined as long as anyone could remember. Except for a brief period when Pringle made a bid for the editorship of *The Times* and found himself rejected – he still winced at the humiliation – his loyalty to his present post had been unwavering.

He reflected on all these things as he adjusted his club tie beneath his stand-up, stiff white collar, put a fresh carnation in his buttonhole as he did every day, a touch of Grecian 2000 on his hair and a whiff of sandalwood behind his ears. That should teach Fisher to wing in off his ranch, smelling of rawhide and bullied beef, thinking that brazen bucks could buy him anything, including civilization. Pringle was not going to let his Daily Newspaper fall into the ignorant hands of some mongrel capitalist as easily as they had capitulated to such opportunist fashions over at the Evening.

Up in the library, he was relieved to find his pet Cabinet Minister opening the sherry and looking forward to a spot of uninterrupted consumption till the House started to sit now that lunch had been cancelled. He ignored the look of irritation on the Minister's face when he caught sight of him.

'Cracking the whip already, is he?' The Minister's tone was mocking when he saw Pringle. 'Got you down on the carpet on all fours with your pants round your knees. Rawhide!' yelped the Minister and slapped the side of his trousers with a snooker cue.

Pringle was momentarily taken aback. 'Something has to be done about this interloper before he makes a rodeo out of the House of Commons, too,' he countered.

The Minister nodded sagely while looking totally unimpressed.

'This newspaper is one of the most powerful weapons of the English Establishment,' Pringle went on. He picked up a copy wrapped round a mahogany reading-room baton lying on the Chippendale table and wielded it like a foil. 'There are elements in this paper that have not been changed since before the French Revolution. For God's sake, we repelled Napoleon with our editorials. Our prose put Adolf Hitler on the run.'

The Cabinet Minister still looked unimpressed. Pringle urged him that questions would be in order in the House if this outsider's projects proved too inimical to the traditional spirit of the paper. He told him he had already heard talk of radical interference in his US publications.

The Minister agreed wholeheartedly, then poured another sherry. 'Willy imports this stuff, you know,' he said. 'His family were palmed off after the Napoleonic Wars with some useless stony Spanish beach and now he rents it off to millions of Danes and Huns who can't wait to take their clothes off. Just goes to show, old boy, you have to take the long-term view in life.'

'How is Willy?' asked Pringle chummily. At the mention of the Secretary of State's name, the conversation worked its way around to parliamentary gossip. They were intrigued to discover that yet another Tory MP was on a morals charge. Several people's children were on drugs. No one seemed to want to go to Oxbridge these days. The old freemasonry was disbanding. The new one only wanted to make funny money.

Then the Cabinet Minister pointed out that it might be an idea to give this new colonial fellow who had bought the paper a bit of a chance to make it work. He hinted that the PM had had some words on the future of the organ with the old proprietor's son when her daughter brought him down for a weekend at Chequers before the old man died. The PM was not altogether against an American sale. She was rather of the opinion that our transatlantic cousins were finally showing some taste in competing for this priceless asset on the open market. The Cabinet Minister himself thought that even an American was a preferable alternative to losing too many jobs in a time of continuing unemployment.

Pringle dismissed unemployment as a side-effect of having a woman in charge of the country. It was something that would right itself with the swing back to traditional values. It was perfectly obvious, he opined, that the distaff branch were a bunch of bleeding hearts who could never balance the books. To realize this, you only had to consider your own experience of women and the housekeeping. However much you gave them, they always wanted more.

'Time to meet with your Yankee pig-sticker, then,' the Minister said as the club clock chimed. He wanted to practise his snooker. Pringle held out his hand to him and proposed a meeting again the following Wednesday, same place, same time, to put the world to rights.

Jeremy Pringle stepped uneasily into his chauffeur-driven limousine. It had not been an altogether reassuring encounter. He checked the time by the gold fob watch he had bought, not inherited, and asked the driver to take the long way back to the office as there was some danger of him arriving in time for Fisher. The traffic was surprisingly light, so he had to ask the man to drive twice round the block so as to waste a few more minutes. Pringle did not want to look too eager to meet this usurper. He took the lift to the tenth floor, entered the boardroom without knocking and looked around for a man with bandy legs wearing a lone star pinned to his chest.

Instead he saw a tall, boyish figure standing eagerly behind the mahogany desk, his long blond hair curling round his starched collar.

'I'm Freddy Fisher,' the figure said. 'You can call me F.J.' He sat down in the swivel chair, took off his tortoiseshell glasses and waved them around as if in a greeting. 'Come in. Sit down.'

Jeremy sauntered across the emerald-green boardroom carpet of the Sunday Newspaper to where a chair was waiting for him.

'I've heard a good deal about you, Jeremy,' said Fisher, 'and I expect you have heard a good deal about me.'

Pringle raised an eyebrow in appreciation. It flitted across his mind that he might get to like this fellow after all. Dammit, it wasn't his fault that his father had been a wildcatter. Or was it a cattle rustler? He extended a hand.

'Delighted to meet you,' he said. He relaxed back into his chair. 'Do you mind if I smoke?'

'If you want to kill yourself, it is a free country,' said Fisher.

'It is a country in which we believe it is the quality of life that counts,' said Pringle pompously. 'Have one of my Cuban cigars.' He offered the fellow his pig-skin cigar case. If you only bothered to educate these colonial upstarts in the proper practices of a civilized people, they were so pathetically grateful. 'You can't get these where you come from, I understand?'

'No use for lethal Commie rubbish,' said Fisher.

Pringle smiled tolerantly and lit up.

'Well, what do you think of me?' Fisher asked excitedly. 'Am I what you expected?'

Pringle did not know what to say. 'I was very shocked by the old man's death,' he tried.

'So was I – I thought he'd never go,' said Fisher. 'I'd been trying to get my hands on these papers for years, and he just kept hanging on. I told him he was wreaking financial havoc by sheer indolence and indecision. He didn't give a damn. I liked him. Still, you'll find me a very different kettle of fish.'

Pringle tried a proper executive hedging look – apprehensive and hopeful at the same time.

'First of all, I am very decisive,' said Fisher. He paused and flashed a charming smile. 'And I have decided to call you here to tell you how pleased I am to own a paper with such an excellent

42

reputation. I've waited a long time for it, so this is a very big day for me.'

Pringle shifted proudly in his seat.

'I'm so pleased,' continued Fisher, 'that I thought I would confine things at the moment to one or two very simple changes.'

Pringle smiled and nodded conspiratorially.

Again Fisher paused, more dramatically this time. 'The first thing I am going to change is the editorship,' he said.

The most terrible thing was that Pringle did not understand for a minute. He was still smiling and then he spluttered into a cloud of blue smoke. His hands went to his old boy's tie around his neck as if it were strangling him. Fisher waved the smoke away with his hands. He crossed to the window and tried to open it. It wouldn't budge. He tried again. Painted shut. He looked back at Pringle.

The former editor was clutching his hand to his breast as he recalled that other awful moment of humiliation over at *The Times* when, omitted as he was from the short-list, he steeled himself to make an application. They called him in for an interview, and it was as if they had done it only to reject him and he felt an overwhelming nausea and shame. He could not believe this could be happening to him again. He could not believe it could be legal, that some cowhand could come here in chaps and summarily dismiss one of the most distinguished buttresses of the English Establishment.

Only the man wasn't wearing chaps. The fellow was a dangerous impostor. The thing was not over yet, thought Pringle. He remembered his friend in the House and thought of the Board which had helped him and Arthur Mitchell over the years to persuade the old man of the necessity of pumping his good money into one of the last bastions of free speech in the world. Freedom to Jeremy Pringle meant that he had been free to edit his Daily Newspaper for all of his mature life. It meant the freedom to send his sons to Harrow, his girls to Cheltenham, like proper people did. He did a quick sum: £25,000 a year is what that little lot cost him. That was well-nigh £100,000 in taxable income. What about his meals at the club? What about his shirts? What about his carnations? He could not relinquish that freedom now.

'I am not going to leave this building, Fisher,' he spluttered. 'You can't get rid of me like that.'

'Good,' said Fisher, unfazed. 'I was hoping you would make yourself useful to me, Pringle. You can tell me a few things about how to get things done round here. How do I get this window open? Is there a carpenter on the payroll?'

Pringle explained smugly that Fisher would have to fill in a chit which would be circulated in the internal mail and that, about two weeks later, someone would open his window for him if he was lucky.

'Two weeks? I have never waited two minutes for anything,' said Fisher.

'I think you can understand that a stiff window does not really come into the urgent category. That is reserved for matters of security,' said Pringle smugly again. 'Indeed, you could say a stiff window is really exactly the opposite of insecure.' He smiled at his own little joke.

Fisher walked back over to the window, took off one of his shoes and broke the glass. 'Now you have a security problem,' he said. 'Tell the carpenter to mend the glass, and while he is about it to ease the window. I love fresh air.'

The air itself flooded in from Fleet Street, damp and grey and so thick you could almost touch it. It mingled with the smoke half-way down Pringle's bronchial tubes. He coughed. 'I think it is only fair for you to tell me to whom you are looking as my replacement,' he said.

'Strictly, I suppose you could say the post is not going to be filled,' said Fisher.

'Not going to be filled?' asked Pringle. 'How can that be? A paper doesn't edit itself,' he said.

'Well, maybe it will one day,' said Fisher brightly. 'Maybe one day we will be able to punch all the news into a machine and the machine will be programmed to sort everything out for itself in order of importance to the public for which it is destined. Maybe.'

'In that case, by all the definitions of the word, you are making me redundant,' said Pringle. Redundancy payments were not subject to tax.

44

Fisher leaned back in his chair and eyed the former editor warily. There was something about this meeting which was bugging him. He should have felt better than he did, and he had decided never to feel bad again. He put it down to the cigar smoke. He waved the blue column away from his face.

'I'm giving you a job outside the office, Pringle,' said Fisher, 'so we can all get some air in our lungs.' He paused. 'I haven't been here long, but I have already noticed there are just two things wrong with this country. One the class system, two the weather. First I'm gonna deal with the class system.

'First thing this country has to do to move forward is to beat it. Envy is behind the bitterness in all your labour disputes. I hear they have a classic one over at the Coote Evening Paper. Find out for me about the way they are all thinking, will you? The way I hear it, they are so old-fashioned over there they are practically writing the paper by hand. They've brought in a new broom, but they're hanging on to the old meanwhile. Where does that get them? Between the devil and the deep blue sea, that's where. Two proprietors, Pringle? What sort of way is that to run a business? I never knew two people agree on any single thing. Ain't nothing in the world one needs two of – excepting girls, maybe.'

Jeremy Pringle winced at the vulgarity of the fellow.

'The long and short of the matter is the whole operation at the Evening Paper needs rationalizing, Pringle, just like this organization did,' continued Fisher, 'and my guess is they will need me to do it for them, too. Find out everything you can, will you? Then, if it suits me, I'll put in a bid for Coote's operation as well. I should think Coote would be pretty well over the moon to find himself the subject of a bid from Fisher Ink.'

7

Extra

Tony Cheever bounced down the stairs two at a time, hair flying and teeth bared, past the Epstein bust of Harry Coote, past the old lino-type machine Harry had brought with him from Calvin's first typesetting works.

He stood on the pavement outside and looked for the surly driver he had inherited from three previous editors. He had made a couple of changes to suit himself, a blue car and a personalized number plate: HACK 1. But he could not see the car at first. It was waiting not in Fleet Street but in the van bay, where it was locked in by three driverless vans.

Next to the vans Cheever noticed a little knot of drivers with their heads together. He looked up at the office clock. It was a famous landmark on the street. It had stopped. He looked at his imitation Rolex watch. Then he beckoned the driver irritably. He was already late for lunch. Why didn't those drivers get their vans out of the way, the idle sods, so a person could get on with what was important in life? The drivers seemed to be holding some sort of meeting. It was probably about a greyhound or a three-card trick, Cheever mused. Nothing that concerned him, anyway. He watched a bald man beckon to them. At the bidding of the bald man the drivers got into the vans, docile as sheep, and drove away.

Still the blue car did not come. Cheever went to get into it. 'I am afraid I can't drive you, sir,' the surly man said. 'Only there is a bit of trouble.'

'Gimme the keys,' said Cheever. He was getting later by the minute. He would deal with whatever problem this man had when he had time. As he put HACK 1 into gear, he nearly ran into a strange figure lurking in one of the recesses of the façade of the

46

wedding-cake building. The man looked like a solicitor or a barrister, for he was very smartly dressed apart from the fact that he was very wet. He was wearing a carnation in his buttonhole, which was the only thing about him which seemed to be enjoying the rain. Cheever shrugged. Some fellow on his way to the Law Courts down the road must have been caught short without an umbrella in an unseasonal storm and stopped to shelter from the weather.

The gloomy prospect of his trip out of town was much redeemed by the lunch Cheever had arranged beforehand. Tony Cheever never lunched in Fleet Street. He spent his expense account in the West End. He had his own corner in a restaurant that had pink tablecloths and was always full of faces. He drank the house wine and always ate the same dish. Though Grant knew Cheever was a vulgar fellow, Cheever thought of himself as snazzy, impeccable and modern. He had read in his own paper, in a pull-out thumb-nail guide to success, that this was a way to establish yourself as a personality. Another way was to date the right women.

Dating women was not something Cheever had any difficulty with. Or marrying them, for that matter. He was already on to his third marriage and there were unmistakable rumbles of discontent from the direction of the suburbs of East Grinstead where the marital home was located. On the one hand, Cheever had bettered himself slightly with each marriage. On the other hand, he had borne the full financial brunt of each settlement. This time he did not think he had marriage in mind. His lunch-date was Sonia Fraser. Leaving the office as he had without bothering to take Grant's phone call, he had no idea anyone else was looking for her.

Cheever's business with Sonia Fraser was twofold. First, he needed to satisfy his own curiosity. Who was it Hamish Grant said her father was? Some doddering member of the House of Lords who had had a whole life of luxury mapped out for him by his ancestry? Cheever knew only that he had been somehow stuck with her as a legacy of the old system which Gold and he were about to change.

Cheever did not rate the system one little bit, and luckily, since the 1960s, he did not need to. With one irksome exception – when it affected him. Where Sonia Fraser was concerned, this seemed to be the case. For one thing he did know was that the little girl's father was a friend of Sir Aubrey Coote. Grant said the two had been at school together. The appointment of Fraser's daughter was a bit of traditional string-pulling, the time-honoured manipulation of the old-boy network – whatever you liked to call it.

Gold, to whom Cheever was indebted for his appointment, had risen from nothing. This should be a blueprint for the future, he reflected as his frustration mounted in a traffic jam, but no one man had any power over posterity. Everyone was in it for himself and the only valid attitude was short-term. He himself might even shortly lose the patronage of the life peer. For no sooner had Gold achieved his ambition of owning, or at least part-owning, a newspaper, than he started to feel awesome symptoms of mortality. He had not been in good shape ever since that night he put a call through to his health guru in Switzerland to ask for some tips on his diet. 'I never eat a meal without Dr Kranz choosing the menu,' he told Cheever. 'Dr Kranz knows everything there is to know about health.'

'I'm afraid you can't speak to Dr Kranz,' someone had said at the other end. Gold had stamped and railed like Rumpelstiltskin, disconnecting his little bald head from his nylon toupé and demanding to be put through immediately as he always was. 'I can't put you through,' came the answer, 'Dr Kranz is dead.'

It was after that that Gold started on his tour of the world's greatest spas. Gold had not been seen in the office since, leaving Cheever to second guess him on every issue. If Gold croaked like his friend Kranz, Cheever would be left high and dry with the other proprietor, Aubrey, still fighting a last stand for the old regime from some tax-haven in the Caribbean.

But what made Cheever's cultivation of Sonia Fraser particularly urgent was the fact that Cheever had heard that Sonia Fraser was seeing Arthur Mitchell. When Cheever first learned that Sonia Fraser was on his staff, he took it with a pinch of salt.

He had enough trouble keeping the peace between Gold and Coote without worrying about the day-to-day running of the paper. No harm in having a pretty face round the office, he thought, especially when it had tits to match.

When Squiffy Spencer, the diarist, complained at conference that Miss Fraser never got in on time, it crossed his mind that she might be a bit of a problem. He turned a blind eye to it, however. But when he heard that Mitchell had got round to courting her, that spelled trouble. Mitchell was renowned for his eye for talent as well as typefaces. If he, Cheever, lost Fraser's daughter to a man who was an acknowledged expert on the contents of newspapers, he could see all sorts of complaints reverberating from the boardroom down. Cheever therefore decided to get to know this member of his staff a bit better and to make sure she did not leave the fold for a rival establishment.

In Covent Garden he ordered himself a bottle of wine and waited. Late as Cheever was for lunch, Sonia Fraser was later. Sonia Fraser was never on time. After she left Arthur covered in mud in front of his desirable bachelor flat, she had tossed a coin. Heads she would go home, tails she would go to Harrods. The coin dropped on to the floor, rolled into the gutter and stopped for a second on a cigarette packet. As Sonia bent to retrieve it, she heard her tights rip. Harrods it was then, to get some new ones. The coin fell down a drain. Sonia shrugged and got into her little black Mini with silver overriders and drove from Limehouse into town. There were wild grey skies on her left, the ones that Turner painted, though Sonia had never heard of Turner because she had turned down her mother's offer of a course on the history of art.

Yet the skies matched her mood. She was angry, thwarted, frustrated. Arthur was such a stubborn, selfish wimp, rattling on about his boring theories and rubbing himself up against you as if it was enough of a thrill just to get a feel of his minuscule erection.

'Shit!' screamed Sonia, slamming on the brakes at the traffic lights. A girl was not asking for a helluva lot out of life. Just a multiple orgasm from time to time and a job that gave her her head.

The skies were full of screeching, dipping, whooping seagulls, and there were cormorants with bottle-brush, oil-slicked feathers bouncing on black buoys, which in turn were bouncing on the tidal waves of the steely river. She left them behind and turned inland towards the financial district of the City, where her route took her between the new glass towers of the City banks and past the post-modernist extrovertist intestinal architecture of the new Lloyds building and the judicial old grey lump of St Paul's, where her mother and father had been married. She gave the cathedral the V-sign and drove on into the common precincts of Ludgate Circus to Fleet Street where newspapers were still written, printed and published.

Fleet Street was a narrow street, quite unsuited to the demands of a motorized society. Thin, narrow, gabled buildings, occupied at street level by building societies and sandwich bars, leaned over and obscured the daring grey light that would otherwise have sped up the river from the open waters of the estuary. Sonia drove past the wedding-cake building and briefly debated going into work. It hardly seemed fair, since she would be lunching with the editor. That was work enough. So far she had got rather less out of her own editor than she had out of Arthur: just a little job, with rarely any byline, and no expense account to speak of at all.

It was raining, and rain always made Sonia want to spend money. A fine grime had settled on the white façade of the wedding-cake building and bitten into the paintwork, making it look as if it had lost all its icing and the fruit cake was exposed. In front of it, trucks and taxis and chauffeur cars blocked the traffic in the narrow street. Sonia could not find a parking spot, so she carried on driving west in the rain. She passed through the Strand where, did she but know it, newspapers first made their appearance to feed the tastes of the gentry. Only with the era of mass literacy and mass circulation had they started their continuing voyage to join the printing trade in the cheaper east, proving they were an industry and not a vanity or self-indulgence.

Sonia did not know these things because, as yet, she did not know she was interested in newspapers. She only knew she was interested in herself. She drove on past Trafalgar Square, noting briefly that it had been boarded up as it always was when a demonstration was expected. London was so badly behaved. Turning into clubland and passing the green open spaces of the royal parks, she felt fractionally safer. She cursed while she sat in a traffic jam in Knightsbridge. She was homing in on Harrods like a heat-seeking missile programmed to spend an allowance she did not have. Sonia Fraser was frustrated at count-down. It was getting to be a habit and she did not like it at all. Unable to park her little car properly, she left it on a double yellow line outside the shop, which was these days less an emporium to the gentry than it was to the most vulgar American and Arab. She took the escalator to the Ladies' Fashion Department and tried on a couple of garments. Nothing suited her. Nothing fitted. She had no money to pay for it anyway. Lots of her impoverished well-born girl-friends ran up their own things, but not Sonia, who had refused her mother's offer of a dress-making course. She wanted to lead her own life, but so far it wasn't working out to her satisfaction. By the time she realized she was late for Cheever she was very late indeed. When she came out of the shop her little car had a clamp on its wheel. She left it where it was and hailed a taxi.

Cheever looked at his watch and concluded The Honourable Sonia Fraser was not coming. If any untitled person had stood him up he would have been furious. Now he entertained the idea that it was somehow his fault. He wanted to wait for her, but he had a train to catch, so he ordered lunch. Then he ordered another bottle of wine. When he saw Sonia Fraser coming towards his table, he stood up and knocked his wine glass straight over her skirt. 'I am terribly sorry you are late,' he apologized.

'Shit, Tony,' she said. 'Be a dear and pay my taxi, would you. I'm right out of small change.'

He went out automatically and paid her taxi. Sonia meanwhile went to the ladies' room. There she took off her wet skirt, put it into her large reporter's handbag alongside her nightdress and all the other things she carried around in case she got a good offer. 'Shit,' she said. She had forgotten to buy a new pair of tights. She went back into the restaurant wearing nothing much more than her jacket. Cheever looked at her legs, which disappeared right up into her jacket. They were long. A fine ladder in her black stockings pointed like an arrow to its quarry up her leg. Cheever shuddered slightly. These women wore what they liked these days, and usually very little of it. Sonia sat down at the table and tried to stop him from apologizing by changing the subject. It did not work. Somehow everything she said sounded to Cheever like a criticism.

'You should have ordered for me,' she said.

'Oh, I am sorry,' said Cheever.

'I'm starving,' she said. 'I can't wait for the menu. I'll have the same as you. Was it good?'

A minute piece of something unidentifiable was laid out before Cheever on a very tasteful bed of warm lettuce. The restaurant was a temple to the nouvelle cuisine. 'I don't know. I haven't touched it yet,' he said.

'It looks like a couple of snails' antennae,' observed Sonia.

Sonia Fraser looked at Tony Cheever as she looked at all men, to see if there was anything in it for her. He was about the same age as Arthur. He was rather more interested in appearances, but his clothes sense was horrible. It was as if he thought that if you signed a garment it became automatically tasteful, even if you signed it Walter or Fred. Yet Cheever was attractive, she supposed, if only he would stop being so fidgety and humble. He still had all his hair and all his teeth. In fact, he had rather too many teeth. He looked as if he had had some teeth added.

'Aren't you going to pour me a drink?' she asked.

Cheever apologized again. He drained the bottle into her glass and she immediately drained the glass.

'Now I feel a whole lot better,' she said. He watched her order another bottle herself without waiting for him to speak to the waiter, and then a double portion of whatever it was on his plate.

When the third bottle arrived, Cheever found himself relaxing a little. He had none of Gold's puritanism about alcohol. He just did not drink in front of the proprietor, that's all. In front of women, drink was a challenge. Cheever now looked at Sonia in the same way he looked at all women, a look that had been noted by the third Mrs Cheever and was not helping his marriage. He thought Sonia was attractive, too, albeit a little bossy. It would

be like pleasuring your mother or your headmistress or the Queen.
'How would you like it, ma'am?' he muttered. Then, even though
he prided himself on being a member of the new generation, he
apologized mentally to the Queen for allowing such a thing even
to cross his mind.

'How are you getting on at the paper?' he asked finally. 'Are
they treating you right?'

'Mmmm,' she said absent-mindedly. 'It's not exactly like
working for *The Times*, is it?'

Cheever apologized again.

'Daddy cut his teeth on *The Times*,' she said.

He noticed she shut up immediately as soon as he looked
interested at this mention of her father. Who the hell did Grant
say he was? You employed these people, you threw money at
money, and they gave you precious little in return – no gossip,
none of the low-down on their friends, no chat from the corridors
of power, none of the basic information that was the stock in
trade of newspapers.

'When was that?' he asked.

'When was what?'

'Your father and *The Times*?'

'How should I know?' she said. 'Ask him. I wasn't around. It
was in the days when they had coal fires in the office and everyone
called each other by their surname.'

'Ah, Fraser,' said Cheever knowledgeably.

'It was long before he inherited,' she taunted.

Cheever imagined Lord Fraser inheriting a magnificent palace
set in a park carved out of vast acres of fertile land filled with
neo-Roman follies and landscaped by Capability Brown. Sonia
did not tell him he had inherited a crumbling ruin with the ceiling
coming down in the main hall and the celebrated round master
bedroom open to the four winds where one of the famous cedars
had crashed through the façade during an electric storm. She did
not tell him about the death duties that also went with the
inheritance. She did not tell him how he had sold the Rembrandt
and opened the park on Sundays or how he had put a sandpit for
visiting children in the espaliered peach garden and donkey rides

on the croquet lawn. It was none of Cheever's business.

'Grant's a friend of his, I believe.' Cheever fumbled through the fog of his limited knowledge about the staff he had inherited.

'Daddy gave him a minute cottage on the estate, if that's what you mean,' said Sonia. 'It was either that or pulling it down. Daddy said it was cheaper to give it to Hamish. Hamish was his fag at school.'

Cheever could not get it into proper perspective. No matter what happened to England, these people, whoever they were, still lived as if they bloody well owned it. They talked about the Norman Conquest as if it were yesterday. In that little skirmish, as in all others, they had been on the winning side. They had distinguished themselves in all the wars England ever got into. They had raped a good deal and pillaged some more. Along the way they bred like rabbits. This was a good insurance policy against the relentless victories of unkind fate. Grateful monarchs gave them rolling acreages on which they built museums to flaunt their families' plunder. Cheever wanted to be bitter about it all. He resented the past terribly. If it was left to him, he would bulldoze Buckingham Palace and erect council flats on the site. Then he would plant a vegetable garden on Constitution Hill.

Except he would not. Something stopped him as it stopped everyone else. Instead of making it impossible for the system to continue by starving the aristocracy out of their grand houses and flogging their plunder to pay for the national debt, here he was employing them for no better reason than that they were still there and there was something about it he was damn well enjoying.

Sonia was amusing. She was pretty. She was privileged. She had a private income. Only the very rich never bothered with taxi money. She would be cheap to keep. She could be the fourth Mrs Cheever. He mouthed it silently: 'The Honourable Mrs Sonia Cheever.' Was that right, or would it be Mrs The Honourable Sonia Cheever, or indeed Mrs Sonia, the Honourable Cheever? Whichever way it was, she would be wonderful for his image. She had her feet in the past, but she moved with the times. Here she was sitting opposite him, using all the buzz words which were music to his upwardly mobile soul: Arezzo, nouveau Beaujolais, GT Sprint. GT Sprint?

'I'm not sure I can quite justify a car like that,' Cheever found himself saying. 'You've only been on the paper a month.'

'You've wasted all that time, Tony,' Sonia said. 'You've stuck me in this anonymous job in the Diary running errands for Squiffy when you know my name counts for twice as much as his. With a name like mine you should put it in the paper every single day. You should blow it up in huge letters so people can read it right across the street.'

'You haven't got much experience,' said Cheever doubtfully.

'I can learn as I go on. Arthur Mitchell says it doesn't matter how many qualifications you've got, there is only one way to learn when it comes down to it – on the job.' She laughed at her double meaning, but Cheever only heard the name Arthur Mitchell. It struck him and hurt him.

'So what qualifications do you have?' he asked.

Sonia was gazing at him with her green eyes. 'What do you want?' she said.

'I suppose you must have an exam in written English,' he said. 'That's the minimum these days.'

'I failed every exam I ever took,' she answered, still looking him straight in the eyes.

'What have you been doing in the time since you left school?' he asked.

'Oh, a little cookery, a little cocaine,' she said.

Cheever looked at his watch. Sophisticated women terrified him and thrilled him. He really did have to leave the lunch table now if he was to catch his train. It made him apologetic again.

'Jesus,' she said. 'I did promise I would go to tea with this friend of mine. Would you drop me, Tony? My car has been clamped. Shit!'

She stood up and dropped her car keys on the floor in front of him and they both bent down together to pick them up. Cheever's eyes rested on the cleavage that protruded outrageously between the manly lapels of her jacket. She straightened up and he was left looking between her thighs. He agreed to drop her. As he drove

HACK 1 away, he saw the smart yet bedraggled man again. He wasn't a lawyer after all. He was in quite the wrong part of town for that. Who was he? He put him out of his mind as Sonia directed him to a very ornate address in SW7. 'Come in with me,' she suggested.

8

Bit Blaster

Freddy Fisher had called a staff meeting. Thirty people in Hush Puppies, sports jackets and ethnic frocks shuffled into the editor's office, where, they had been told, something very important would be announced. Those who had already heard of Freddy Fisher's interest in the paper warned everyone else and told them to be on the look-out for a vulgar-looking foreigner, weather tanned from cattle rustling. They were totally unprepared for the clean-cut man, smelling of Aramis, who faced them and told them of his plans and of Arthur Mitchell's new post as editor of the first seven-day-a-week newspaper.

'That's all I have to say,' finished Freddy Fisher triumphantly, 'except that this is the proudest day of my life. Whenever I acquired a newspaper in the United States, it was this one I was looking to. I have acquired hundreds of newspapers back home. Well, now I have acquired you, too.'

Thirty people looked apprehensive.

'Some of you have been here a long time,' he continued. 'You'll have had some good times, and some bad times too no doubt, but the past has a habit of looking rosier than it was. I don't want any nostalgia. I am only interested in the future. Your loyalty is to me from now on. And I have quite a simple motto. If you are not for me, you are against me.'

He paused meaningfully. It was a habit of his which, together with his manner of holding his gaze, made each of the staff feel he was looking at them in particular. 'What's that, Arthur?' he said suddenly.

Mitchell jumped to attention. He couldn't see what the man meant.

'That,' said Fisher. He was pointing at a typewriter.

'It's a typewriter,' said Mitchell uncertainly.

'I've never seen one like it before,' said Fisher.

Thirty people looked at each other. Then they looked at the typewriter. It was a plain, ordinary old-fashioned mechanical typewriter of the sort which had filled British newspapers for years. What did he mean, he had never seen one? The man was pig-ignorant. It was just as they suspected all along. He had no familiarity with the basic tools of the trade. Even without his six-shooters and bull-whip he was clearly a dangerous illiterate.

Fisher carried on, though he changed the subject. 'I need your support,' he said winsomely, 'and I can tell you right now that I am worth supporting. I am one of the very few people in the modern world who has made a business out of newspapers alone. I have been able to do it because I know what the public want. I know what they want even when they think they want something else. I wasn't born wealthy and influential. In fact, I was born dirt-poor and no one ever gave me a helping hand. I have survived by hard work and my own judgement, so you see it may be that I am worth listening to. Any questions?'

'This newspaper has always had a strict policy of managerial non-interference,' a man in a yachting cap began timidly. 'It is a British institution with two hundred years of tradition behind it. So far you have made more changes overnight than it's known in two centuries. To begin with, you have single-handedly eradicated the Sabbath. I think these sort of sweeping changes are something that should be considered rather carefully before being put into practice. It is usually taken into consideration, when dealing with a sale of this nature, that a suitable candidate has the intention of injecting funds into the enterprise rather than withdrawing them. Yet with one fell swoop you have saved yourself maybe £100,000 a year in editorial expenses.'

'You think that is what is behind this?' asked Fisher. 'That's cheese-paring. Wait and see what I've got up my sleeve.'

'Cheese-paring, then asset-stripping?' said the man in the yachting cap, who was growing bold. 'I am not entirely sure you can do what you have just done.'

'I've just done it,' said Fisher.

'Do you plan as active an interest in editorial policy?' asked the man in the yachting cap.

'Damn right, I do,' said Fisher. 'You know why?'

Thirty people looked apprehensive.

'I paid the piper, that's why,' said Fisher. 'I'm calling the tune.'

Arthur Mitchell winced. This wasn't quite the idealistic forward-looking meeting he had envisaged when he realized, after lunch, that he was appointed chief of this heady new enterprise.

'But what about the freedom of the press?' asked an idealistic young researcher with an unwashed fringe and bad acne.

'You have the freedom to say anything you can get away with,' said Fisher excitedly. 'You can try anything you like. That way we will have fun. But, in the end, you can only get away with things if you have a paper to say them in, eh? First rule of the game. What's your name?'

'Me?' she asked.

Several of the assembled throng looked at her with a mixture of disapproval and jealousy.

'Yes, baby, you,' said Fisher.

This time she reacted to the words as if he had raped her. Fisher did not flinch. He looked straight into her eyes as if he was trying to divine what she might be called.

'Sukie Smith,' she answered finally, shuffling her flat shoes expectantly among the spilled coffee and pencil sharpenings.

But, instead of saying anything else, Freddy Fisher changed the subject and immediately ignored her.

'The way I see it,' he continued, 'is very simple. The digger's a mucker maybe, but he has not got it quite right over at *The Times*. To start with, he was landed with a bunch of superannuated flower-children, all pretending it was going to be 1965 for ever and ever. It's a generation that has never grown up. It's going straight from the cradle to the grave, both subsidized in your country, I understand, and missing out all the really interesting bits in between. What he did was put a couple of sergeant-majors in charge to stop them grumbling and get the paper out on time, but no one's thinking for themselves except the man in charge. If he's not careful, they'll turn *The Times* from a dying institution into a dead institution. If he's not careful, I'll be taking over *The Times* myself next. But all he has to do to stop that is to go back to basics. Basics are what people all over the world understand. You can try and argue otherwise, and I might listen to you on a slow day, but you'll be wrong.

'Basics are what we are going to get back to over here. People have been reading this paper, as you, sir, pointed out, for a couple of centuries. English gentlemen were doing the crossword on the back page when Americans were skinning Indians and Murdoch's kith and kin were cutting stones.

'Now, history is fine when it is old, but there is history which is not old enough. I don't want any member of my staff writing about recent history, looking back with longing to the days of free love and feminism. There is nothing so uninteresting as the ageing trendy. I am not in the business of funding a socialist broadsheet, neither have I any interest in running an establishment newsletter. I expect my journalists to be ahead of the times, so to speak.

'As a matter of fact, that's as good a slogan as any for this paper. Write that down, Arthur. Ahead of *The Times*. I want every member of staff on my papers to be in tune with what is going to happen *next*. That's the way with newspapers. We don't publish them yesterday or today, we publish them tomorrow. Since we are stuck with the future, let's get into it.

'You won't find me difficult. If you have any questions I will always be available to you. Do you have any questions?'

He looked at his watch. It was Sukie Smith who spoke, though first she inhaled a lungful of nicotine from the cigarette dangling between her brown and broken fingernails. 'I thought crosswords did not come in until the 1920s,' she said.

Again Fisher did not flinch or appear to give her a second thought. He wound up the meeting and wished everyone the best of luck. As he left the room, he gave Sukie Smith a backward glance: 'Would you come with me for a moment?'

Now that the editorial meeting was starting to break up, the staff were gathering in little huddles in various corners of the office. Sukie looked around for guidance and then decided to do as Fisher asked. She followed him into the corridor and then down it.

'Come this way,' he said. He opened a side-door. It was a kitchen.

'But that's the kitchen,' she said.

'Ain't that the truth,' said Fisher. 'Glad to see you girls still recognize one when you see it.'

He held the door open for her, but when she did not move he stepped right in. He was only looking for privacy and he did not care where he found it. Sukie followed him in reluctantly.

'What's eating you, sister?' he asked.

She said nothing.

'Do you mind if I give you a piece of advice?' he said.

She looked curious.

'Come here,' he said.

She came. He took her hand gently in his. She noticed he had a small hand for such a big man. He looked at her hand and then he turned it over. Very gently he took the cigarette from between her fingers. Then he flushed it down the sink grinder and ran his fingers under the tap till they were perfectly clean. 'That stuff's killing you, baby,' he said.

He maddened her with his patronizing attitude. She looked at the floor and still she said nothing.

'Do you want to tell me what's wrong so we can deal with it man to man?' he teased. When there was still no answer he continued: 'Or shall we take the other route?' He pronounced the word as if it meant a massacre.

Still she was silent.

'OK,' he said. 'I'm sorry to have to do this, but I have no use for trouble-makers. Either you tell me what is on your mind or you're fired.' He paused. 'You're fired.'

9

Late Extra

Beautiful girls, Cheever couldn't get enough of them. The room was absolutely filled with them. They were all especially beautiful, thought Cheever, and he smiled at Sonia gratefully with all his teeth.

What's more, they all seemed to be about thirteen. It was amazing how young they came on stream these days. All that welfare milk and orange juice had them popping out of their bomber jackets before they could do the two-times table with their calculating machines. The world had become a more physical place since the days when Cheever had grown up. In those days it was too cold ever to get all your clothes off. People liked to reminisce about their knee-tremblers behind the bicycle shed, but they forgot that millions of legitimate sex acts had been committed in scarcely more congenial circumstances. Generations had been conceived in a hot muddle of heavy petting between stinking, steamy flannelette sheets, unimaginable milliards of determined sperm finding their way through some tiny gap between the Chilprufe vest and regulation fleecy navy knickers. Most people never knew beauty or the touch of skin, but these kids in this room were no strangers to any silken seductions. The sexual revolution was taking off right in front of Cheever's eyes, and no scaremongering could stop it, even as the 5.40, which he should have been on, was pulling out of the train station. How could he leave? In public in this front room somewhere in SW7, the whole orgiastic point of life was being released, and all because of central heating and welfare orange juice.

Cheever could not believe what was happening right out in the open here. A beautiful girl came up to him and offered him a chipped mug of something.

'What is it?' he asked.

'Champagne and SpeBee,' she said.

He did not know what she was talking about.

'Special brew, daddy,' she said. 'And supermarket bubbly.'

Cheever sipped the stuff. A couple of beautiful girls flew into each other's arms in front of him. They were practically naked. They shimmied front ways on in greeting, crotches touching, breasts lurching. Then they turned round and shimmied with their backsides. They were both wearing heavy gold ankle chains. Cheever leered at them, but they turned on their Minnie Mouse shoes and lurched off together into the shadows, casting him a contemptuous backward glance. It was a world in which he had no maps, but he was determined to do some surveying.

'How much is your allowance, then?' one beautiful girl was saying to another.

'Not telling you,' came the sullen answer.

'See if I care what your miserly father gives you?' the first girl said. 'I don't give a nipple. It's obviously peanuts or you'd be telling me.' Then, 'Look what I got.'

'What's so special about them?' her friend asked.

'Banana-flavoured johnnies,' screamed the girl. 'They're wicked. You can suck them all night.'

Even as he looked, Cheever was catapulted out of the guilt-ridden Stones Age which had been his youth into the ever-expanding Age of Rubber. The blow-up economy was responsible for the latex rubber society just as it had been for the puritanism that had insisted he keep his dick to himself throughout his horny teens. The Pill was not the reason these children were all over each other. No one was on it any more. All these nymphets carried round rubber johnnies pressed between the covers of their schoolbooks. They boasted about them in public, took them out and put them on display. They blew them up and tweeked them, snapped them, slapped them, waved them around their heads. They had slogans inscribed on them, they came in many colours, they were embossed with ridges and dots and furrows and whorls,

63

they were quilted, patterned, bumped and lumped, pleasure-prolonging, sensation-seeking, consequence-avoiding, little balloons of ecstasy. They were their badges of initiation in a world dedicated to consumerism, besides which an oral contraceptive was a small, private and therefore useless thing. These kids masturbated at their school desks. They saw no harm in it. They got off with each other in public over a Coke. You could not choose between these girls, each one more nubile than the next, Tony Cheever thought, so the only solution was to have them all. You only had to look at them, their skin-tight skirts pulled up over their bulging buttocks, everything spray-on tight. Everywhere he looked he seemed to be surrounded by French letters. This was the age of Condom Culture. Cheever had some catching up to do.

There was one girl on his left whom he had noticed the moment he came into the room. What a stunner she was. She looked as if she would put out for anyone or anything. Cheever looked at himself in the mirror. He still had that hair, it made them come just to touch it.

It was second nature to Cheever, when he was having these thoughts, to look round guiltily for his wife. What excuse had he given her for not being at home? What excuse had he given for her not coming to town? He tried to recap their last conversation. Had he said it really wasn't worth coming all the way to London from the outer suburbs for the evening's entertainment? He usually got away with that so long as he wheeled her in once a week for a movie. She liked to hear him say that, if she stayed where she was, he could make her absence his excuse to leave the party early and get back to her and they could finally have that early night.

Then he remembered. He wasn't supposed to be going home to East Grinstead at all. He was free, in as much as going out of town on business was free. As long as he was at his destination by Saturday morning, it would be all right. First he would enjoy himself. He snatched a look at the girl sitting on his left. Yes, she was beautiful. Back in East Grinstead he would have said something amusing like, 'Last one into the sauna is a sissy', but

Cheever wasn't quite sure how, in SW7, a sauna rated on a scale of ten. He waited for the girl to speak instead.

'Who's the wrinkly?' the beautiful girl said to Sonia.

Cheever looked around to see whom she could possibly mean.

'No one you need worry your little head about,' said Sonia.

'He's got to have bread,' the girl said. 'Have you seen that suit? He must have ironed it all over to make it shine like that. And have you seen that signet ring? Jesus! His taste is where he sits. He must be good with his plonker.'

'Shut up, dickhead, will you,' Sonia hissed this time.

Cheever took another look at the girl, who had been speaking about him. She was as pale as paper, almost transparent, with wild black Pre-Raphaelite hair down to her shoulders. Apart from the hair, she was wearing very little else. She had on a sort of minute black jersey sarong round her bursting hips and another round a pair of breasts that were still finely cantilevered in defiance of gravity but already on their way down. These kids kept coming off the conveyor belt, legs splayed ripe for the taking, each with the life-span of some iridescent mindless butterfly. He would have to move quickly.

'What's your name, darling?' he said.

Instead of answering, she turned to Sonia. 'I suppose you are so late because you have been screwing him all afternoon,' she said.

'Wrong,' said Sonia. 'I've been working.'

'I don't know why you have to work for a living,' the beautiful girl said. 'Your father must be a real arsehole, making you put out for those prats. Mine's given me a Gold American Express card. And he's promised me a new car. What car did you say you were driving now?'

'Same one,' said Sonia, remembering crossly that it was clamped.

'My father's buying me a black BMW convertible latest registration just as soon as I pass my test,' said the girl. 'You'd think yours would be ashamed to see you rattling around town in that poxy hairdryer of yours. What's wrong with the old fart?'

Cheever was getting the message slowly. These kids were not reacting to him as they should. He was out of place in this room full of young things, but by everything that was reasonable in this world, he should not be. Instead of them having heard about him, here he was right in the middle of something *he* had heard about. Normally, when he went out at night, everyone knew who he was due to his countless television appearances, but these children did not seem very interested in him. He asked the girl whether she watched television.

'Good grief, no,' she said. 'Not unless it's my dirty video day.' She turned to Sonia again. 'Dirty old man,' she said. 'Who does he think he is? He can't take his eyes off me. Doesn't he know I don't put out for just anyone?' She carried on. 'Hugo's here,' she said. 'He is *so* horny. I've had it off with him three times already. Toby caught me at it. He's absolutely furious. He fancies me like crazy. Who's that?'

It was Simon Lawrence Caulfield.

'It's only Simon Lawrence Caulfield,' said Sonia dismissively.

'Boy, is he flossy?' said the beautiful girl.

Cheever looked round to see whom she meant. She wasn't looking at him but at a boy with dyed blond hair cut very short, except for on top, where it flopped winsomely over one eye. The flossy boy was young, whatever flossy might be.

'What does he do?' breathed the girl

'Simon? He says he wants to be writer,' said Sonia.

'Psst, psst, Sonia, introduce me to your editor, darling,' said Simon Lawrence Caulfield to Sonia. She did. 'Go on, tell him,' he whispered urgently in her ear. 'You've left something out.'

'You didn't tell me he was your editor,' the beautiful girl said admiringly to Sonia.

'Simon is related to D.H. Lawrence,' said Sonia.

Cheever nodded sagely. He could not stand writers, all temperament and principle. The worst part of an editor's job was having to consort with them.

'Just a distant relation,' said Caulfield modestly.

'Who's D.H. Lawrence then?' asked the beautiful girl.

'How the fuck should I know?' said Sonia, who had refused her mother's offer of a six-week holiday course in twentieth-century culture.

'Writing is in the blood,' said Simon Lawrence Caulfield. 'I'd love to write a piece for you,' he said.

Suddenly everyone looked at Cheever expectantly. He ran his fingers through his lovely hair. This was more like it. Cheever prepared for his turn on stage.

'I think I am going to be sick,' said the beautiful girl with impeccable timing so that everyone turned their attention to her instead.

'Not now, Diana,' said Sonia.

She ignored Sonia, now her competitive instincts were aroused. 'Would you like to take me upstairs?' she said to Cheever.

It seemed to Cheever as if the beautiful girl was opening everything even as she spoke, her lips, her breasts, her legs. Cheever blushed.

'Second on the left,' said Simon Lawrence Caulfield. He placed himself in between the girl and Tony Cheever and pushed her without him in the direction of the stairs. 'I'd like to show you some of my work, Tony.'

'Do you think she'll be all right?' said Cheever anxiously. 'Do you think Diana will be all right?'

'She spends every night in the bog,' said Sonia.

'What shall I write for you, Tony?' persisted Simon Lawrence Caulfield.

Cheever did not know what to say. Even as he read the signposts of this world he had started to inhabit, they were being repainted right before his eyes in a seemingly totally arbitrary language. These young people were so casual on the one hand, so ostentatious on the other. He felt brutalized by them. If it was a parrot language, he would have to learn it like a parrot, for youth was surely where it was at. These young things were so pampered, so practical. He turned to another beautiful girl sitting opposite. 'What would you like to read in the paper, darling?'

'Who? Me?' she said. 'I never read the paper.'

Cheever did not demand that they read it, just that they buy it. These young people whom Sonia Fraser knew were representative of the new generation Cheever had heard about. It was a generation committed to careless consumption and proud of it.

This was the youth factor for which all the advertisers were looking. Their talent was for competitive and aggressive spending. In Cheever's day, it was young men who made empty boasts and put their biceps on display. Now it was young women. These young were different from everyone else. They had always had money in their pockets. They didn't give a fig for anything but themselves. They wanted filofacts to facilitate their expenditure. It was entertainment they were after, for they had heard all the news, bad and good. They had lost all innocence long ago and there were no facts that could startle or chasten them now.

Cheever needed beautiful girls like this to pick up the paper from the stands every evening. Then he would have a queue of old men picking it up as well. It would do wonders for the figures. Old man Gold would give him a bonus for coming up with a formula for the future. The old man would be able to have a different operation every day of the week if he wanted to. He'd already had his quadruple by-pass, his prostate, his hernia, gall bladder, kidney and hair transplant. He could have himself totally replaced bit by bit now Cheever had hit on how to keep the money coming. He could devote himself entirely to finding the secret of eternal life. He could take himself off *ad infinitum* on his world tour of health resorts. He would be able to plug himself in for ever to his drip of sheep's placenta and royal jelly.

The young were the only way to stay in the race and Cheever, with his hair and his teeth, had stumbled on this brilliant idea. He would have the gratitude of Gold and Coote. Hell, he would promote Sonia Fraser, with all her connections, from diarist after all. He would make sure she got a column in the paper. Arthur Mitchell did not know what he was fucking with. Arthur Mitchell could go fuck himself. He looked round to tell Sonia the good news, but she had disappeared.

At the moment when Cheever made his momentous decision there was a sound as of someone screaming coming from upstairs. Cheever rose to his feet immediately and then sat down again. No one else had moved anything except their eyes, which they directed at the ceiling. A long silence settled into the room.

'What was that?' asked the beautiful girl who did not read the paper. The scream was obligingly repeated, allowing everyone to consider it anew.

'It sounds like someone screaming,' said her girl-friend.

'Yes. I would have said it was someone screaming.'

Cheever said nothing. The pace of life in SW7 was something alien to him. It went with high ceilings. The higher the ceilings, the slower people seemed to fill up the space in between. This generation appeared to have turned everything inside out. They wore their underwear on the outside and put the boiler pipes on the façade of their buildings, yet when it came down to it they moved in a sort of aristocratic pavan as if the centuries were frozen rather than passing. This was the detachment that a familiarity with money gave you. Even the poor had it today, but it was something that Cheever, from another generation, just did not possess.

'Would you like to read my Santa Fe memoirs?' asked Simon Lawrence Caulfield.

'What?' asked Cheever. Now all was quiet upstairs. 'Where is Sonia?' he asked Caulfield.

'I don't know,' said Caulfield. 'I can have the manuscript to you by Monday.'

Cheever went up the stairs. He opened several doors till he came to a room which was occupied. It was the bathroom. In the mirrored bathroom two girls were lying on the floor in a mess of tumble twist and hair. One was Diana, the other was Sonia trying to breathe some life into the pale girl. On the handbasin was a mirror, some white powder and a razor blade.

'Jesus!' said Cheever.

'Christ!' said Sonia. 'What took you so long, Tony? I screamed as hard as I bloody well could. You'd think you would want to know what was going on. I thought you were supposed to be a newshound, for Chrissake.'

Cheever looked at the scene. The beautiful girl still looked beautiful but she also looked dead.

'What is going on?' he asked.

'The little idiot's O-deed, of course,' said Sonia. 'And I've got to get out of here. There'll be a hell of a stink if Daddy hears of this. He'll have a beni, for Chrissake. The Prime Minister will have an epi. You'll take her home, won't you, Tony?'

Without waiting for an answer, Sonia left. She pushed past Cheever and was gone. Cheever looked at the girl whom he had fancied so much only moments before. She still looked dead. Now what did he do? He did not want to call the police any more than Sonia had. If the puritanical Gold got hold of this, Cheever's days as a salaried person would be numbered. He would never survive to tap into his pension fund, there would be no golden handshake, no offer of a consultancy to a publisher. Cheever would have to solve this one all by himself. He slapped the girl across the face and was relieved to see a little colour momentarily flush to her cheeks – and just as soon drain out again.

'Can you stand up?' he asked. He hoisted her to her feet and she rocked queasily backwards and forwards.

'Sit on my face,' she murmured. At least she had spoken. It was a good start.

'You're coming with me,' he said. He put his arm round her and dragged her down the stairs.

'What address shall I send the piece to?' asked Simon Lawrence Caulfield, who was standing between him and the bottom of the stairs.

'Come to the office on Monday morning,' said Cheever.

'Does that mean I am hired?' asked Caulfield.

'I've got to go out of town,' said Cheever. 'I've got a train to catch.'

'I love to fuck on trains,' yawned the girl, coming to slightly.

'Someone's got to get her home,' said Cheever. He did not know what to do.

'Put her in a cab,' said Simon Lawrence Caulfield. 'What's her name?'

'Diana,' said Cheever. As he said it, it struck him as a piece of irony. 'Diana's the name of my wife,' he said helplessly.

This time Simon Lawrence Caulfield looked at the girl more carefully. She was about nineteen, with eyes like two burned pieces of coal and strange excited mannerisms. Her skin was bleached quite white and her hair was very black, though not crudely so, thought Caulfield, who was given to practising his prose in his head. Although she looked like a painted doll, not one of her colours was artificial. She had two feverish spots on her cheeks. She was burning with the brightness of reckless youth. She turned a peculiar look on Caulfield and he felt his insides fester. His mouth hung strangely slack. She offered him her hand, and he was aware there were little beads of perspiration on his palms. She was the editor's wife.

'I'll take her home for you, if that would help,' Simon Lawrence Caulfield offered.

'No, thank you,' said Cheever coldly. 'Stay here, Diana,' he said.

He propped her up against the doorpost and went out into the street to try to get his car. In the shadows something moved. Probably a cat. He looked back. The beautiful girl was sitting at the doorpost, watching him vacantly. Simon Lawrence Caulfield was sitting with her. Cheever drove HACK 1 right up to the front of the house and left the engine running.

'I'll help you,' Simon Lawrence Caulfield said.

Caulfield, with his stringy figure, picked up the girl's arms and Cheever picked up the girl's legs. There was nothing of either of them. That was another thing about the well-fed young. They were thin. It must be the excitement of modern life, thought Cheever. Together with Caulfield, he shovelled Diana into the back seat of the car. They propped her up against the upholstery and Cheever was relieved to find she stayed sitting up.

Caulfield sighed. The editor's wife. 'Monday then,' he said. 'What time?' But Cheever had already slammed the door in his face and activated the central locking device.

Cheever looked in the rear-view mirror. The girl was still sitting up, staring vacantly into the darkness. 'Diana,' he said. Then he realized he had no idea what her last name was or where indeed she lived. He asked her, but she didn't answer. What did he do next?

'Would you like to sit on my face?' she sang instead to a tune Cheever knew with other words, 'or would you rather some other place?'

Cheever put HACK 1 noisily into gear. It was with mixed feelings that he realized he had no alternative except to take this beautiful young girl with him to the train station where he might just make the night-train.

10

Newtech

'What's that?' asked Fisher. He and Arthur were walking through the machine room. Fisher was looking at a lino-type machine.

'It's a lino-type machine,' said Arthur. 'It makes lines of type. In hot metal.'

'Fuck me,' said Fisher. 'I think my grandmother once saw one of those. How does it work?'

'You punch out the letters like on a typewriter. They are set in lead.'

'Show me some more,' said Fisher.

'You put the lines of type in this tray. Then you bolt it up with this key so they are nice and tight and won't fall out. You can run some ink over it and press a piece of newsprint on it and make a tear sheet. When it's all set up how you like, you make an impression in papier mâché. It's flexible and it's called a flong,' said Arthur. 'You pour molten lead into the flong and make a rigid semi-circle. It wraps round a cylinder on the presses. Look.' He picked up a half-circle of papier mâché. 'Flong,' he said.

'Flong?' asked Freddy Fisher.

'Flong,' repeated Arthur.

'Where's the tablets?'

'Tablets?' asked Arthur.

'The stuff is old as the Ark, Arthur,' said Fisher.

Arthur looked wounded.

'Forget it,' said Fisher. 'Let's see the blockmakers.'

This was Arthur's favourite department. He still did not quite understand how a picture could be wrapped round a wire machine half-way round the world, broken down into dots, transmitted over invisible airways into his offices, reinterpreted on to metal

73

plates and the dots broken down in baths of acid so they, too, could undergo the same printing process as other black-and-white marks on the paper which were the words. It was a miracle every time it happened. On this miracle his whole professional life had been based. He showed Fisher the great baths of acid needed to create letter-press plates.

'How long does that take?' asked Fisher.

'Three quarters of an hour, maybe,' answered Arthur.

'Jesus, they could assassinate your Queen while you're just waiting to print,' said Fisher.

'You get a jolly good picture,' said Arthur.

'Life's an impression,' observed Fisher. 'You never do get to fill in all the dots.'

Arthur looked tragic.

'Sad but true,' said Fisher. 'Show me your presses,' he continued.

He pressed the button for the lift, but when it did not come immediately he changed his mind. He bounded down the backstairs into the bowels of Fleet Street with Arthur trotting behind. The machine room was the size of an aircraft hangar. The presses made a deafening noise and the two men had to shout.

'How many copies in an hour?' asked Fisher.

'Six thousand,' said Arthur proudly. 'It folds the pages all by itself.'

'Fucking brilliant!' said Fisher.

Arthur was relieved. At last he had shown the new proprietor something that impressed him.

'Only trouble is I'm not in the origami business.'

Arthur looked puzzled.

'Forget it,' said Fisher. 'I bet with your circulation you have to start printing two days in advance of distribution.'

'Three, some pages,' said Arthur proudly. 'We print more than a million.'

'When I was a kid I'd hear a story in the morning and I'd have it on the street by lunch,' said Fisher. 'I was very proud of that. Course, I had no circulation to speak of. I'd never have thought circulation could be a problem. You always got to aim at the direct response, not get bogged down by the bits in between.'

'The printing process does take time,' agreed Arthur thoughtfully.

'This is the challenge,' said Fisher. 'Unless we get it right how can we hope to compete with television? We will get it right in the end,' said Fisher. 'Any time you have an idea, Arthur, I want you to tell me. Good or bad, whatever the idea is, let me be the judge of it. We must get it right in order to compete. Life's a competition.'

They inspected the entire premises. Fisher had no respect for the practices they had been developing for more than a century, still less affection for them. Apart from the sort of mild curiosity he might have shown to a stuffed dodo in a museum, he didn't show any interest in them at all. 'This has all got to go,' he said. 'Immediately.'

'I'd say immediately was pretty well impossible,' said Arthur.

'Impossible is not a word in my vocabulary,' said Fisher.

'Trouble is, over here you're in a cleft stick,' explained Arthur. 'We are stuck with the infra-structure of another age. In order to change the system, you have to shut it down. If you shut it down, you lose money and then you can't afford to change the system.'

'You edit the paper and leave the mathematics of what we can afford to me,' said Fisher.

Again the lift did not come, and Fisher set off up the backstairs towards Arthur's office on the editorial floor with Arthur panting behind him. 'I want you to start thinking of running right up against a very late deadline,' he was saying. 'I want you to have the paper all set up ahead of time, but ready to change right until the last second, and then again during the run if necessary. I want you to come up with some ideas about streamlining things here, and in order to help you do that, I want you to see how I do it back home,' said Fisher. 'I want you on the plane with me first thing tomorrow morning. Be ready for the limo at six.'

Frederick Fisher took his hand-held portable telephone out of his pocket. He pressed just one button, which summoned its digital memory. 'Four p.m.,' he said into the phone. No more and no less. He clicked off the machine. 'Dallas,' he said. 'Clear as a fucking bell. Cost me less than a dollar. That's technology. Now let's edit the paper,' he said.

As they climbed the stairs towards the editorial floor, the smell of ink from the big machines in the basement gave way to the unmistakable sour smell of human sweat. It was lingering all round the editorial offices, yet there seemed to be no one in the offices to whom it belonged.

'Where is everyone?' asked Fisher.

Arthur was puzzled, too. It was not nearly early enough to go home. He slipped to his desk and tried to make an internal call, but there was no answer. Then he tried to call Sonia. He had no idea how he was going to be ready to go to Dallas the next day, but he knew he had to let her know. There was no answer from Sonia either. He called Nora. She was in. No matter what happened in their lives, his wife was always sitting by the phone.

'Laurie's home for the weekend,' she said. 'You can't go to Dallas now, Arthur. You promised. I don't matter, but you can't break your promise to Laurie.'

'You are going to have to cope,' said Arthur. Immediately he felt guilty. 'Even you can see that this is a set of unusual circumstances,' he told his wife.

'The circumstances are always unusual,' she said.

Patiently he explained to her that the Sunday Newspaper had been taken over and that their livelihood and Laurie's depended on him making a good impression on the new owner of the paper. He tried to call Sonia again, but she was still not there, so he called Nora back.

'I'll sleep at the flat tonight so I can go straight to the airport,' he said.

'What for?' she asked.

'To catch a plane,' he said. The woman was completely stupid. 'What else do you do at an airport?'

'You didn't say anything about that this morning,' she moaned.

He wanted to shout at her, make her feel small and stupid, and point out for the hundredth time that in all the twenty years he had been a high-flying executive in Fleet Street she had never

76

learned that the job demanded flexibility. Instead, because he felt guilty, he bit his tongue. 'I have only just found out myself,' he said.

'When will you be back?' she asked.

'I don't know. I'll call you,' he said.

'But Laurie . . .' she began.

Again the goddam guilt-trip. 'Look, I don't want this any more than you do,' he said. 'I'd have liked nothing better than to have fed the ravens with you and Laurie at the Tower. We could have gone to one of those old pubs round there and had a shepherd's pie overlooking the Thames. Instead, I have to sit closeted in a plane for the whole day just to wind up in a country I can't stand with a megalomaniac Texan millionaire whose own country is not large enough for him. He wants to run the world.'

There was silence from the other end. That had shut her up. Arthur felt a lift in his mood. Then, almost immediately, he felt guilty again. It wasn't just her he was letting down, it was Laurie.

'You know how the Americans make me sick,' he continued. 'You know how they make me cringe with their "Have a nice day" and their chocolate-box face-lifts. You know how fussy they are about their health. I won't be able to smoke, I won't be able to drink, I bet I have to have a salt-free lunch. God knows what other perfectly harmless ingredients they have outlawed since I was there last. It'll taste like polystyrene foam. At least, if you stay at home here, you can eat well.'

He looked up. Fisher was standing at the door, leaning on the doorpost and listening to his conversation. Arthur had no idea how long he had been there. It was so unfair, the way the man blended everywhere. Arthur would have recognized him if only he had been wearing his chaps and his cowboy kerchief, but with that pin-stripe suit he could pass for anyone. How could you trust such a man? Whatever would he think of next?

Next Fisher thought he wanted to play at editing. Just as he had gone through all the stages of the printing process, now he wanted to see all the pages in their various states of readiness. Arthur showed him the notes on the spikes, the copy in the typewriter, the corrected proofs. He showed him the art department with its

researcher in this organization. She is a very hard worker.'

'How much does she want?' asked Fisher.

'How much of what? Oh,' Arthur was taken aback. 'Money?' he said. For a minute it came to the forefront of his mind that his own contract had not been discussed. He must call Bleidenstein and have his law firm run the rule over the terms. Still, he did not want to introduce such a sordid note as finance at this moment in time. Surely that could wait. He was getting on too well with Fisher for anything to go wrong. 'Sukie Smith doesn't mention money,' he said. 'It'll be a question of her pride. Why did you pick on her?'

'She's not good-looking enough,' said Fisher. He grinned. Then he changed his tack. 'That's true, but it's not the reason,' he said. 'I didn't pick on her. She picked on herself.'

'Trouble is, over here she can't really be fired,' said Arthur.

'Is that so?' said Fisher. He took a step back and put his hands on his hips.

Arthur could have sworn he saw him fingering his holster in the half-light. If he looked down he would see his spurs. In a tone that approximated to apology, he explained the Employment Acts, redundancies, quotas, unionization, maternity leave, job-sharing, time-serving.

Freddy Fisher put both hands up. 'Stop right there,' he said.

'You see what I mean?' said Arthur, scenting a victory. 'Trouble is, I am afraid there can be only one outcome to this chapel meeting. Too many people's consciences will be pricked by her fate.'

'Too many people's interests coincide, is what you mean,' said Fisher. 'But not mine. I have an idea, Arthur. Follow me,' he said. He went out to the lift-hall again, punched the button and once again changed his mind. He pushed through the fire-door and took the backstairs down two at a time.

Arthur followed him out of breath. Coming up there was a bedraggled figure who looked as if he had been left out in the rain all night. His hair was plastered down on his face. He was wheezing so badly he seemed to be spewing up rust. Arthur was not aware of ever having seen him before, which was just as well, because Pringle had no intention of being recognized.

'What news of the Evening Paper?' Fisher asked the figure.

'Still on strike,' squeaked Pringle, keeping his back to Mitchell. 'It's been out all day now. What's more, according to his secretary the editor's left town.'

Fisher looked curious but said nothing.

'He was booked on the 5.40 from Euston to Liverpool,' Pringle continued.

'Cheever must be on to a good story,' said Arthur. 'I'll send a man up there immediately, Frederick, to find out what he's up to.'

'I've got a line on the story, too,' said Pringle, feeling his competitive hackles rising. 'When I last saw Cheever he was with a girl,' he said. 'And I am pretty certain I know who that girl was. It was old Jock Fraser's daughter.'

This time Arthur did not mean to react like he did. He could not help himself. He coughed and spluttered and choked with the insult he felt to himself at the mention of Sonia's name. What was she doing with Cheever away from the office? Why on earth would she go to Liverpool? Were they on a story together? He had to get in touch with her before he went on to Dallas.

Fisher looked at him uneasily. 'Women are a whole lot of trouble, Arthur,' he warned. 'Better forget them. In fact, forgetting them is the best thing you can do with women.' He had changed his mind about going to the chapel meeting. 'Talking of which, you tell little miss whatshername . . .'

'Who?' said Arthur urgently. 'Who?'

'Little feminist girl.'

'Sukie, Sukie Smith,' he said.

'You give the little feminist girl a message from me,' said Fisher. 'Tell her if she wants to go to chapel, I'll make certain she has something to pray about. Six o'clock tomorrow morning, Arthur, OK?'

11

Splash

Crumm was seated next to Mrs Crumm in front of the twenty-six-inch television screen in its walnut consul fitment. On top of the set was a bowl of plastic tulips, a fighting bull from Spain and a velvet-covered matchbox.

Crumm had had a brainwave. When he first saw Sonia Fraser in the van bay, he had been exasperated by the sight of a good pair of legs being brought in by someone other than himself.

At the outset he had only wanted to give the boy who did it a little moment of discomfort for upstaging him. He wanted to watch him squirm a little, just as he liked to watch his worms squirm when he twisted them on to his fishing line of a weekend. Crumm applied the squirming principle from the bottom of life to the top. He liked to make things squirm from pain now he was of an age when he could no longer make them squirm from pleasure.

It was good for discipline to make things squirm. Crumm made the cat squirm, and the dog. He even made the budgie squirm, and as for Mrs Crumm, she had squirmed for so long he had her nicely under control. Mrs Crumm scarcely bothered him at all. 'Shut up, you daft bird,' he said to her whenever he felt like it, and pretended he was talking to the budgie, which was always trying to assert its independence.

The brainwave was a landmark in Charlie Crumm's life. Was squirming on an individual basis enough, he asked himself now, if by its mass application you might achieve immortality within the trade-union movement? Crumm felt the finger of destiny. His moment had come. Something he said to the boy in the van bay had struck a more resonant chord as he drove his own van home

81

through the rush hour: 'Our contract is to carry papers, and your job is not to exceed your contract . . .'

Perhaps, after all, the contract could be extended to exceed present specifications. Perhaps it could be rewritten to extend rights of transportation in any of the firm's vehicles to editorial staff, and clerical staff, and front-hall staff, and managerial staff, and boardroom members for that matter in a real emergency, though they might form the basis for a special clause of exception.

Crumm was not thinking, of course, of the service he could render to the editorial staff and the clerical staff and the front-hall staff and the managerial staff and the boardroom members. He was not thinking of the good of the Evening Newspaper as a whole. He was thinking of what might be in it for him. He soon saw that this transportation service he had invented might be extended for a fee. The terms would have to be laid down as to under which circumstances such a thing would be allowable – an emergency exactly defined, for instance, the ingredients analysed which constituted it – otherwise you would have bloody journalists thumbing a lift all over the show.

Naturally there would have to be some sort of control, especially over any possible impromptu violation of the privilege, since the blighters were especially given to this, being congenitally lazy, forever on the make and as likely to cut corners as look at you. Crumm had that from his father and grandfather for starters. Now it was up to him to redress the balance. He looked forward to a monumental tussle with the National Union of Journalists in which his personal victory would be assured by the pendulum of history. The NUJ would be a pushover. Then there was the string of other unions, NATSOPA, SOGAT, NALGO, bloody-minded all of them, but Crumm had right on his side. He had more than that. He had to acknowledge that he was that rare thing, the right man in the right place at the right time. He took his hands off the steering wheel, rubbed them together with anticipation, and nearly sailed into a brick wall.

But he didn't. The brick wall was intact and so was Crumm. It was an omen. Nothing could faze him tonight. His scheme was inspired. There would be no end of paperwork involved, of course, but Crumm liked paperwork. A signature, an explanation, and compensation would be metered out to the driver depending on the distance involved, much as a taxi-driver charged for his time and service. Crumm would go down in history.

By the time Mrs Crumm brought in the evening Horlicks, Crumm was well pleased with himself. Not only had he evoked a whole scale of circumstances spanning the nature of the emergency which the van drivers would be servicing and the distances involved, which he jotted down on the bosom of the day's Page Three girl in the *Sun*, but he had also worked out a formula about the time of day, the day of the week, whether traffic was inward or outward bound and the density of this traffic, and he was working on a system of variable compensation according to the identity of the person carried, with boardroom members right at the top of the remuneration chart.

Obviously a name writer whose copy was needed for that day's edition was of more value than a typist who worked on the Letters' Page. Or was this so? Were they not all equally interdependent? Was not that the true meaning of democracy? Exactly what was the pecking order to be, if any, in an institution such as a great city's evening paper? Crumm wrangled with himself as he silently dipped his ginger biscuits into the hot nightcap. Would it affect the insurance clauses he had in mind? Was the managing editor, Hamish Grant, who was a figurehead within the organization but anonymous without, more crucial at any one point to the operation than, say, Joe Rizzi, the greaser photographer who specialized in catching personalities unawares like any other bastard *paparazzo*, and who sold papers on the results?

The equation was obviously too difficult for Crumm to solve on his own. The possibilities seemed endless. They would have to be hammered out at a meeting with all the lads and submitted to the union officials. But Crumm must keep control of it, for this was his chance of fame.

He saw it now – the clause in each driver's contract from now on, heretofore to be known as the Crumm Amendment. The great thing was not to miss any tricks. Not to miss any tricks was

Crumm's special watchword, for he suspected the people upstairs of being guilty of just that, not missing any tricks. This was something they did at the expense of the people downstairs by trying to put one over on them and pull the wool over their eyes.

As he was about to fall asleep, he sat bolt upright, struck by the sudden thought that Sonia Fraser's apparently innocent and irresponsible gesture in climbing aboard one of his vans in Fulham, though not his personal van, might not be the aftermath of a long lunch after all. Nor might the true explanation be that at that time of the afternoon it was very difficult to get a taxi. Supposing Sonia Fraser had been planted there, as Crumm was beginning to suspect? Planted by the management with an eye to saving taxi fares in future, not just for Sonia Fraser but for all the people upstairs? Supposing she had been the guinea pig planted there in order to judge the fibre of the people downstairs? 'The Honourable Miss Fraser', Grant had said. That meant she was someone's daughter, not that Crumm knew whose. All he knew was that there was nothing honourable about Miss Fraser if she could put into operation a plan like that.

At this point a whole new notion entered Charlie Crumm's fevered brain. Supposing he had quite simply been made a fool of? Supposing Charlie Crumm had been used in the most cynical possible way by those penny-pinching snobs in the boardroom who were forever looking for ways to do an honest working man out of a decent wage packet?

Supposing the self-made Emmanuel Gold, who said he was on the side of the man in the street, but who was driven right past him in a Rolls-Royce nevertheless, and that decadent ponce Aubrey Coote, who chugged round in traffic jams in his overheated Ferrari, had entered into a conspiracy to find a way of shaving expenditure throughout the organization, claiming it was hard pressed but keeping their own jumped-up life-style none the less and boosting company profit to boot? Supposing, what was more, in their infinite wisdom on the fifth floor they had seen fit to use against the working man one of his few acknowledgements of brief pleasure in this life of toil, his appreciation of the Page

Three figure, which they just happened to have on their side upstairs in the shape of Sonia Fraser?

Mrs Crumm, in her hairnet in the opposite bed, seeing her husband in this mood, put aside the interesting possibility of a heart attack and decided to say nothing at all since there was a memorial late-night rerun of her favourite weepie. The rare luxury of her silence allowed Charlie Crumm slowly to come to the evening's conclusion that this whole business must not be allowed to wait until the next chapel meeting, but that Hamish Grant must be approached immediately and an extraordinary meeting called. He already had the lads on his side, since he had explained to Mike Green the devious inner working of the minds of the capitalist classes.

Crumm lay down again and pulled the pink candlewick bedspread up to his nose, which was how he liked to sleep. At the back of his mind was the soothing conviction that there was absolutely nothing to lose. Even if all his notions were thrown out all along the line, he would still achieve a ruling on the subject, which always took a great deal of time. What Charlie Crumm liked best in the whole world, better than paperwork, a go-slow or an afternoon off, was a ruling. A ruling could waste perhaps a week, perhaps two, or even a month if he was lucky. He would be a hero among his peers. It was a good time to go for a ruling now the allotment needed planting.

If the management refused to make concessions to the drivers for the privilege of extending their transportation facilities to other members of the organization, then Crumm's least achievement would be a clause inserted into each man's contract, specifically defining that they were *not* allowed to carry any other members of the organization whatever the pretext. In preparing for this eventuality, Crumm did not think the specification should be extended to members of any other organization, or indeed to members of the general public (otherwise known as family and friends), given as the van drivers were to taking their nearest and dearest off on weekend picnics, or to Southend or the Zoo, in their vans as the cheapest form of transport at their disposal. No, a simple clause defining their responsibilities, or lack of them, their relationship towards this particular management or any future management was the thing to aim at, not least to wave at such members of the organization who might be inclined to, or in real emergency be driven to defy it, and could therefore be persuaded to make some small *ex gratia* payment to a van driver, or indeed a foreman driver, for the privilege of being transported by him wherever he liked in default of any other available means of locomotion.

Crumm slumbered, fitfully secure in the belief that he had stumbled by this lengthy process of ratiocination on the unique manner in which an organization in the late twentieth century in England could be forced to work against its own best corporate interests, thereby preserving the unique rights of the individual. He made a last mental note that the Crumm Amendment, typed out possibly by one of the Crumm daughters, Miss Kerry Crumm, should be on the managing editor's desk first thing after the weekend.

12

Lead

'Yaahoo!' Frederick Fisher drove his pick-up truck right up to the ranch-house and put it into a skid on the gravel drive. He leapt out and hugged the pretty girl who was standing on the porch. 'I got it,' he said. 'I got the newspaper and I got five hundred of the goddam British working for me.'

'What are they like?' she asked.

He didn't answer her at first. Just looked at her. She was wearing blue jeans and a cotton top, and on her brown forearms she had soft down that caught the light, and she had long shiny auburn hair. He held her at arm's length and whistled a cat-call of a wolf-whistle to show his approval. 'You look great, baby,' he said. 'You really do. What did I do to deserve you?'

'What are the British like?' she insisted.

'What are they like? I'm gonna fuck the lot of them,' he said excitedly. 'Civilization is a sitting duck. Just wait till you meet them, honey. I've brought a couple for you to see.'

They walked arm in arm into the house. It was dark after the sun outside. A barrage of cold air greeted them from the air conditioning.

'Home,' he said. 'I love it. Didn't I always promise you I would always try to come back on weekends?'

He always went straight to the kitchen, opened the refrigerator door and poured himself a grape-flavoured Kool-Ade. This time was no different. He leaned against the refrigerator while he drank. The girl watched him as if happily mesmerized.

'You should spend more time here,' she said.

'I'm planning to,' he answered. It was his far-off dream. 'When I've got enough newspapers.'

'Tell me the story of the first one again,' she said.

'Oh, just let me relax, honey,' he said. 'I've been a long way. It's good to be home.'

He wandered into his den, prowling around as he always did to see if anything had been put out of its place in his absence. Then he sat down and switched on the television and she sat at his feet. He took the remote-control switch and zapped all the channels in turn.

'Bullshit,' he said. 'Hey, that's one of my channels. Bullshit,' he repeated. Then he switched off the sound with the remote-control switch.

She put her golden head in his lap. 'Go on, tell me, Dad,' she said.

'You've heard it all before, honey, you must know it by heart.'

'Please, Dad.'

He never could resist her. 'You've been lonely, haven't you, while I've been gone?' he said.

'Edith and I are fine,' she said.

Edith was the black housekeeper who had looked after her since she could remember. She knew her better than she had ever done either of her parents, and it was on Edith's dogged persistence in dealing with the smallest tasks that she based her expectations of family life. Edith was the reason why Fisher was free. Melanie expected from her father the parenting of inspiration.

'Tell me the story, Dad,' she nagged.

'OK, you win, baby,' he said, stroking her hair. 'Where shall we start?'

'At the beginning, like we always do,' she said happily.

'The first one was the *Gulf Gossip*.' He ran her auburn hair through his fingers till he got right to the end of each strand, then he picked up another strand and began again. 'The *Gulf Gossip* is what I called it, anyway. I was just twelve years old. I was walking down by the water's edge on the Gulf of Mexico and it was so fucking hot I thought I would die. It was so hot the heat was a living thing. It was so hot it was like the air had one purpose and that purpose was to climb right down your throat and suffocate you. It was so hot I thought what do people do when it's hot like this? And I thought there isn't a helluvalot they want to do. They don't want to move a finger, they don't even want to move a toe, they don't want to cut their nails or look at their face. Hell, they don't even want to procreate, 'cos procreation's too damn sticky, they just want to stay in close to the fan and do nothing. But doing nothing gets boring, so what do they do then?'

'What do they do, Dad?'

'That's when I figured they tell each other things. They just lie around and tell each other tales, 'cos talking's all they got the energy to do and they ain't barely got the energy to do that. All over the world, I thought, all the time, whatever else they are doing, they're just telling each other things. I thought there's an awful lot of gossip in the world, and most of it, everyone's telling each other for free. I thought I am going to write it all down. That way they can read it themselves if it is hot, which it surely was, and they don't have to get into a lather because their lips don't even have to move. So I did. Most people reckon nobody reads when it's hot, but that ain't true if you pitch it where it's interesting.'

'How do you pitch it where it is interesting?' asked Melanie.

'You tell 'em what they want to hear,' her father said. 'You tell 'em what they know already.'

'How do you get them to buy it when they know it already?' asked Melanie.

'People like to be told what they know,' he said. 'Leastways, they liked what I told them and they told each other to buy it all right. Like I said, you can't stop people gossiping. The gossip just spreads itself around. Gossip reassures people. I said that if they bought one copy of my newspaper they could have one for the neighbour for nothing. Zilch. Zero. Something for nothing. Always works. Then I just doubled the price anyway. I charged them a dime but I was into profit at a nickel so the readers paid for both.'

'Then what did you do?'

'I invested the profit. Weren't much after I'd paid the Xerox machine. But I had no overheads. Rent was paid and my sources were everyone in town. They told me what I needed to know and

they were flattered to be in the paper. Don't anyone ever tell you
the opposite.'

'Neat,' she said. 'What did you invest in?'

'An ice-cream machine. I made a fair bit of money with my
ice-cream machine. Well, it was fucking hot in town. It's still hot
now. Freshen up my drink, honey, that's my girl.'

She got up willingly and went to the refrigerator. She loved it
when her father came home. She came back quickly with the
drink, put it into his hands and hugged him. He looked tired, but
she wasn't going to let him go yet. He looked so thin when he was
tired, as if the energy of which he was made and which had
temporarily drained out of him was a tangible thing. It was only
when he was tired that she could make him stay put for a while.

'Tell me some more. Tell me about Tyler,' she said.

'Come on, honey, you know the rest.'

'I forgot.'

'The *Tyler Times* was my first real paper,' he said. 'Just a little
local paper, but hell, it meant a lot to me. The day I walked into
Tyler, honey, I thought I'd bought the *Washington Post*. It was a
little brick shack down by the tracks out of town, no rent to speak
of at all. No one else wanted the place, a shack on a piece of dirt in
the middle of nowhere. We just bundled the stuff on to the tracks
on one of those little machines, what're they called? One of those
little hand-pump jobs, and rode them right into town for free,
courtesy of the railroad line. Then we sold 'em in main street out
in the open right by the movie theatre opposite the courthouse,
and we cleaned up.

'I'll always remember Tyler,' he said. 'It was good to me. It
was good to me in the winter when it snowed, it was good to me
in the summer when it was hotter 'n hell. But a place is just a
place, honey,' he said, twisting her hair through his fingers.
'Don't ever let anyone tell you a place is what counts. A place
ain't the reason why a man does something he has to do. The
reason's himself. I always wanted to do things my way. First thing
I did in Tyler was fire the editor. Mean-looking man. I just done
that again.'

'Why did you do that, Dad? Didn't he know his business?'

'Maybe he did, maybe he didn't. I didn't wait to find out. When you got two papers under the same roof and two guys who have been around a long time, one of them has got to go, otherwise next thing you know they're in the men's room together, tearing you apart. I don't ever want anyone tearing me apart, you hear that.'

She squeezed his knees together. 'Gee, I love you, Dad,' she said.

'My way you get hundred-per-cent loyalty,' he said. 'Pringle will never speak to Mitchell 'cos he's too fucking ashamed. Mitchell will never speak to Pringle 'cos he figures he's top dog. They woulda spoke all the time.'

He stretched his long legs and arched his back with tense fatigue. She shifted from one knee to the other till he was comfortable again.

'I've always been an outsider, Melanie,' he said. 'An outsider's not an easy thing to be, but there's one advantage to being the way I am: I don't owe nothing to no one. So when I look, I see. Just now I see that foggy little island in the North Sea working its arse off for me. They don't know what they got over there, honey, they're just giving it all away. They've got circulations bigger than any place in the world. They got literacy and they got lethargy. I can clean up in a place like that. You really love me, baby?'

'I said so, didn't I? Tell me about the house.'

'Which house?'

'The house like the dinosaur,' she said.

'Come on, honey,' he said.

He did not like it when the conversation turned to this. Sometimes he got away with it when they had their little talks and Melanie stopped her questioning, but every now and then she would turn it round again. He tried to get to his feet, but she wouldn't let him. She clasped her hands round his knees so they were held tight together and she laid her chin on his thighs and looked up at him with those eyes. He felt that uncomfortable feeling again. It was like the one he had felt with Jeremy Pringle.

'You said the house was like a great dinosaur rotting by the edge of the forest,' Melanie said. 'You said the rafters were sticking up through where the roof used to be like bony spines through dried-up flesh. You said there were just a few tiles left on the envelope of the house like skin on the bone. You said a house is a living thing and when the family leaves it the soul of the house starts to roam. You said sometimes it finds a home and sometimes it doesn't.'

'Did I say that?' The silence grew uncomfortable again.

'Tell me how you met Mother, Dad.'

'I can't, honey, I don't have time. You know the story.' He tried to make it better. This time he got to his feet. 'I have a dinner with the Brits.'

'Where are they?'

'Mitchell's most likely still at the airport waiting for his goddam luggage. Mitchell's the editor I kept. Always keep one so he can fill you in on things. Arthur Mitchell, CBE. That's some goddam badge of courage of Her Majesty the Queen herself. When you get it, you kneel down in front of her in Buckingham Palace and she taps you on the shoulder with a sword just like Queen Elizabeth I did to Walter Raleigh when he discovered America or whatever it is he did.'

'Walter Raleigh did not discover America, Dad.'

'He discovered bowling.'

'Francis Drake discovered bowling.'

'Raleigh discovered something.'

'He discovered smoking.'

'Now why would Queen Elizabeth make him into a knight for discovering something lethal like smoking?'

Playing dumb was one of Fisher's tricks. She was supposed to laugh, so she did.

'Anyway,' he said, 'I think Mitchell's brought his badge with him. I think he's packed everything he owns.' He sighed. 'Getting him out of the place was like getting a pig into a slaughterhouse. There is something he is afraid of and not even he knows what it is. They're all a bunch of poofters. I tell you, that they don't know what they are all sitting on over there, honey. They don't know the difference between their balls and their brain cells. They need someone to put some lead in their pencils, and that someone's me. They don't know whether it is today or yesterday. I wonder if he will make it in time for dinner?' He looked at his watch, then he looked at his daughter. 'You look great, honey, you really do. I wouldn't do any of this if it weren't for you. You know that, don't you?'

She shrugged.

'What have you been doing, Melanie?'

'I went to the horse show,' she said. She stood up and did a funny gangling little pirouette in her blue jeans. 'I won a couple more rosettes. I stuck 'em on the end of my brass bed. It's all filled up now. No more space. I got to move on to a new hobby.'

'I don't want anything else on your brass bed, you hear?' he said.

'No, sir,' she said.

He looked at her for a long time as if trying to remember everything about her. For a moment he had an uncomfortable feeling again. 'I'm gonna lose you one day, aren't I, Melanie?'

'Not yet awhile, Dad,' she said. 'I've been real good. Do you wanna see my prizes?'

'I'm tired,' said Fisher. 'Later, baby. Just now I'm gonna take a shower.'

He kissed the girl quickly on the cheek and went upstairs. He himself never travelled with luggage, so there was nothing complicated about his homecoming. He kept six separate identical wardrobes in six key cities scattered throughout his empire. Now he stripped off his formal clothes and threw them on the bed for Edith to wash. He looked out some easy clothes to wear that night. Then he looked at himself in the mirror. He was still a good-looking man, tall from birth, firm from exercising every day. He was as tough on himself as on everyone else. He had no choice. It had to be that way because inertia bored him to death.

He started to run the shower, then changed his mind. He poured bubble bath into the tub and eased himself into the hot water. He stretched, he laid back, he was more tired than he knew. He felt his stomach, he felt his thighs. That felt good. His transparent sheets of paper placed over the simulated pages. He showed him the typefaces and even started to venture a couple of his theories about public response to the look of the product, the unconscious identification with type as it had been used in the past, the effects you could achieve, for instance, with an appeal to the subconscious memory and the rich culture of association by the use of Gothic or Teutonic faces. He started to expound on the language within language.

'What are you going to say with all this language?' asked Fisher drily.

'What do you mean?' asked Arthur.

'What's the story?' he asked.

The phone rang.

'Oh, no,' said Arthur into the receiver. He sounded dismayed.

Fisher looked excited, as if he had been waiting for this all the time. At last something was happening.

'So that's why there's no one here,' said Arthur into the phone. He put it down and put his head into his hands. 'Frederick,' said Arthur portentously, 'this might change your mind about leaving first thing tomorrow. This is important.'

'Finally something important,' said Freddy. 'Shoot.'

Arthur took a deep breath. 'Sukie Smith has called a feminist chapel meeting tonight,' he said. 'That's why the office is empty. That's where everyone has gone.'

'Now hold on a minute,' said Fisher. 'Feminist I know. We'll deal with that crap in a minute. Chapel meeting, Arthur? You didn't tell me you were running a bunch of religious nuts.'

'You know that chapel means a branch of our union, Freddy,' said Arthur. He loved it when there was something he could tell him. 'The printing trade has termed it that ever since the eighteenth century.'

'Gee whiz,' said Fisher. 'And who's Sukie Smith?'

'Sukie's the little girl you fired this afternoon,' said Arthur. 'You remember her. I didn't realize you had fired her, Freddy. That sort of thing we should liaise about in future. Sukie could be big trouble. She has the sympathies of all the clerical workers. She's worked herself up all the way from secretary to fingers strayed. With one hand he slowly jerked himself off. With the other he punched out the number of the *Tyler Times* and the *Beaumont Bugle*. He always kept in touch with all of his newspapers at least once a week. Tomorrow and the next day he would show Mitchell what he expected of an editor. Then he would let the guy go back home and sort the lot out. Fisher would move on. He would get himself on a plane to Tokyo and lay plans for the first truly global news-sheet. He wanted it all and he thought the time was coming when he could get it. You could have editors all over the world tapping universal information sources and putting together local and international news in a formula designed to suit their own particular local readership.

The new form of truth would be called the Fisher Standard. How would such a truth work? He thought about this often. Would there ever be such a thing as the real truth? Was the real truth something you could ever encapsulate in words, or did truth have as many points of view as there were people on the planet? Truth was an element, he thought, like water or air. It was protean, like water and air, but was it constant, for unlike water or air there had never yet been a formula to describe it to the satisfaction of everybody. Was that formula the end result of it all? When it was found, would that be the end of the world? Who would get there first? Would it be he?

He dialled the hotel where Arthur Mitchell was staying and was pleased to find he had already checked in. 'Welcome to Texas, what's the news?' he asked. 'Gimme the headlines.'

The headlines, from where Arthur stood, spelled out that a very small room had been booked for Arthur at a very ordinary hotel in a part of town which looked like a building site, and that when he checked in the receptionist, who had not so much as bothered to take her eyes off the computer at the desk, asked him how he intended to pay.

'Frederick Fisher booked me in,' he said.

'Yeah, but you have to settle direct,' said the girl. 'Fisher always does that.'

Arthur was plunged into a grim mood. He couldn't swank in front of Sonia or get her for free. She'd already cost him a plane ticket. While he took the American plane with Fisher, she had taken the British plane. Fisher had made him travel economy, which he had found humiliating. The new proprietor sat next to him in the best of moods, but that had not reassured Arthur. Then Sonia's plane was late. Arthur had waited for her long after Fisher had taken his pick-up truck and left the airport. He told Fisher his luggage had not arrived. That put Fisher in bad mood. It put Arthur in a bad mood. Adultery was expensive, he realized, and it was not his only problem.

Once more he had wondered how he could bring up the subject of money with Frederick Fisher, but Fisher was gone before Arthur had time to ask him about his contract. It had been like that ever since they met. Every time he wanted to ask about it, Fisher made it seem somehow paltry or money-grabbing or irrelevant. Even as he wondered about whether he should and how he could, Fisher would leave the room. He said he would always be available for whatever might happen. But although he said it, in fact his methods were those of the completely unmethodical, or at least the unpredictable. He would issue an order, or what sounded like a threat, and without waiting for any reaction would quite simply disappear. Then he would reappear just as he had now.

'Tell me about my first British edition. Monday morning,' Fisher was saying. 'What are we leading on?'

That was another problem. As soon as he had checked in to his hotel, Arthur had managed to reverse the charges on a call to the paper which no one had answered. It was the early hours of the morning in London. Still, there should be someone there to hold the fort till the print-run was through. Then he had found himself forced to pay for a call to his deputy editor at home. The news was not good. There was no print-run. They had lost the week's Sunday edition because of industrial action.

'Pray God we have a paper to lead on by Monday,' said Arthur Mitchell to Freddy Fisher. 'Sukie Smith's got it in for all of us.'

'Sukie?'

'The little girl you fired,' said Arthur. 'Your remember, sir?'

'She's a little fool,' snapped Fisher.

'That may be,' said Arthur. 'But her chapel meeting was a great success. Now she's called a branch meeting for tomorrow. She's got all the girls out canvassing support, and it looks as if there's a lot of sympathy for them in the circumstances.'

'What's the matter with them? They all want to be fired?' asked Fisher incredulously.

'They say they are not working until Sukie gets her rights,' said Arthur.

'Oh yeah, what more can I do for her?' asked Fisher. He was listening attentively.

'She wants an apology.'

'You have got to be kidding!'

'Sukie Smith says you have every right to fire her but not to call her baby.'

There was a moment's silence.

'She should be so lucky as to have someone call her baby,' he said.

'She says it's a sexist remark,' persisted Arthur.

Again there was silence.

'You should write all that bullshit in your paper,' Fisher said. 'Your readers would not believe it.'

'Trouble is, even if we had a paper, that is not the stuff they would print,' said Arthur. 'If the writers wrote it, the typesetters when they read it would refuse to set it. If it got as far as the presses, the printers would refuse to run them. One way or another it looks as if we've got a strike on our hands.'

There was a silence at the end of the line once more.

'You'd better get back there and sort it out, Mitchell,' said Fisher. 'Momentum is the great thing in this business. I don't want it stopped for a moment. Wait a minute,' he said. 'It's too late to do anything now, and anyway it's the middle of the night back in England. Get a good night's rest, and if I pick you up before dawn we can go down to my place, I can show you everything I want and I'll still have you on the first plane to New York. You'll get something from there that will get you into London while the Dallas plane is still changing crew.'

'I don't know what I'll find back there,' said Arthur. 'Sukie

Smith is pretty determined. It's not just the feminist chapel, it's the whole union climate at the moment. They already have one strike on Fleet Street, so now they are talking about the tandem approach into the future. Sukie Smith wants our paper publicly declared a sexual-equality newspaper.'

'She's got that already,' said Fisher.

'What do you mean?' Arthur was puzzled.

'I mean you are all a bunch of sissies,' Fisher said.

13

Lino

On Mondays it was Hamish Grant's habit to pick up his Morning Paper at the station on his way in from the country. He would read it from cover to cover on his way in to Paddington and then feel well enough informed to fool most people by the time he arrived at the offices of his own Evening Newspaper. This Monday, however, there was no Morning Paper there. There was no paper there because the paper had not been delivered. The old lady who ran the newsagent's informed Grant that the wholesalers had informed her the paper was on strike.

Even without his own industrial problems, this sort of thing always made Grant out of sorts with the world. A chap had to be able to rely on doing the crossword in the Morning Paper before getting down to a day's work. Instead, he had to look out of the window at the housing estates. Acre upon acre of blasted grey brick boxes, their feet bogged down in grubby clay and H-antennae reaching as if for help into a sodium sky. He could not help thinking things were going to get worse.

On Monday morning, the amended Crumm Amendment was on Grant's desk. He read it through with incredulity. What had been one of Tibbet's frivolous hiccoughs on Friday night now revealed itself as a veritable leprosy of the extremities during the course of the weekend. What it boiled down to was that this fellow Crumm, a minor employee to whom no one had ever given a second thought, not content with all the benefits he had of secure employment and employment for his family, had dreamed up of a way of hyping up his boring life by charging the management twice for his time and that of his staff. Grant could dispute it, and he would, but dispute took time. Time was always on the side of the employee. The situation was such that, until this matter was settled to Crumm's satisfaction, he and the rest of the people downstairs decreed there would be no distribution of the paper.

Grant's last thought on Friday night was still his first best thought on Monday morning. Cheever knew how to handle his own kind. Get him to do something about it. He walked over to Tony Cheever's office.

Frank Morley was in it. 'I'm editing the paper today,' Morley announced smugly.

Actually, he seemed to be trying to move the refrigerator. He did not seem to care one jot that there was no paper to edit. He was balancing the refrigerator on the corner of the desk.

'Tony didn't tell you he was off to a course on the new technology then?' Morley was a master of one-upmanship. 'Lord Gold is anxious for us to move with these push-button times.'

Grant experienced a certain amount of enjoyment, watching Morley push and shove the fridge on to the desk, keeping a bright look on his face although the work was hard.

'At level three of management you are allowed a three-star freezing compartment in your cubby-hole,' Morley said, putting his finger next to his nose, the bewildering gesture of the street-wise. 'Am I right or am I right? How many stars have you got, Grant?'

Grant took his leave without bothering to answer. He would abandon Morley, electrical equipment still in mid-air, to his fringe, or should it be fridge benefits. He would make the direct approach to the man Crumm himself. He rang Crumm's extension.

The man sounded as pleased as Punch, as if he had just painted the Sistine Chapel single-handed overnight. He could hardly contain himself. 'What do you think of the Crumm Amendment, Mr Grant?' he said.

'I'm giving you the chance to take it all back,' said Grant. If he was the only remnant of sanity left, and it looked as if he was, he was going to nip this trouble in the bud with a firm attitude right now. 'If you can persuade them all to go back to work by the time of the morning edition, I promise you there will be no disciplinary measures for anyone.'

Crumm sounded disappointed. 'I can't do that, sir,' he said after a pause. 'Only it's not just me that's involved. It's out of my hands now.'

'You needn't be involved at all,' said Grant irritably. 'You can pick up your cards on the way out.'

Crumm wasn't in the least bit cowed. 'That won't get you anywhere at all,' he said, coming back quick as flash. 'You're living in the Dark Ages, if you think that's the score. You fire me and they'll all come out anyway.'

Grant sighed. Next thing he knew Crumm would start listing all his rights, and he didn't feel like listening to that. 'You are missing the point, Charlie,' Grant said wearily. 'You know and I know that you can put the entire print out of action, but what good will it do you if you kill the goose that lays the golden eggs?'

Crumm thought about that one. 'Of course, I am prepared to come to the table,' he said cautiously. He had heard this phrase used, though he did not quite know which table was meant.

'How about in the canteen in half an hour?' Grant suggested. To his relief it sounded OK to Crumm. There were plenty of tables there.

As Hamish Grant climbed the backstairs, he, who had resigned himself to imminent retirement, could not really believe he was taking such decisive action, but there was such a thing as being pushed too far. As he puffed up the stairs he saw a shadowy figure coming down them, trying to turn its face to the wall. It was wearing a raincoat with the collar turned up and a trilby crammed down on the head as if it had picked the props off a peg on the way to a film set and was playing the part of a private detective. Yet, for all the disguise, Grant was sure he recognized the gait. There was something familiar about the figure. It was the carnation in the buttonhole.

Then Grant did recognize him. It was Pringle Minor, the most narcissistic boy in school. He had first seen him in front of the practice nets in his Somerset prep school, all kitted out in brand-new whites by his *arriviste* family as if he were advertising some washing powder. Grant had never trusted Pringle's insistence on the appearance of things, thinking such people only skin-deep. All the same, other people had been taken in by him because Pringle had become editor of Britain's Oldest Newspaper. What on earth was he doing in this building now? As they both drew closer, Grant snapped to attention in a left-over ritual from those days.

Pringle straightened his old-school tie and threw back his shoulders. 'Where the hell is Cheever's office?' he asked. 'Reception sent me on a wild-goose chase. Some little girl with a degree in hairdressing.'

'Cheever's not there,' said Grant.

'Well, where the hell is he?' demanded Pringle.

'In Liverpool, at a course on the new technology,' said Grant, and immediately regretted it. One newsman could never withhold information from another in case it was thought there was something he did not know. This time he realized there was something he did not know. There was something extremely irregular about a situation in which Jeremy Pringle was creeping up the backstairs of the Coote building, his Jermyn Street shirt covered in ink. He looked a mess. What on earth was going on? Pringle Minor had never even been seen with the slightest grass stain on his cricket whites.

Grant's uneasiness made Pringle uneasy. 'See you at the point-to-point Saturday, will I?' said Pringle reassuringly, and continued his grimy way down the stairs.

Not for the first time since this strange set of circumstances began, a memory knelled in Grant's grey matter. Hamish had seen Pringle furtive like that once before and long ago. But it was no use lingering on the past. He had work to do. He put it out of his mind and carried on up to the canteen.

It irritated Grant to find Crumm was not yet there. He bought himself a cup of tea and tried to do *The Times* crossword but couldn't. It was not the paper he always bought which was part of his reassuring routine. There was nothing reassuring about anything this Monday morning.

Crumm was out of breath when he arrived. He was overweight, but it did not stop him ordering a bacon sandwich. He ate it by dipping it into his tea so that the white fat melted and left little greasy bubbles on the surface. Grant had to look away. He continued to gaze at ten down.

'What do you know? Trouble over at Fisher's place, too,' said Crumm jubilantly in between bites. He had altogether recovered his aplomb. 'That's why I am late,' said Crumm. 'That's why there are no morning papers. Do you know why there are no morning papers?' He leaned forward conspiratorially. 'I got it on the hotline. Industrial dispute,' he said triumphantly.

Grant shuddered inwardly and wished himself back in Little Nelling where he had spent all weekend trying to get his queen down from his apple tree. It had been a lot easier than anything he was doing now. He should never have left the place this Monday morning. The weather was lovely for the time of year.

'Damn Yankee, it's no more than he deserves,' continued Crumm. 'He'll have a full-scale shutdown before he can say Paul Revere. Coming over like that and trying to teach us our business. No one likes that sort of thing, you know. You should have 'eard 'em on the beaches, sir. They thought they won the war.'

Hamish sighed. 'This is forty years on, Charlie, let's get to the point.'

'This is the point, Mr Grant,' said Crumm. 'The point is industrial action's very contagious. You can't do nuffing about it once it starts. Industrial action is like wildfire. It's like a snowball. It grows and it grows and it grows, and pretty soon it's too bloody big to shift as much as an inch. I should know. My brother-in-law's in charge over at Fisher's paper.'

Grant nodded sagely. He knew all about the freemasonry of the underdog. 'Come off it, Crumm,' said Grant. 'I've heard of Spanish practices, but this won't wash.' Since the working classes had started going to the Costa Brava for their holidays it had given a new meaning to the old phrase. Every fiddle that every foreigner had ever dreamed of seemed to have been brought into play right here in the heart of London on English territory.

'This is not Spanish, this is not even Common Market,' said Crumm. 'This is American. Do you know what Fisher's done?

He's only folded the two papers into one. He's only fired the editor. If he can fire the editor, who else can't he fire?'

'Fired the editor?'

Now Grant did take notice of the fellow. Fired Pringle. This put a new aspect on him wandering round the backstairs. He did not know whether to be pleased or sorry at the sudden thought that, next time he went into Cheever's office, he might find Pringle in the editor's chair. Even the new boys had to watch their backs in this time of change. You only had to go out for a packet of cigarettes and they had your desk cleared out. If only they would clear his desk out, he could go home, always supposing the price was right, of course. If only he could be sure of that, but the fact of the matter was he could not be sure of anything any more, and though he had nothing at all in common with Charlie Crumm, he had that in common. He would appeal to their common interest now. Crumm had already said he remembered the days when every Englishman, no matter what their background, had loyalty to a common ideal.

'This makes it all the more important for us to stick together, Charlie,' he said. 'We've been through a lot together in our time, you and I,' he said. 'Remember all we've been through? Remember all those times we licked the competition, all because we got our newspaper on the streets first? Remember that? We got it out half an hour earlier. We did that together. Your lads drove their vans like kamikaze artists. Sir Aubrey was very pleased with you over that.'

'So he bloody should have been, pardon my language,' said Crumm. 'I did him a bloody great favour. I got 'em to get it out on the streets.'

'I organized everything upstairs,' said Grant. 'I got them writing earlier.'

'And they got bloody paid for it. They got an adjustment that year all right,' recalled Crumm. 'Bloody writers.'

'We couldn't do it without them,' said Grant.

'Bloody prima donnas with pens, that's what they are,' grumbled Crumm. 'There's more to a newspaper than writing.'

'You're right there,' said Grant. 'A newspaper is a very delicate equation of which you are a very important part, Charlie, and now more than ever before. Fleet Street is under fire from all sides and we newspapermen can only resist it if we put up a united front. We have always done that in the past. Haven't I communicated with you each new marketing *coup*? Haven't we put on circulation together as a result? Together, that is the word, Charlie. We were a team, upstairs and downstairs. It was a triumph for both of us.'

'You'd have never got the paper on the streets without my boys being agreeable,' squabbled Crumm. 'They bent over backwards to accommodate you over the years.'

'The reason they were bending so far is their pockets were weighing them down,' said Grant. He was losing patience with these reminiscences. 'We've had to pay a fortune for extra runs, extra circulation. Does that form part of your memories, Crumm?'

'Every penny I have contributed you have seen reflected in the share price, Mr Grant,' he said.

Hamish softened slightly. 'There's always cash in hand in it for you, Crumm.' The truth of that stung him not for the first time. Whatever he did, no one crossed his palm. His future was entirely tied up, his cash-flow petty, his luxuries gambled on the outside chance of Rum Baba running in a straight line past the winning post one day. To Crumm he simply said: 'Together we have solved it all. Let's solve this one, too, shall we?'

'Well, what do you think of it, then?' asked Crumm, leaning forward eagerly. 'My Amendment?'

'You can't decide the merit of a thing like this overnight,' obfuscated Grant.

'I can wait,' said Crumm.

'Everything takes so much longer than you think,' argued the managing editor. 'You and I may not even see the benefit before we retire.' As sure as he knew he lived in the past, he was sure the working classes lived in the present. 'Our lawyers will want to take it apart.'

'I'll get legal advice,' said Crumm.

Hell's bells, the man was not going to be put off. 'You do it your way,' Hamish said, 'and I'll do it my way. We'll win in the end. You can't win, Crumm. You don't generate anything.'

Insults were getting them nowhere, except well on the way to losing the next edition. Squabbling was useless. Challenge was no good. Grant tried pathos.

'You are going to get me fired, Charlie, and no one else is going to see you all right like I did.'

He turned sadly back to his *Times* and doodled with his fountain pen on the racing page. Neither of them knew where to go from here. Crumm felt strangely ashamed. He had nothing against Grant. It was true they had worked well together.

'Weather's nice for the time of year,' said Charlie.

'It is,' said Hamish. 'I've got my sweet peas in already.'

'Really?' said Charlie. 'Isn't it a bit early for sweet peas?'

'Mrs Grant likes to try to get them ready for the vicar's birthday,' he said.

'You could be unlucky with the frost,' said Charlie.

'Frost certainly looks bad for Bigcanter on Saturday,' said Hamish.

'That could do you a great favour, sir,' said Crumm. 'Rum Baba's never going to win.'

'You don't think so?'

'I know who is. I've got it from the horse's mouth,' said Crumm.

They looked down the list of runners.

'You might as well stick a pin in, the way you are going on,' said Crumm. 'That's your boy.' He pointed to a horse called Tough Nut.

'Really? How do you know?'

'Let's just say I know,' said Crumm. 'If I'm right, you owe me one, sir.'

'Look,' said Grant amiably, 'I think it is a good Amendment. I really do. I think there is something in it.'

'You do?' said Crumm. He was all right. Grant was all right after all.

'Yes, I think management will see very interesting break-through possibilities of the entire workforce co-operating in this sort of common venture when they hear about it upstairs,' said Grant, obfuscating grandly once more. 'I think there will be a promotion in it if you get them back to work, a promotion with increments. I'll see to it personally. What do you say, Crumm?'

Crumm did not know what to say. He was certainly tempted.

'Will you think it over?'

'I'll think it over, Mr Grant.'

Grant watched him leave, round and fat and suddenly responsible. He himself idled down the backstairs, stunned by modern life. In the past there had always been a set pattern to man's affairs even in the unpredictable arena of newsgathering. Some of the flashier graduates hoped for a war in a far-off place to distinguish themselves. Most contented themselves with showing off in the bedrooms and boardrooms in town. News reporters came up from their apprenticeship in the provinces. Secretaries, vans, sweepers, were local. Management took the global view: Aubrey's from an airliner somewhere over the Western United States, Hamish's from Little Nelling, ninety minutes down the motorway where the seasons passed as they always had done and the vicar's wife made apple jelly.

It was inconceivable that Crumm should break the mould. OK, he had shown a bit of initiative and that had fooled them all for a while. But he would not show stamina. He would not have the imagination to envisage the future. Five editions was all Grant would lose after all. In his heart of hearts, Crumm would be afraid of events over at the Daily Paper. Grant was a little more confident now he thought he could see a chink of light on the horizon.

14

Spike

'Good morning,' said Squiffy Spencer at the top of his voice, exactly three hours, fourteen minutes and three seconds later than he should have. Five little heads looked up from five ancient typewriters and five piles of dirty newspaper clippings. Five bottoms eased themselves back on their green swivel plastic-covered chairs and three pairs of hands lit cigarettes. Five pairs of knees crossed themselves in anticipation of the cabaret act they knew was to come.

Spencer was in an ebullient mood after a weekend in the country which had begun early on Thursday morning so that he had missed all the developments at the paper. Now he snaked out of his weather-worn, once-blond gaberdine great-coat with its brown velvet lawyer's collar and hung it on the peg along with all the other soiled outer garments. Fleet Street was a grubby place. No matter how much they earned, everyone in it looked slightly second-hand.

Under the coat, the lining torn but the Gieves & Hawkes label carefully stitched back in, Spencer was wearing a dirty blue pin-stripe suit of the same near-historical period, the trousers so tight that the outline of two handkerchiefs easily showed at the crotch. To complete the outfit he had chosen a heather-coloured lamb's-wool sweater and a cravat he had picked up from a wedding in Dorset stained with 1986 Windeshafenbundesfahrtenschattenhofen Frühlingsspätlese.

'Up from Snodgrass and Snoring, into the sun all the way,' he was explaining. 'Bad enough to begin with, what? Got up at 6 a.m. specially and I wasn't in bed till 4.30. You think I look bad; you should see Penelope. Shafted her up against the china

107

cupboard in the green drawing room, Sèvres old boy, 1742, the whole thing smashed. There she was flat on the floor, me on top of her banging away, right up in there and in comes the old man . . .'

'Her father?' asked the Skunk, wide-eyed. He was called the Skunk because of the strange way his black hair grew in a white streak over his forehead.

'Her father indeed, Skunky, who else? I don't mess around with the minions.' Squiffy lapsed into an imitation of an old man's voice, ' "Making the devil of a din someone, Spencer, think it's in the servants' quarters, distinctly heard the smashing of china. Good Lord, old boy, this *is* the servants' quarters. Didn't know you fancied the upstairs maid. Good for you, old boy, give her one for me. Must remember to sack the housekeeper. Won't have her hiring young gels with loose elastic." '

'I swear to you, Skunky, there I was putting it to his daughter and he never recognized her – never recognized his own flesh and blood with my immense member inside her.'

'Oh yeah?' said Beano. No one knew why he was called Beano, but it suited him. 'Pull the other one.'

Squiffy ignored him. 'Quite a houseparty I've been to while you were all mowing your lawns and clipping your hedges,' he said. 'Flicker Coote was there.'

'Flicker Coote?' they all said in unison. 'Not *the* Flicker Coote? Our very own Page Three girl? You don't mean the proprietor's wife?'

'The very same,' said Squiffy proudly. 'Flicker Coote burbling on about her long-lost son.' Now he parodied a high-pitched voice supposed to be Flicker's. 'Where was Michael Coote? Why didn't he do his duty? You brought children into the world, you fed them and nurtured them and gave them their freedom and what did they do with that freedom? They used it, ungrateful bastards. I like Flicker, but not in her maternal mood. Besides which I had other fish to fry.'

'Out of the frying pan into the fire,' rumbled Beano. 'You're late, old boy.'

'I can explain all that, Beano, old chap,' said Squiffy. 'The M1 closed, wouldn't you know, fog in the early morning. Devil of an inconvenience. Calculated I had only six traffic lights between me and the Rising Sun garage and there was the damn motorway closed. You know what? Guess how many gears I had? Two. And you know which? Fourth and reverse. You try driving up from Snodgrass and Snoring with just fourth and reverse when the motorway's closed. Shot three traffic lights just to get on to it, missing buses, milk floats, mothers with prams, Monday morning the whole bit, but at the fourth I had to stop. Had to or else curtains, finished, forget it, fucking great ten-ton lorry trundling across at right angles to me.' Squiffy made a lot of angular gestures with his hands. 'Suddenly I've got first gear back, now I've got fourth *and* first. I can start it in first with my foot on the clutch and off it goes *chug, chug, chug*, and every time I stop I have to do it again, 'cos it stalls, then straight into fourth, no control of the machine, and the M1 closed in front of me, so off I go twice round Breezing, down the castle hill in fourth, old boy, disaster, no first again by this time. By the time I'm coasting past the airport I'm in a real lather. At least £600 worth of damage, I figure. I thought it was a bit odd on the way out when the clutch fell out. For God's sake don't tell Penelope. It's her car!'

There was silence among the diarists. From the distance, through the glass partition that divided this office from the sports desk, came the thundering of an authoritative voice.

'Keep your fucking voice down, Spencer,' said Beano. 'Today of all days is not the day to create a disturbance. You should have been here three hours ago. Now pull your finger out while you are still fortunate enough to be an employed person.'

'Three hours ago! You're lucky I'm here at all,' responded the irrepressible Squiffy. 'I could be lying excessively close to the concrete on the M1 under a tangled heap of metal.'

'More like excessively close to Penelope under a tangled heap of bedclothes,' said Beano. 'Get on with it!'

'Jesus Christ, what a lay,' persisted Squiffy. 'I don't mind her hot, wet little body wrapped round mind any time. What's the matter, Beano? Jealous of my past?'

'Don't you notice anything different round here, Squiffy?' asked the Skunk timidly.

'Yes,' Beano took up the theme. 'Anything changed since you've been trying to screw the upper classes?'

'Not trying, old man, you misheard. Succeeding where others fear to tread. I don't have your hang-ups, you see,' said Squiffy. 'Phew, what a scorcher. Those titled girls go like trains. Talking about titled twats and all that,' he said, 'where's the Hon. Son. Fraser?'

No one could think of an answer to that one, and for a minute or two all the cacophany of newsgathering, the ringing telephones, the clacking typewriters, the barely repressed temperament which had been so much background noise, now came into aural focus.

'There are a great many people who would give a great deal to know the answer to that,' said Beano finally.

At this moment the door opened and a young man with a blond quiff walked in. Everyone stared.

'I'm Simon Lawrence Caulfield,' said the young man eagerly. 'I'm the new boy.'

They continued staring.

'I am the new appointment of Tony Cheever.'

The diarists all looked perplexed.

'Cheever, your editor,' said Simon Lawrence Caulfield brightly.

'Ugh,' said Squiffy.

'Ugh,' repeated the diarists all in unison. They had never been able to accept the appointment of Cheever to editor since he could offer them, of all people, nothing at all. No gossip, no connections. Cheever thought a connection was not missing the 10.58 to East Grinstead.

'We might need a second opinion about that,' said Squiffy. 'Where's Hamish Grant, our beloved managing editor?'

Beano explained that Grant had also not been seen that morning and that this was part of the problem.

'Name again?' said Squiffy looking at the newcomer.

'Caulfield,' the young man said. 'As in Holden. Simon, Lawrence as in D.H.'

'What is he talking about?' Squiffy asked Beano.

'Beats me,' said Beano. 'What are you talking about?'

'D.H. Lawrence,' said Simon Lawrence Caulfield. He was persistent. 'I'm related to him. I'm a writer. Writing is in the family.'

Five little people sat with their mouths open.

'If writing is in the family, sit down and write something then,' said Squiffy. 'Look at this overmatter. I'm supposed to print this? This stuff is about as topical as last week's shopping list. What we need is a lead story. This is your chance to prove yourself, D.H.'

The phone rang. Squiffy, who always answered other people's phones when he was bored, answered this one. 'That's a terrible story,' he said into the phone and put it down again. 'These publicists think you were born yesterday. They think the free press exists as an arm of the glorious modern drive to self-advertising.'

Squiffy looked satisfied with himself for one moment. Then he was on the move again. He looked around for the man who was called a boy whose job it was to fetch newspaper cuttings from the library and generally act as messenger and gofer for the writers and editors. He was asleep on the radiator.

'Boy! Get me the cuttings on the Maharajah of Gungapoor!' He threw the remains of a paper cup of coffee at him to wake him up.

'Marjorie who?' asked the boy.

'Is everyone pig ignorant around here?' said Squiffy. 'No wonder this is such a fucking failure of a newspaper. No wonder they are losing circulation.'

The phone rang again.

'Where's the fucking secretary?' asked Squiffy, who was already bored with the telephone game.

'Putting her tan on in the loo,' said the Skunk.

'Very, very idle, useless and ugly,' said Squiffy Spencer. 'OK, I'm taking bets on Grant's first words back,' he said. 'D.H.? What do you say?'

'The telephone is ringing,' said Simon.

'If the bloody telephone is ringing why don't you bloody answer it?' said Squiffy. 'Or do you expect me to do it? If so, you are going to wait a long time. I'm not your fucking slave.'

Simon answered the telephone. He looked momentarily pleased.

'Who is it, D.H.?' asked Squiffy. 'What's it about, D.H.? If it's a story, don't forget to check your facts.'

Simon put his finger to his lips.

'Don't sssh me, shitheap,' said Squiffy. 'Who's on the phone? What's the story, Simon?' Squiffy persisted, but Simon still did not answer. 'You don't even know what you are doing, Simon,' said Squiffy. 'One, write everything down in your reporter's notebook. Two, don't ever throw anything away. Three, spike all your notes when you have finished with them. Four, check the spelling, Simon. For Christ's sake get it right.

'Simon's on to something important,' teased the implacable Squiffy. 'Who is squealing to Simon? Which taxi-driver, which doorman? Or is Simon walking in the corridors of power? Tell me who it is Simon or I'll put the phone down on you.' Squiffy swung his padded trousers on to the desk next to the Skunk and held his hand up above the telephone like a guillotine. 'Simon can't take a joke,' said Squiffy. 'Simonpure. Who's Simonpure talking to? Is it the Archbishop of Canterbury?'

Squiffy's next move was to pick up the waste-paper basket. Then he did a little dance in front of Simon as if he was going to hurl its contents across the desk. Simon ducked in anticipation, but instead of hurling the green tin waste-paper basket, Squiffy turned it upside down on the newcomer's head, raining half-empty coffee cups and pencil sharpenings all over his blond quiff. Then, before he could fight back, Squiffy jammed the bin down over both his head and the receiver. When Simon earnestly continued with his telephone conversation, Squiffy's next move was to grab the sticky tape and wrap it round and round Simon, the telephone and the bin so that he was trussed up and could not move.

'Right, I'm making a book on Grant's first words back,' said Squiffy. 'Beano, you're on.'

'Get a bloody move on,' said Beano.

'Skunk?'

'Scoop, scoop,' said the Skunk.

'Simon?' There was no answer. 'Simon!' Still there was no answer, which, though hardly surprising in the circumstances, seemed to madden Squiffy more. Now he took the pen out of the new reporter's hand and then he took the notepad and threw them both out of the window. When there was still no reaction from beneath the waste-paper basket, he took a copy of *Burke's Peerage* from the shelf and aimed it at the side of the green waste tin. It missed and followed the reporter's notebook out of the window. 'Howzat!' he yelled. Squiffy seemed incensed. Next he took the typewriter in front of Simon and threw that out of the window, too. At this point everyone except the unfortunate taped Simon rushed over to see where the typewriter would fall. It fell down in the van bay where the van drivers had just finished having a meeting. Although they had finished the meeting they saw it fall.

When the diarists looked back, a most inelegant Simon Lawrence Caulfield was banging his little feet helplessly on the bottom rung of his green stool and waving round his grotesque green head while from it came the sound of a muffled yet magnified sob.

'Hold that just as it is!' said a voice from the door. It was Rizzi, the *paparazzo* photographer. 'Say cheese,' he said and flashed his camera at the waste-paper bin.

'Do you want to join our sweepstake, Rizzi?' asked Squiffy. 'Grant's first words back in the office? A fiver and you're in.'

'Scoop! Scoop!' said Rizzi.

'We've already done that one.'

'Very, very idle indeed,' said Beano, spotting the secretary returning from the loo, her face orange from man-tan.

'Very, very idle, useless and ugly,' said Squiffy. 'You do do shorthand, do you?'

She nodded sullenly, staring from the Skunk to Beano to Squiffy to the waste-paper basket.

'Right, make the book then. Grant's first words back.'

'Get on with it,' said Beano.

'OK. "Get on with it." Where's your money?' asked Squiffy.

Beano produced a five-pound note and put it on the table.

'Do you want in?' Squiffy asked the secretary. 'You can make £30 if you get it right. Lunch-time drinks on you.'

She was still staring helplessly at the apparition with the waste-paper basket on its head.

'Place your bets,' urged Squiffy.

Still the secretary could not speak.

'What are you?' Squiffy asked her.

'Very, very idle, useless and ugly,' she answered automatically. The book stood at:

Squiffy: 'Scoop, scoop.'

The Skunk: 'You're all fucking fired.'

Beano: 'Get on with it then.'

Rizzi: 'Lies, lies and damned lies.'

'The strike's still on,' said the secretary. 'That's what the managing editor'll say. That's all he's been saying for days,' she said.

'What strike?' asked Squiffy.

The door opened and Hamish Grant walked in. 'Who's Caulfield?' he said.

Squiffy scooped the money up from the desk. 'No win. This goes in the accumulator kitty. I get the use of it meanwhile. My sweepstake, my rules.' He put the money in his pocket.

Grant looked at the apparition wearing the waste-paper basket. 'What's that?' he said.

'Oh, that,' said Squiffy. 'That's Caulfield, the new boy.'

'Good,' said Grant, trying to remain calm. He was normally reassured by the freemasonry of their silly prep-school rituals, but now even the old order of things was letting him down. Pringle out of place and out of sorts, Aubrey's inaccessibility, Crumm's defiance – if worker–management relations had seemed complicated when he left the canteen, they now seemed impossible.

'We'll need an extra hand,' he said wearily, 'because you, Spencer, have some serious work to do. Ten minutes ago I would have been able to tell you that I had just come back from a successful meeting with Charlie Crumm, the van drivers' foreman,' he continued irritably. 'I was going to say that our little strike was over and you could all get down to writing some good stories for the readers, which is what you do for a living, I believe.

Unfortunately I can't do that now. I was all set to get the buggers back to work when something happened which was extremely ill-advised in the circumstances. The fact is one of Crumm's lads in the van bay narrowly missed getting killed by a flying copy of *Burke's Peerage*, hotly followed through an upstairs window by a Remington Upright,' expanded Grant. 'I am not asking who threw the offensive items because I can guess.'

It was all true. Grant had just got back from the betting shop where he had put some money on Tough Nut when Crumm had waylaid him in the stairway.

'I am sorry to have to tell you this, sir,' he said, 'but there has just been an attempt on the life of my lads.'

'Hell's bells, Charlie,' said Grant. 'Speak plainly. Whatever can you mean?'

'The fact of the matter is, sir,' Crumm said, 'one of my lads in the van bay has been the target for some flying missiles launched from an upstairs window of the building. It was a second-floor window, sir, leading me to conclude that the items came from the editorial floor. Not surprisingly, sir, the lads have decided to take this attack personally and there is nothing I can do about it,' Crumm concluded.

'Charlie Crumm has added danger money to the Amendment of his Amendment, based on evidence that there have been threats to the lives of his van drivers,' explained Hamish Grant to the diarists. 'Hell's bells, I've done all I can to stop the strike spreading. Now Aubrey will have to decide just how much his newspaper means to him. You have put in some time on the country-house circuit, Spencer. When did you last see Aubrey?'

'I've just seen his wife,' said Squiffy Spencer. 'She was burbling on about him selling the newspaper.'

'Find Aubrey,' said Hamish Grant.

'That'll be four-figure expenses,' said Squiffy, quick as a flash.

'Just get down there before the cashiers pack up as well as everyone else,' said Hamish.

Suddenly he was aware of standing awkwardly with a packet in his hand in front of a man wearing a Sellotaped waste-paper basket on his head. 'If you are Simon Lawrence Caulfield,' he said, 'this package has come for you.'

15

Fisher Ink

One way or another, Arthur was standing in the brown dawn at the front entrance of his hotel in Dallas the next morning to await the promised arrival of his new proprietor, Frederick Fisher. He was looking for a limousine. What arrived instead was a pick-up truck. There were four shotguns battoned on the back. At the wheel was Fisher himself. He was wearing jeans, ostrich-skin boots and a blue shirt that was so clean it looked as if it had been bought that morning and still had the cellophane on it.

'Get in, Arthur, what are you waiting for?' he said. 'You've got a plane to catch.'

Arthur got in. He was staring at Fisher, a very different Fisher from the man he thought he knew in London. His blue eyes were like two keen beams reflecting the colour of the shirt, but that was not what made him different. All this Fisher needed was a ten-gallon hat.

'Oh,' said Fisher as if he divined what Arthur was thinking. 'My clothes? Always blend in with the landscape, I've always done that. I don't ever want anyone knowing anything about me, not unless I tell it them.'

He drove with one hand on the wheel and the other he used for changing the radio stations. He seemed to like country and western music. He seemed to be looking for a particular song. He roved round the dial after it and whenever he tuned into the news he said 'Bullshit!' and tuned immediately out again. He swung on to the tollway, throwing some coins into the machine from a collection which he kept rattling around on the dashboard. Between the two of them was a telephone and a caddy for carrying

116

drinks. They were held rigid so they did not spill. Fisher had prepared two plastic glasses full of ice and purple liquid.

'Have breakfast?' he asked.

'No, actually,' said Arthur stiffly. He had had no time. Now he was hungry, apprehensive and out of sorts.

'I eat on the hoof,' said Fisher pointing to the caddy. 'Kool-Ade. One for you.'

'Oh, good,' said Arthur. He reached for his glass.

'Not now,' said Fisher firmly. 'Save your ammo. You'll be thirsty enough when the sun comes up.'

As he drove, the light was just coming over the rim of the horizon and spreading across the city. It changed from brown to pink. Just now it had a purple look. Fisher kept up a running commentary, looking around him all the while. His subjects were history, demographics, politics, housing, the poor, all delivered like a barrage of gun-fire against the melancholy twanging of the western guitars on the truck radio.

'I love this country,' he said. 'Couldn't live anywhere else in the world. Your place is sitting in the dark compared to this. You gotta let some light in. You really do. I mean it in more ways than one,' he said.

They were driving out of the city now towards the east.

'Down there's my ranch,' Fisher said. 'Two hundred acres, small for hereabouts, but big enough for me. We're not going that way today,' he added. 'My home's my own and I don't ever let anyone in, not ever.' He drove on. 'I shoulda shown you our only tourist attraction,' he said, 'where a man died at an assassin's hand. You remember that, Arthur? A man who was President of the United States?'

Arthur looked back apprehensively through the rear window to the buildings he was leaving behind. As the buildings got sparser, he felt more and more insecure. He was heading out into Indian country with a man whom he thought was crazy. A man who had no rules but his own. He had broken down the past into easily assimilable thoughts and had become a self-appointed prophet of the future. Nothing seemed to hold any complications for Fisher. Arthur looked at the telephone. It was his only contact with the outside world. He felt as if he were riding in a pressure cooker on a hotplate which was the whole hyped-up state of Texas.

Again it was as if Fisher divined what Arthur thought. 'Telephone won't ring unless Melanie's in trouble,' he said. Now he sounded tender. 'Melanie's my little daughter. She's the only one can call this line. Relax, Mitchell,' he laughed. 'You think I am crazy, don't you? You aren't the first to think that and you won't be the last. If I'm crazy, the whole goddam place is crazy. I grew up in this state and I know everything about it, but it ain't so different from any place in the world when it comes down to it. Leastways, the people in it aren't any different. Men are what they are, Arthur. Mostly they lie to themselves, but I don't make that mistake. I'm different. All my life I've made it my business to know about men. But really to know, Arthur. No illusions. Do you think newspapers are about making a better world, Arthur, or reporting the one we have, warts and all?'

'A bit of both,' said Arthur, hedging his bets as usual.

'Wrong,' said Fisher. 'Warts sell newspapers. Warts have built me everything I have. You know what, Arthur? I hate people, but I love their warts.'

Arthur thought that a very cynical thing to say, but he said nothing.

'People are shitty, cowardly, feeble hypocrites. Men are fickle and women are inconstant. They are all cheats, fools, liars and self-deceivers – and what's more, they will do anything rather than admit it.' He laughed at his joke.

Fisher continued driving. By now he had reached the open road, going like a bullet out of a gun into the rose dawn in the east. Faced into the rising sun on a level with the windscreen, Arthur could see nothing. He could only feel the motion and hear the whirr of rubber on concrete beneath him. He hung grimly on to the dashboard of the pick-up truck. Big bold cars sidled comfortably past them on either side.

'I've never had any use for fancy automobiles,' Fisher was saying. 'Never had any use for fancy anything. Always have driven one of these ever since I had my first permit to drive,' said Fisher. 'That's when I started up my first delivery service. Every night before I went home I piled as many papers as I could into the truck and drove 'em all round the neighbourhood. 'Most everyone subscribed to that service. I put the subscriptions in the bank and that helped me buy my next newspaper.

'I learned a lot of things just driving around, Arthur. I love to drive on the open road. It reminds me how life's a raw ribbon and man just a tiny fly-blown speck on it. Ain't nobody gonna do a thing for him unless he does it himself. Not everybody knows that, Arthur, but that's what they should know. You know why I love it here in this part of the world? Because that's what the geography of this place teaches you. I take my instructions from it. Most folks sit on their porches all day long waiting for something to come to them. You can see them doing that if you drive around. I don't sit and wait. Not me. Ain't nothing gonna come to you, Arthur, not unless you meet it more'n half-way. I built my own porch. I fix my own air-conditioning. It wouldn't matter to me if I was the last man on the planet, I'd fix myself up somehow. Meanwhile I just drive around. I just drive around and keep my eyes open and that's when I see life. That's when I hear the stories men weave to keep themselves alive.

'When I bought my first newspaper I always brought in some story for them to print the next day. That's how I started my syndication service, too. Fisher Syndication, so fucking simple it was a piece of brilliance. Every paper I bought bigger 'n the last I syndicated the news right back to all the little ones. That way I opened up their sights and cut down all my expenses. You can draw on Fisher Syndication back in London, too,' he said. 'Make up your inside pages well ahead of time, concentrate on hitting them with the late news.'

On the horizon was a second patch of light like another sun in the wrong part of the morning sky. As the truck approached it, it grew bigger and bigger, filling the open space till Arthur could see it was a building. It was made of green glass and it rose like a greenhouse out of the flat, bland, arid countryside. Suddenly Fisher veered off the highway and was careering across the front courtyard of the building. One side of the building, with its grid of glass panes, caught the rising sun like a ball in a basketball net and held it suspended there. That was the light Arthur had seen from afar.

'Look at it, don't you love it?' grinned Fisher.

He slammed on the brakes of the pick-up truck, locking the wheels into a skid and turning it neatly round through ninety degrees till it came to a full stop in front of the entrance. No sooner had the truck stopped than he was out of it and through the automatic doors. Arthur ran behind him. In Fisher's hand was the plastic mug from the truck caddy.

'Wait a minute, I'll get mine,' said Arthur.

'Later,' commanded Fisher. As he walked he drank a bit and rattled the ice round in the liquid. 'Fisher Ink,' Fisher threw over his shoulder, barely turning around.

They had entered a marble-lined atrium full of plants, each one as tall as a house back home. The fierce sun shone through the roof, but inside the climate was that of a pleasant English spring day, slightly on the chill side. There was even bird-song. It was recorded. On one wall of the atrium stood a bank of lifts. Frederick stepped inside one which was waiting just for him and produced from inside his pocket a small key that he inserted into the control panel.

'Your little girl settle in all right?' asked Fisher once the doors were closed behind them.

Arthur shot him a look. Did he mean Sonia? Who else could he mean? But how did he know about her? Arthur could not think of anything to say. He was aware that Fisher was looking at him intently, as if consumed by all the possibilities of the answer. Arthur felt guilty. Then he felt jealous at the thought Fisher might meet Sonia. Then he felt better because Fisher had said he had no dealings with women.

Arthur did not know that Fisher had built a tower round himself. That it was a tower built of glass and bricks and pre-stressed concrete and all the materials of the buildings of all his empire, of the balance sheets and the computers and the scraps of daily news that fed them. That he had padded it with the minutiae of his own daily routine, with airline timetables and the baseball game, with the meanest task that needed doing on any part of his estate, all with the single objective of being totally independent in life. That he did indeed think that women were insane and men were greedy, but the knowledge did not stop him longing for perfection and a pact between the two. Arthur knew none of this. He only thought that Fisher thought he was guilty of bringing a woman into these things. Arthur feared Fisher as he feared everything, because of what he thought he thought.

As luck would have it, he was saved from having to answer the proprietor by the arrival of the lift at the penthouse floor. The doors opened into a huge close-carpeted room filled with three banks of computer screens.

'This is my centre of operations,' said Fisher. 'I can call up anyone anywhere in my buildings anywhere in the United States on these screens.'

Arthur thought perhaps this was how Fisher had learned about Sonia. Though the man talked all the time, facts, figures, theories, memories, he never fleshed himself out. Arthur realized uncomfortably that it was as he himself had warned, that he knew nothing really about him.

'So far that excludes the London end of the operation,' Fisher continued, 'but it won't be long now. Look,' said Fisher.

He settled himself at one of the screens, spread his long legs out before him and keyed in some instructions. The lean figure of a middle-aged man appeared on it, his skin pickled and pocked with sun. He was sitting at a desk with his feet up, surrounded by screens and telephones and eating popcorn out of a giant paper bucket. There was Muzak in the background.

'That's the editor of my Beaumont paper,' said Fisher.

Arthur winced. Just how could anyone write fine prose with Muzak playing? You had to have dirty linoleum on the floor. Preferably the roof had to be leaking. Good prose meant bad debts, he was sure that was how it was done. You had to suffer for art.

'He can't see me on his screens, but I can see him,' continued Fisher. 'That's the beauty of it.' He switched to another screen. 'This here is my circulation manager in Wyoming. They had a good break there. A mass shoot-out in a shopping centre. Some kid went crazy. I can either ask my manager the figures or I can cue them in myself. That way I double-check. Look. This is how I send a message to him.' He pressed a single button. 'Right on there!' appeared on the screen. 'Here's another: "Up yours, buster!" I have a bank of messages like that. Sometimes, very occasionally, I add a new one. Then they really know they have gotten to me. I have a whole in-house newspaper on these screens,' he said. 'A notice-board, a message desk, births, deaths and marriages, the transitions of all my employees. They can switch jobs, house-swap, there's even a dating bureau. Pretty good for a guy who started out life with nothing but the good fortune to be the nosiest kid on the block?

'You wait, Arthur, till you are in on my system. The beauty of everything I do is it is so simple. Simplicity will make your life a whole lot easier, too. When we have this system working over there I can call you up in person wherever I am. My plans are pretty far advanced. You see, I always knew I was going to get your paper. I had a premonition, a flash, a dream, a memory almost. Yes, it was like a memory of something I already had. You wanna know how I knew, Arthur? I knew because I always wanted it. Do you have a son, Arthur?'

The man could not seem to stick to a train of thought. It was what made Arthur fear him. He was sure he must be dangerously stupid.

'My son is a haemophiliac,' Arthur said.

'A what?' said Fisher.

'Like the last Tsarevitch of Russia,' Arthur explained, although it did not explain anything at all. It brought back uncomfortable memories. 'He's at special school. Today's his half-day.'

How far away that all seemed, the conversation with Nora and Laurie's outing to the Tower of London. How long ago it was, too. Yesterday he had been editor of a different paper.

'I never had a son,' Fisher was saying. He was thinking what on earth did Russia have to do with anything? Unless this guy was a Commie. That would explain it all. He might be a double-agent, a goddam spook, for all Fisher knew. It would explain all this indecision, this trying to do two things at once, which in Fisher's book was beginning to border on immorality. It would explain why Arthur hated America. He had heard him say that back in London on the telephone in his office. Now he was trying to pursue an affair and learn a new job. The guy wanted everything both ways. He put the thought on hold for the time being and continued speaking.

'But if I had had a son,' said Fisher, 'apart from the gift of health I would have wished one other thing on him, that he should know what he loved. It's easier that way. I have always had that going for me. I know what I love.'

He switched subjects again. 'Come, I'll show you what is going to happen to the London end.' He picked up the telephone. 'That reminds me,' he said. 'What's the time in London?' he asked. 'How many hours' difference?'

'Six,' said Arthur.

'Whole world should be on the same time.'

'Then half of them would be in darkness all day,' Arthur said.

'They'd adapt,' said Fisher. There was a pause. 'Humans always adapt,' he added darkly. He punched a number. 'What's new?' he said into the phone. Jeremy Pringle, who had been waiting to get this call over with so he could go and complain about Fisher at his club, told him Tony Cheever was at a conference on the new technology.

'Shit,' said Fisher. 'The Evening Paper's on to the new technology already?' He did not bother to explain anything to Arthur. 'I gotta move faster than I thought.' He put the phone down, cued up a file on the bank of computers and produced a set of architectural plans and finished drawings of a glasshouse set by the Thames. It was a blue glasshouse this time, and it rose right up out of the blue water into the blue sky like a cathedral made of light. It did not look like a newspaper office at all.

'Fisher Dock,' he said. 'Good name, huh? It's as if it was always meant to be. We are going to get you out of that mausoleum you inhabit. I'm going to build you a palace, Mitchell, a palace of technology. You're going to love it.'

'We've done pretty well in our mausoleum,' said Arthur defensively.

'Shit!' said Fisher, taking no notice of him. 'Goddam. System's crashing. Look at that.'

Arthur looked. The screen had gone blank but for a ribbon of computerese instructing everyone to log off.

'Technology,' said Arthur smugly.

'Ain't nothing wrong with technology,' said Fisher. 'Trouble lies with stupid people who can't figure technology out.'

16

Lady Chapel

While Arthur was trying to get a proper night's sleep in Dallas, Sukie Smith was finding it all too easy to fill her chapel meeting in London. It was a Sunday and no one had anything better to do. This was the best entertainment around.

The feminist branch came in force. Even those women who had not been working for years were delighted to lend their support to a really important cause. Just for starters, everyone on maternity leave turned up. The room was full of suckling mothers, of fathers with babies strapped to their backs in aluminium frames, of crawling infants spread out on chain-store sheets decorated with teddy bears or flailing their chubby limbs with frustration in striped pushchairs. They were joined by everyone on sabbatical, and everyone on sick-leave who had miraculously risen from their beds.

Sukie's acne had flared up since this American sex-maniac dared to call her 'baby' in the kitchen. It was not just the insult, the man had also cost her money. She had had to call her alternative doctor and go on a Vegan diet to counteract the collective poison released into the ether by all red-meat-eating males like this Frederick Fisher. The guy obviously ate half a cow for breakfast. He would follow that up, no doubt, with sausages, bacon and eggs sunny side up, the whole lot covered in maple syrup and washed down with a couple of pints of milk. It was the accumulative aggression of this macho diet that had led him to do the sinister thing of which he stood accused. He had tried to subvert the morals of an impeccable British thinking female by insinuating that both he and she were tarred with the same brush. Why else would he have called her sister?

This was just the beginning of Sukie Smith's long saga of woes. She thought something ought to be done about it. Fisher ought to do something about it. Fleet Street ought to do something about it. But most of all, the government ought to do something about it. The Prime Minister herself had a lot to answer for. Sukie went methodically through the agenda she had drawn up for the meeting of the feminist chapel, and when she had finished she received a standing ovation from all those who had somehow managed to stay awake. A vote was taken and carried unanimously that the complaint would be put before the Equal Opportunities Commission and the following recommendation made, subject to discussion.

1. The word 'baby' must not be used in the newspaper or in the building in which the paper was produced, no matter to what or whom it might refer.

Even the reference to a person smaller than adult could not be condoned since such reference was a form of discrimination against small people, implying, as it did, that the person had less experience than another person and therefore less competence and was somehow small of mind as well as body.

There was a bit of a problem over spin-off or compound words containing the suffix or prefix 'baby'. 'Tar-baby' was completely out on several counts, though mainly because of racism. The word 'babywalker' posed a completely different kind of problem. No other alternative readily came to mind to describe this method of infant locomotion, which was demonstrably popular at the meeting itself with several kamikaze kids careering round the floor in their plastic vehicles while their mothers wrangled against the din. The word 'infant' itself was a problem. You could, of course, indicate the passage of a being through life by mentioning his or her or rather its age at every juncture. In the old days, indeed, this would have been recommended to students of journalism as handily providing a thumb-nail sketch for the readers as to the subject's experience and appearance. Nowadays, however, this sort of pigeon-holing could give rise to the accusation of ageism.

It was therefore recommended that any concept giving rise to any such form of prejudice be radically avoided and another word be substituted altogether for the word 'baby'. Now all that remained was to decide which word. To use the word 'small' about a person was inevitably to belittle them, therefore small would not fit the bill. To use the word 'child' was to invite the adjective 'childish', which was a form of denigration. After much toing and froing it was decided that the only acceptable substitute was the word 'person' itself. The motion was carried unanimously.

2. The word 'sister' should henceforth be deleted from the vocabulary of Fisher employees and the style book of Fisher newspapers.

At first it was thought the obvious substitute would be 'female brother' until it was pointed out that any qualification of the word 'brother', especially through the addition of adjectives normally reserved for the distaff branch of humankind, would somehow imply a lesser or younger brother. For a while the term 'sororial person' seemed a possibility, yet again the sticking point was the diminution through qualification. A sororial person was not a fraternal person, and the distinction immediately invited some form of comparison and therefore discrimination.

The feminists were hopeful they had hit on a solution with the word 'sibling' since it could describe a sororial sibling or fraternal sibling, but after a while there were various factions who were unhappy with sibling since its most usual overtones were those of sibling rivalry. It was felt it was essential to indicate to this sheriff from Texas, who was in danger of mistaking the West End for the Wild West, that competitiveness of any sort was considered directly against the policy of this newspaper. No sort of excellence could be condoned unless everyone had some of it. Some trouble-maker was worried about the definition in this case of the word 'excellence', and this occasioned a popular move to accuse the word itself of élitism and have it banned from the dictionary. A discussion was launched about wordism at this point, but this discussion was wisely shelved till later because there were several people whose nappies needed changing.

So, after much discussion, it was decided that the only acceptable substitute for the word 'sister' was the word 'person' itself. Once again the motion was carried unanimously.

The motion having been debated to this conclusion, it was obvious that Fisher had been guilty of sexist discrimination in uttering the words 'baby' and 'sister'. These insults would never have been addressed to a male member of the staff, thus obviating the necessity for Sukie Smith's reaction.

It was further agreed, moreover, that Fisher would never have dared to insult any male employee by taking him into the kitchen and trying to humiliate him by firing him expressly in such domestic surroundings. At this point in the discussion, a most interesting dilemma arose. In order to eliminate any possibility of this sort of humiliation in the future, there would seem to be two obvious courses of action. One was to eliminate the word 'kitchen', the other was to eliminate the object kitchen. At first this second course of action seemed altogether preferable. But though the kitchen itself should be eliminated, provision could still be made for those endless cups of tea and coffee without which a newspaper would never make it to the presses. It was agreed that the kitchen could be eliminated by the provision of a vending machine in any open space with no specific designation.

On the other hand, it was pointed out, the end-result of the provision of such a vending machine was that some employee, usually female, would regularly be sent to said vending machine to bring back those polystyrene cups of beverage invented to save the humiliation of washing the dishes.

The fact that females tended to volunteer their services to perform these mundane tasks only served to underline their perennial exploitation activated by years of sociologically inspired masochism. It was decided that this masochism would always be perpetuated unless every employee had it written into their contract that they had equal, indeed compulsory (say, every half-hour) access to the vending machine. It was important to make it compulsory, otherwise the more kind-hearted would offer their services and be exploited for the offer, and the betting was the kind-hearted would be female. To get round this, a secretary and an editor, any employee in whatever capacity and indeed a proprietor should all fetch their own coffee on the half-hour.

At this point someone put their hand up and objected to the word 'employee' as a word that implied a form of formalized subjugation open to exploitation and discrimination. Someone else suggested the word 'personnel' rather than 'employee', but yet again it was agreed that a slight aura of inferiority attached to this word as well. It was therefore suggested that the only suitable word for use in these circumstances should be 'person' and the motion was carried unanimously.

Now the question remained from what source this person should fetch a cup of coffee. Even a vending machine had to be placed in some area, which, if it were not called 'kitchen', had otherwise to be defined and was likely to be defined as menial the moment it was put to practical use.

A good hour was spent summoning up all the associations of the word 'kitchen'. A kitchen, it was generally agreed, invoked by historical definition the image of a servile female busying herself with menial tasks. The feminist chapel asked themselves what synonyms they knew for the word 'kitchen'. Some idiot suggested 'scullery' and was cried down. A scullery was even worse, for it was the province of a poor lowly creature called a scullery maid. The word 'bar' was discussed for a while and then rejected because of certain overtones of heartiness which might encourage any lingering macho streak, if there was such a thing in any newspaper person.

Finally the chapel came up with the word which was irrefutably perfect because it had no overtones at all. The word was 'room'. A kitchen and any other division of space such as lavatory would henceforth be known as room. The motion was carried unanimously.

There remained one task. It was to get the objection down on paper, after which it could be sent to Frederick Fisher. Now it was important to describe precisely what had happened and between whom. The feminists, however, found it impossible to address Frederick Fisher as Frederick Fisher since the first name, with its exclusively masculine associations, immediately invited some contrast with the name Sukie, with its exclusively feminine associations. Even the reduction to the formal Mr or Ms invited the same comparison. A satisfactory solution was finally found in referring to Fisher as Fisher and Smith as Smith, whereupon the incident could be described to the satisfaction of everyone present. Until someone raised their hand with another sticking point. This was that, since Fisher was known to be the proprietor of the newspaper and Smith known to be his employee, even to use this basic nomenclature on top of this knowledge was to prejudice the issue. In order to reduce this to its barest unprejudiced bones, it was agreed that any such appellation was impossible. The only logical thing to do in the circumstances was to describe Fisher as person A and Smith as person B. Whoops, no, that would not do, since the one came alphabetically *after* the other. For a similar reason, in that the one came numerically after the other, person one and person two were no sort of a solution. Neither could there be any question of a person and another person, another being an adjunct and an afterthought and therefore inferior.

They decided to adjourn the hour of decision while they discussed the right and wrong of Frederick Fisher interfering with Sukie Smith's personal habits, namely, her right to smoke a cigarette when and where she wished. It was generally agreed that smoking a cigarette represented exactly the same sort of right as wearing your personal choice of clothes to work. If the right to smoke cigarettes was not preserved, then pretty soon Fisher would have them all in uniform. If, indeed, he was allowed to dictate any part of their daily intake, whether it be into their lungs, their stomachs or even their minds, this represented a form of manipulation that would very probably end up in something completely unacceptable, namely, overt censorship. Frederick Fisher had tried to patronize Sukie Smith by telling her that smoking was bad for her health. It was Sukie Smith's opinion that she should be allowed to take strychnine in full view of everyone if she so wished.

She now expounded at length her theories of personal liberty. It was her view that the age of personal patronage had died because personal relations between people could be guaranteed to bring out the worst in them. Sukie Smith maintained that satisfactory relations could be forged only with a satisfactory ideology which must be reinforced by law. There was no law against cigarette smoking, even if it killed the lot of them. Sukie Smith felt that there was only one way this could be made quite clear, and that was by upholding right up front the right to kill oneself as one of the inalienable rights of any contracted person. Not only would they have the right to a proper funeral and memorial service at the expense of the newspaper, but their heirs should have the right of inheritance of the vacated job.

It was all becoming excessively complicated. People were having temper tantrums, demanding toast and Marmite and clearly needed to be put to bed. The feminist chapel decided to confine themselves for the time being to the description of the main incident. This was how the incident, in which Sukie Smith had been taken into the kitchen by Frederick Fisher and there fired, was finally described to the satisfaction of all present:

'A person in a room had addressed a person and called this person a person. He' – whoops, the 'he' was struck out and replaced by the gender indeterminate word 'person' – 'This person had furthermore addressed this other person as another person.' There was still some dithering to do over those 'others', nevertheless the memorandum finished up triumphantly, 'What was the person going to do about it?'

17

Stone

The packet was full of amyl nitrate, hash, coke and qualudes. It had arrived even before she put the phone down and was immediately cleared by security. Simon Lawrence Caulfield, now extricated from the green waste-paper basket, looked at it in dismay. How could he explain to Sonia that, even with her veritable cornucopia of recreational aids, he still had not done anything about his passion? He picked up the telephone to East Grinstead. Every time the phone had rung since he met the beautiful Diana he had rushed to answer it. But it never had been Diana. How could it be? She did not have his telephone number.

He had spent a terrible weekend. He took out his boy-friends, he took out his girl-friends. He grew pale with frustration and dull with lack of inspiration. He could not concentrate even on his writing career because he could not put pen to paper without composing poetry to the beautiful Diana. He wondered not what his lusty namesake, D.H. Lawrence, would do, but just how he would manoeuvre himself into position to do it. SLC knew that girls were made vulnerable in order to be defiled, but just how, in this world which had moulded him into a cool dandy and master of brinkmanship, should he regain, feel familiar even with those anarchic, primeval urges?

In his quest for a solution to all this, he wrote again and again with his fountain pen in his brand-new reporter's notebook the name DIANA CAULFIELD. He made anagrams of his name joined with hers and discovered that, within the two, lay the erotic words 'more sin laced in a field', apart from other more banal variations. Prompted by this, his idea of bliss became to get Diana Cheever in his clutches in a rural situation. When the

132

telephone rang on his first day at the Diary on the Evening Newspaper, he had thought it might be her. It was Sonia.

'You've got my job if you want it,' she said, coming straight to the point as she always did. 'You can tell them as far as I'm concerned they can stuff it because I don't need it any more. The great Arthur Mitchell has whisked me away from all that bullshit,' she boasted. 'He's made me into features editor on his brand-new Weekly Newspaper. Someone told him Cheever wanted to promote me and the next thing I knew he had forced a plane ticket into my hand.'

'There is just one problem,' Simon Lawrence Caulfield answered. 'I've fallen in love.'

'That's wonderful,' said Sonia.

'It's agony,' he spluttered, for it was at this point that the waste-paper basket was jammed down on his head.

'What is wrong with you?' Sonia said impatiently.

'There's still a problem,' Simon said. He was trying to breathe.

'You haven't fucked her then?' Sonia had said.

'How do you know?' He was breathing heavily because the waste-paper basket would not move.

'If you had, you wouldn't be behaving half so wetly,' said Sonia. 'You've got to do it, Simon, one of these days.'

'What do you mean? I did it with you.' He couldn't get the damn thing off.

'No, you didn't.'

'Yes, I did.'

'No, you didn't.'

'Yes, I did.'

'Well, if you did I didn't notice,' said Sonia. 'On the whole, a girl likes to notice if she is getting laid.'

'She's not that sort of girl,' wailed Simon. It was too much for a poet to be treated this way, inhaling bits of polystyrene coffee cups and pencil sharpenings.

'Don't be silly, darling, everyone's that sort of girl,' said Sonia. 'At least, everyone I know is.'

'You'll get an unmentionable disease with your behaviour,' Simon said.

'Nonsense,' she laughed. 'I'm being good. Well, quite good. I've bought a condom for my vibrator. Well, who is she then, Simon?' asked Sonia.

Very painfully, under the circumstances of sitting with a waste-paper basket on his head, which made him feel even more masochistic than usual, he outlined the fact that she was a married woman and listened to Sonia's peal of derisory laughter come down the phone. 'Married women like getting laid best of all,' she guffawed. 'Listen, I know all about married men, darling. They never pay any attention to their wives in case it saps the energy they need to fool around. The more successful they are, the worse it gets.'

'Poor darling Diana,' said SLC with feeling.

'Successful men think a dull marriage is the highest compliment they can pay to a woman.'

'I'm going to save her from all that,' said Simon Lawrence Caulfield. He meant to just as soon as he could untangle his present situation.

'Tell me who she is and I will help you,' said Sonia. 'I've got some brill new stuff.' Then she had called her friend on the other line and had the packet of stimulants couriered over to the wonderful white wedding-cake building. 'The editor's wife! Brill!' she said. 'It'll be a super scandal.'

'I doubt it,' said Simon tragically. 'Nothing really terrible will happen, you'll see.' He sighed. 'I'll probably go off her. Oh, if only I didn't. You know me, darling, I never want anything unless somebody else has got it.'

When everyone sloped off to lunch he took his courage in both hands, removed the waste-paper basket and called Diana.

'Diana Cheever speaking.' She had an amazingly experienced and throaty voice over the phone.

'You probably don't know who I am,' stuttered Simon Lawrence Caulfield, and then added his full name for good measure. 'That's Caulfield like Holden Caulfield and Lawrence as in D.H.'

'D.H.?'

'Lawrence.'

'D.H. Lawrence?' the throaty voice said. 'Are you trying to sell me something? If so, I've got it. I've got the *Encyclopaedia Britannica* and the *Reader's Digest*. I've got the hundred best poems in the English language. Goodbye.'

'Diana,' Simon wailed. He thrilled to her irony. Who would have thought as much of such a beautiful girl, or that she should live in East Grinstead? Simon Lawrence Caulfield's world stopped at the World's End in Fulham. No matter, he loved her more than he could say, and love, so the poets said, conquered all. He was specially thrilled to be speaking to her on the very instrument her consort had placed at his disposal; this was a form of cuckoldry: to think that somewhere within the mysteries of the PBX all three of their voices might be simultaneously wired up, and that he, her dauntless lover, was sticking her oafish old man with the bill.

'Who are you?' she snapped. 'What do you want?'

'I have written you a poem, Diana,' said Simon Lawrence Caulfield.

There was a silence.

'Are you calling from the paper?' she asked. She knew it. The guy was a nutter, just like everyone else on Tony's staff. 'If you have a problem, don't bother me, tell my husband, will you?' She sounded affectionate, almost as if she were smacking a baby's bottom. 'He's not here now.'

She had to get this loony off the phone because she had left some fish fingers under the grill. Just who was this jerk, and why did Tony leave his private number lying around the office as if it was the hotline to the local bin? She didn't want to be in charge of the strait-jackets. The democracy of newspapers was all very well, sure, anyone was supposed to be able to get hold of anybody at any time, but from the kitchen she could smell the fish fingers burning.

'I know he is not there, Diana,' said SLC. 'That is why I am calling you. This has nothing to do with your husband.' He took a deep breath. 'I think I am in love with you, Diana.'

This time there was another sort of silence. It spelled out that Diana Cheever was interested. 'Hold on, there's someone at the door,' she said. The fish fingers, what there was left of them, were levitating in the form of ashes into the open-plan hall.

'When's tea ready?' asked a childish voice.

'Watch television,' she said. 'You're not having any.'

She snapped off the grill and returned to the telephone, passing the hall mirror as she did so. Fuck domesticity, she thought. She was a good-looking woman and this boy was telling her what she wanted to hear. He had noticed her when she had not noticed him and that was at least a step in the right direction. When could it have been? At the Evening Newspaper drama awards or the annual Woman of the Year lunch? One function blended into another. For Sonia was right, although Diana Cheever did not know Sonia. Mrs Cheever could count her marital rights over the past few months on the fingers of a double amputee.

She never complained, although she was considered awfully unliberated by the other members of her local self-help therapy group. She tried old-fashioned methods like white satin night-gowns slashed to the waist in both directions. She whispered erotic endearments into her partner's ear. Tony flicked her away like an annoying mosquito. He remained blind and deaf and fell asleep muttering things about morning conference, circulation boosts and whether the company could be persuaded to allow him a German rather than an English car. She didn't complain because, contrary to what the group-therapy classes thought, it wasn't sex she really wanted, at any rate, not the sort of sex she was likely to have with Tony. She wanted passion. She wanted the insane whisperings of two unrealistic romantics. That was what you did not get when you were an older woman, which was why she would now handle this boy very carefully, in case there was anything in the situation for her.

When she came back to the telephone she sounded very young and eager.

'Let me meet you again,' begged Simon Lawrence Caulfield. 'We could have lunch together. The moment I saw you I thought you were the most beautiful girl I had ever seen. I was consumed with envy that you should be going home with Tony Cheever and not with me. When will you lunch with me – tomorrow, Diana?'

18

FOC

Crumm had been confused when he left the canteen after speaking to Grant. For a while, he had been tempted to see management's point of view. Had he overstepped the mark by challenging the Establishment head-on as he had done with his Amendment? Were things more complicated than he ever dreamed in the candlewick comforts of his bedroom, safely tucked up next to Mrs Crumm? At the instigation of a mere Crumm, the great presses stood still and the vans were motionless in their loading bays. As Crumm came down the stairs, he could see the drivers next to the vans, toasting their idleness with a crate of Four X. They were playing cards on upturned boxes and listening to their Sony Walkmen, resolved to do nothing more onerous till management took a clearly conciliatory position over the stoppage. The realization made Crumm more than a little afraid. Surely all he really wanted was a quiet life? Was it not better, as Grant and he had discussed, to cultivate sweet peas than unrest? He was tempted to call the lads off. It was Monday; they could get off to a fresh start and pretend all this never happened.

It was as Crumm had stepped out on to the van bay thinking these things that a copy of *Burke's Peerage* landed at his feet, hotly followed by a Remington Upright. He looked up. The book and the typewriter must have come out of the window on the editorial floor. The buggers were raining missiles on the workers now. Not content with suppressing any enjoyment they might have in life, they were trying to kill them off once and for all. Crumm felt a shaft of betrayal to his heart. How could he have ever entertained the thought that the men upstairs were on his side? He felt his wavering resolve strengthen. He turned right round and met

Hamish Grant coming out of the betting office, where he had sent
him with his tip, but he had no smiles for the managing editor
now. No way would he give Grant the go-ahead he wanted to get
the presses moving again. Instead, Crumm went back upstairs to
find Tibbet, the circulation manager, in his office, determined to
add to the Crumm Amendment a draft clause about danger money.

'I think you have had a stroke of genius here, Crumm,' Tibbet
said, slapping him on the back. 'I am proud of you, my son.'

Crumm preened himself and pushed out his pouter chest.

'With any luck I think we can bring the whole bloody lot to a
full standing stop for the whole of the summer,' said Tibbet.

Pinned on the wall behind Tibbet's desk was a map of the
metropolis. It was big. It was so big it gave you pause for thought.
Crumm took a felt-tipped pen and marked the Evening Paper
offices with a red cross to show his achievement so far. He looked
at the main artery of Fleet Street running parallel with the river
and the side-streets which led off it on either side at the edge of the
City limits. This was the heart of the newspaper business, and had
been for two centuries.

'Like a spider in its web,' Crumm said. 'Fleet Street,' he said.
'Why do they all stick together?'

'So the people upstairs can control it better,' said Tibbet. 'They
all went to the same school. They all think alike. They all meet in
the same clubs and pubs. If you could just separate them up, think
what would be in it for us.'

'Here's the body, here's the legs.' Crumm pushed his metaphor.
With a blue felt-tipped pen he marked the routes the vans took
from the various newspaper offices scattered down the side-streets
above the River Fleet to the mainline stations where they put the
bundles of papers on to trains to distribute all over the country.
'It's a money spider,' said Crumm.

'A fucking great money tarantula from the size of it,' said
Tibbet. He rolled up a copy of the newspaper and gave its image a
swot.

Crumm imagined the huge money spider squashed and oozing
money into all the gutters along the route and everyone bending
down to pick up its life-blood, which ran gold, like money itself,

and stuffing their pockets full of the stuff. 'I need a drink,' he said.

'You deserve one.' Tibbet offered him a can of beer. 'I like the irony of it, Charlie,' he continued, stroking his moustache. 'There's something neat about a transport union bringing the whole paper to a grinding crashing halt.'

Crumm snapped the ring on the can and enjoyed the drink. He did not usually drink on duty, but today he was aggrieved. He was thinking. 'I've been thinking,' he said.

'Easy does it,' said Tibbet. 'It's an ugly thing, brain strain.'

'What I've been thinking is this,' he continued, ignoring him. 'I've been thinking we ought to act quickly.'

Ever since that cosy little chat in the canteen with Hamish Grant, Crumm had been disconcerted, and that was before he had narrowly escaped with his life from the onslaught of murderous missiles from the editorial floor. He had realized how easy it was for something to go badly wrong with his plans. In among all the brotherly love and pulling together, what Grant had really pulled was rank, which was always the way out of the bosses. If Crumm allowed himself to be intimidated by that, which was easily done by the workers, all would be lost. All through British history they had never really made the final push. At the last minute they had sunk back into lethargy and thought somebody else would handle it all.

The same thing could easily happen now. The spider would wriggle out from under the newspaper and go on its merry way. The Crumm Amendment would be torn up and thrown into the waste-paper basket. Crumm's finest hour would be as the twinkling of an eye. He would lose his chance for immortality. He must not let this one go. He figured a fate that had taken Cheever out of town to Liverpool must be on his side. If Cheever was there, Cheever might just handle it. Now it dawned on Crumm that he did not want it handled. He did not want it smoothed over. Crumm had been given another break by fate, and that was the dispute at Fisher's Sunday. Industrial action was in the air, it was fashionable again.

Again he thought about the conversation with Grant. Lawyers, the managing editor had said. Management had them coming out of every orifice, trying to confuse the workers. In order not to be confused, Crumm needed professional advice. To get professional advice, he needed the solidarity of his brothers to let him take his Amendment to headquarters.

'This is just the tip of the iceberg, Tibbet,' Crumm said. 'You know that, don't you? It's been given to me to see the writing on the wall. As the future got closer, we have all been wondering what will happen to us. The printers have been wondering loudest of all. Us vanmen have hardly had a look in all this time. Now I, a mere vanman, see you can't hold back the future, lads. We got to stare it in its ugly face. The way I see it, they got us all on the run with the new technology,' he stated slowly. 'Mark my words, it will come. I mean, if they can put men on the moon, they can print without printers, no problem.'

'That's right, my son,' agreed Tibbet. 'There is no doubt this is just another example of the sort of exploitation we have had to deal with ever since the days when printing began.'

'They will print without printers and they will distribute without vans,' Crumm said. 'I don't know how they'll do it, but they will. We got to nip it in the bud right away. They may be cleverer than us, they may be richer, but we still got our rights.'

In the canteen he had seen just how deviously clever they were. Hamish Grant pretended to be discussing horses and sweet peas, but what he was actually doing was working on an offer which Crumm would not be able to refuse. To achieve the immortality that was his due, Crumm must put the strike beyond Grant's reach and beyond the reach of everyone at the Evening Paper.

'Our only safety lies in numbers,' he said. 'One paper is not enough,' he said.

'You're right there,' Tibbet cheered him on again. 'If we can only get a sympathy ruling from the other outlets, you are on to a sure-fire winner. You're half-way there with those feminists down the road.'

'Yeah, well, I don't trust them,' said Crumm. 'In my experience, last thing you need is a woman on your side.'

'There's still some real men around,' said Tibbet. 'If we have

140

got them on our side we can use them to crumble the others. We can take out the telly companies by some judicious interpretation of the agreements. They need a lot of transport. We can take out the limo drivers. We can stop deliveries of the pork pies to the canteen. You watch those pinko lefties squeal if they have to pay pub prices out of their secure salaries just like everyone else. You've blazed a trail for the van drivers of this world, my son. Pretty soon the whole bloomin' universe will know about you.'

'You've got it,' said Crumm. 'This definitely calls for a sympathy strike. We gotta take it to the union. We must arrange a vote. We need leaflets. We'll need a text. We need some inspiration.'

The beer crate was empty. As Tibbet and he were about to go off to the Printer's Devil for a celebratory noggin, the telephone rang.

'It's for you, Crumm,' said Tibbet. 'It's only the bloody telly,' he said, put out that it wasn't for him. 'Fuck me if you're not famous already,' he said.

'Crumm here,' said Crumm. He did not really like talking on the telephone, but this was going to be one of the burdens of the mantle he had made for himself. His medium was the soap-box, personal contact, the beery sweat and disgruntled monosyllables of the downtrodden. 'Yes,' he said. 'That's right . . . Do I get paid? . . . Right, you're on.' He put the receiver down. 'They only want me on the bloody box,' he said.

'I told you you were famous,' said Tibbet, full of resentment. 'What do they want your ugly mug on television for?'

'I told you the Crumm Amendment is going down in history,' said Crumm.

'History! We're a part of history already, Charlie,' said Tibbet. 'Dead and gone. The whole world of print, and that includes you and me. You're a dinosaur, Charlie, like the rest of us.'

'Not actually,' said Crumm.

The germ that had germinated just before the telephone call was popping in his mind. So far it was no bigger than a tiny alfalfa sprout, but it was there all right. He would not explain it to Tibbet till it was a piece of perfection. He could already feel the envy in the air. That telephone call in front of his colleague had been badly timed, yet there was another sense in which it had come to push him just when pushing was most needed. Crumm realized that he was being worried by destiny because he was a man of destiny. Destiny had its teeth into the seat of his overalls, he mused. He might as well admit to himself that he was on to a very fertile streak. He had no idea to what he should attribute this run of luck, but he knew it was his turn to run with the ball. He couldn't quite put his finger on what he was thinking yet, but he knew there was something there. Something Tibbet had just said had fertilized the little sprout. Something about being a dinosaur, because he was a man of the print and television being the world of the future.

'That'll be the logical end of it all, no doubt.' He looked mournful. 'I might as well get some practice in now. The logical end of the new technology is to stick it all on the TV screen. Ceefax the whole blooming lot of it and leave the trees standing where they are. By rights, in a hundred years or less, we shouldn't need paper any more.' He could feel his argument coming on. 'But for one thing,' he said. 'Your intellectual classes are not prepared to do away with paper, see. Your intellectual classes want it all down where they can see it, where they can keep it in their stuffy libraries gathering dust. I mean, what's so great about the Dead Sea scrolls? Because they were scrolls they were great. It wouldn't be the same had they been Dead Sea silicon chips.'

'That's a point,' said Tibbet.

'It is a point. It's very refined point,' said Crumm. 'I mean Dead Sea silicon chips aren't worth nothing without a Dead Sea computer, are they? I mean, haven't we got a case in point upstairs? I mean, didn't they put the whole goddam library on microchip when previously they had been stuffing the cuttings into paper envelopes for one hundred years, and didn't they have to dig out the paper envelopes again to satisfy the intellectuals? Yes, they did. Your intellectuals wouldn't use your bloody microchips, see. Your intellectuals don't dig microchips. You know why?'

'Because intellectuals have got bad eyesight,' said Tibbet.

'That's partly why,' agreed Crumm, 'but there's another reason, too. You've got to get inside their minds to understand the reason why. You've got to roam inside the grey matter. It's because of their egos, that's why. The way they look at it, anyone can have a computer, and if anyone can have it there is no ego gratification involved. We got a big job ahead of us, brothers. It won't be easy but, if we stick together, we'll win. There's safety in numbers. We got to get that sympathy vote,' he said.

In a straight fight between personal egos, Grant would be bound to win, but not if Crumm summoned the collective ego of the working class. Crumm realized that he was going to have to tell Grant there was no chance of a deal. 'This is Union business,' he would tell him importantly. 'You can shove your newspaper up your arse.' Well, that's what he would like to tell him, anyway. How dare the managing editor think he could buy a man like Crumm away from his destiny with a few tips on sweet peas?

19

Flong

Simon Lawrence Caulfield was determined to take Diana to the trendiest restaurant in town, which happened to be her husband's favourite also. The moment she stepped out of her taxi in Covent Garden, she had an odd premonition that her life was about to change. It had been so long since she had done anything like this that she was horrified to find herself completely befuddled by the big city.

This had been becoming more and more apparent even as she dressed for this important lunch-date, which had come completely out of the blue. First she tried on her blue suit, then she tried on her green dress. If she wore the green dress, could she wear it with the blue shoes? On the other hand, if she wore the blue shoes with the blue suit, did that look overdone? She washed her hair three times. Then she chopped a bit off the front. How were they wearing it in London these days? Never mind, it was raining anyway. The shoes, the hair, her beige coat, everything, would undergo a watery change.

Would he recognize her when she stepped in out of the rain? For by now she had convinced herself she really had met Simon Lawrence Caulfield before. She looked at all the pictures of the young reporters in the newspapers she used to line her larder shelf. She hadn't been able to find his name. As she handed her folding umbrella to the head waiter, she wondered for an instant of panic what she was doing there at all. Perhaps her husband himself might not be safely tucked away at a conference on the new technology in Liverpool but lunching right here at the very next table. Perhaps they would all be found out.

'I'm Mrs Cheever,' she explained to the greeter guiltily. She chided herself immediately. How clumsy she was to reveal lovers' secrets. Of course, Simon Lawrence Caulfield would have made sure they were alone.

'Mr Caulfield is already here,' the head waiter said, and she blushed as she thought she detected a look of conspiracy on the man's face.

She did detect a most peculiar look on the face of Simon Lawrence Caulfield as she joined him at the table. She blinked at him in the half-light. He was a fish-like young man, and she knew as soon as she looked at him that she had never set eyes on him before. Her heart went out to him immediately, for he looked even more vulnerable than she felt. The moment he saw her he seemed to be searching around for help as if he was about to succumb to a heart attack or a strangulated hernia or both.

'Mrs Cheever,' the head waiter obliged.

Simon Lawrence Caulfield extended one limp white hand fragilely in her direction. He seemed to gag on his own oxygen supply, then he turned his blushing face to the pink tablecloth. The head waiter settled Diana in the booth opposite Simon Lawrence Caulfield and put a huge menu in both their laps which prevented them having to look into each other's eyes, indeed, made such a thing physically impossible. Diana's heart beat faster in this clandestine situation. After a while, she tried peering round the menu. What she saw made her certain she was on the brink of romance. The child opposite her was still hiding behind his menu, overcome with embarrassment in the presence of his love-object. Where had they met and why had she forgotten it? For an instant she felt like a very young girl again, with no idea what lay ahead in the script. Then Simon Lawrence Caulfield put aside his own menu and raised his watery eyes. She smiled. Even in the bad light she could see that he returned her trust with a look of ecstasy. Or was it ecstasy? It looked more like frustration. Then it turned to disappointment. Then, not to put too fine a point on it, to hatred. Diana Cheever, in turn, at that moment hated all men.

'I'm overcome,' said Simon Lawrence Caulfield.

'There's some mistake,' admitted Diana.

'I didn't say that.'

'Wrong girl?'

'What are you eating?' said Simon.

'The most expensive thing on the menu since Tony is paying for it,' she said.

Simon Lawrence Caulfield looked momentarily interested in her hatred. 'Tell me all about yourself,' he said. As a reporter, he would have to cultivate a sympathetic interviewing technique. They ordered a very small meal which was an age in coming and she had plenty of time to trot out her small life.

'I'm a housewife with two children,' she said. 'What more is there to say? On Saturday I go to the supermarket, on Tuesday I go to the gym, I do pottery on Wednesday, and group therapy on Friday. There's nothing wrong with any of the group who go to therapy. They only wish there was. I live in a mock-Tudor house conveniently near the crematorium. I am not the most beautiful girl in the world.'

'That's not true,' he lied.

'Don't lie,' she said. She couldn't eat a thing. She did not care to finish her expensive fish dish.

'Would you like something else?' It was a *tour de force* for Simon Lawrence Caulfield to show such sustained interest in someone other than himself, but after all, she was the editor's wife. Or was she? 'Aren't you enjoying your lunch?'

'No, since you ask,' she said. 'As a matter of fact, I don't like any of the things my husband pays for.' She found herself saying it just like that. How had it come to this? She had been bored but content. Now she was frustrated and full of vengeance. She was driven mad with it.

'I am the wrong girl, aren't I?' she said.

'You're not the wrong girl for anyone,' said Simon Lawrence Caulfield.

'I'm not the one you fell in love with?' She did not wait for an answer. 'Do you normally fall in love over lunch?'

'All the time, I am afraid,' said Simon Lawrence Caulfield. 'Each time I pray it will be the last time. I'm such a horribly untrustworthy person.'

'Was she very beautiful, the girl you fell for this time?' asked Diana.

'Exquisite,' Caulfield replied.

'A young girl?'

'A young boy-girl.'

'About how old?'

'A nymphet.'

'A working girl?'

'A free spirit.'

'Dark? Fair?' Diana Cheever rearranged her tight blonde curls.

'Darker than dark. A passion fruit. Exotic.'

'But who was she?'

'I know nothing about her but her first name. Diana.'

'Like mine. How convenient!'

'A coincidence.'

'He introduced her as his wife?'

'He introduced her as Diana, I just assumed.'

'Creep!' said Diana.

'No, I'm not, really I'm not,' said Simon Lawrence Caulfield, who always assumed people were talking about him.

'I'm sure you're not. I'm sure you are very sweet.'

She didn't blame this idiotic young man, she blamed herself, her own gullibility, her own curiosity, no, her own wishful thinking. She looked at her watch. If she had been her own person she would have been playing bridge right now in East Grinstead. Or was today the day for the gardening lecture? Or was she supposed to be buying gnomes for the old lady in the almshouse to stick next to her crazy paving? Or was she quilting for Jesus that afternoon? Or collecting for the Scouts? It was a stupid life she led. That was the conclusion her curiosity had led her to, coming into town like this, hoping she was going to take a lover. She must have been wanting to prove to herself how stupid her life was because she had been planning to chuck it all along.

Despite her romantic notions, Diana Cheever was a practical girl who had married Tony after an ugly divorce suit by his first wife because she thought it was one way to get out of the typing pool. She had married against her mother's wishes. 'If he leaves one woman, he will leave another,' were the older woman's most conservative observations. Diana had tried to be loyal to her original hopes and dreams, but now she had that feeling that every woman dreads, that her mother was right after all. She was unused to the smooth tones of young socialites, and she wasn't at all sure what Simon Lawrence Caulfield wanted, but as she listened to him she knew what it was she wanted. Her husband Tony, whose hair and teeth made every woman swoon when he made his television appearances, had a social life she could only imagine in East Grinstead, but in East Grinstead the imagination of every woman was rife. Now she knew what her revenge for that would be. To begin with, it would be to live her own life.

The charmless child opposite was trying to say something. What was it he was trying to say?

'You're very sweet, too,' was what he was trying to say. 'I mean, you are quite fanciable really.' He took her hand over the table. 'If you want to go to my place I don't mind.'

What was it Sonia told him he had to do with the amyl nitrate to turn himself on? With the hand that wasn't holding Diana Cheever's, he fished in his pocket for the instructions.

'What?' said Diana Cheever.

'Shall we go to bed then?' he asked.

'I think I am going to be sick,' said Diana Cheever.

'Oh, for Christ's sake, not here,' said Simon Lawrence Caulfield.

20

Binned

'This is too boring, darling,' said Flicker Coote to Squiffy Spencer when the number seventeen failed to come up on the roulette wheel for the sixth time. 'Let's go some place for a night-cap.'

'What a good idea,' he answered guardedly. He tried to look at his watch without her noticing it. After his long weekend, he was supposed to be in the office by 7.30 in the morning for his turn on the stone, and by then Grant was relying on him to come up with a solution as to the whereabouts of Flicker's husband Aubrey. He had just six hours to do it in and, given the amount of energy he had been expending in the country, he was exhausted already.

Flicker noticed him looking at the watch. There was not much she missed, although she had had three Tequila Sunrises at the Zanzibar, two Harvey Wallbangers at Langans, a Manhattan at the Groucho and had repaired for two bottles of champagne while they had been gambling, leaving her dinner totally untouched. She was on a diet.

'You're right. It's awfully late, Squiffy. Let's go to my place. I've got some Moët & Chandon on ice. Vintage.'

'But what about Aubrey?' Squiffy began hopefully. He knew Flicker would never tell him anything directly, but perhaps he had stumbled on a way of flushing him out. 'I mean, he probably wants to get some sleep. What with the bloody strike and everything.'

'Darling, since he's discovered sex he never sleeps.' She paused. 'What strike?' she said.

'Oh, Flicker.' She really was too much. 'The paper. The paper's on strike,' he said. 'Your paper. Aubrey's paper. The family paper. Not that that's any problem for me. While the presses gather dust, I gather material. Race you to Tramp.'

149

'The paper on strike?' said Flicker. 'I thought I read it in the hairdresser this afternoon.'

'That was last week's,' said Squiffy.

'They all look the same to me. It's a frightfully boring paper anyway,' said Flicker, flicking her hair out of her face, which was how she got her name. 'The trouble with Fleet Street is it doesn't actually know anything at all.'

Squiffy looked at her sharply.

'I'm right. They always get the wrong end of the stick,' she said. 'No one ever finds out what the real people are doing. Aubrey, for instance.'

'What do you mean?' Squiffy was filled with hope again.

'How the fuck should I know what I mean?' said Flicker. 'I'm drunk. If I could read what I mean in the paper it would be worth buying. What I mean is, I don't want to see Aubrey ever again,' she said. 'What I mean is, I don't ever want to see his name again. In print. I never want to see his name in print. And if you write about him I'll go straight to Bleidenstein and sue you.'

'Oh, come on. Aubrey likes to keep his name in the news,' said Squiffy.

'Leave me alone,' said Flicker. 'There's no story.' She was smearing lipstick, without the aid of a mirror, way beyond the outline of her large mouth. 'What do I look like, darling?'

'Lovely,' he said reassuringly.

'I didn't take off my clothes all my young days for all those sex-mad lensers only to be plunged straight back into the orphanage when they had finished drooling all over me,' she said.

Now what was she talking about? Squiffy leaned back in his chair and pretended to draw an invisible violin bow across some invisible strings. In all the years he had been escorting Flicker when she couldn't find anyone else to escort her, she had stuck to this ridiculous story of herself as a Dr Barnado's child. But none of the facts checked out. Flicker had reinvented herself the minute she met Aubrey.

'Come on, you were never in an orphanage,' he tried again.

'How do you know?' she said.

'You're a liar and my heart bleeds.'

150

'I'm not going to lose out now, Squiffy. Aubrey is not going to do this to me. Come on, let's go home.' She leaned out into the road and hailed a taxi. He thought she was going to fall flat on her face into the gutter, but at the last minute she righted herself. In the taxi, she said: 'Anyway, what happened to you, Squiffy Spencer? Why do they always call you Lady Di? Why don't they ever see you with any other women? Why don't you ever get married? Or are you just in love with me?'

Flicker was in her three o'clock in the morning mood one hour early, which filled Squiffy with some hope. There was only one problem: in all the years he had known her, however drunk she got she never seemed to spill the beans.

'You know I am in love with you,' he said as he always did. 'There's only one problem with you, why did you ever marry Aubrey?'

To his surprise, Squiffy Spencer saw Flicker Coote become strangely emotional at this point, emotions which he could not necessarily put down to her phenomenal consumption of alcohol.

'Aubrey. I really admired him,' she said. 'I wasn't much of a catch, actually. Just a Page Three girl and lucky to be on page three. OK, I was beautiful. I was ravishing.' She took out her lipstick and missed her mouth once more. 'We were both beautiful. We were young. I adored Aubrey. He hated his family. I hated mine. We wanted to fuck all of them. You see, we had a lot in common. I guess I wanted him as much as any man before or since.'

Squiffy Spencer squirmed. True Confessions of this nature were not what he expected. He peered out of the taxi into the night. Mayfair, where she lived, was a long way away yet. She might still spill the beans in this mood.

'He was tall and straight as a die,' she was saying. 'That's the upper classes for you – nothing if not well-made. He used to say, "You are magic, my little Felicity." Aubrey was the only one who ever used my real name. Flicker, Fee, Flickarse, they all called me. Not even my mother used my real name. I didn't want much from Aubrey at first. Just to touch him, and not his bloody cock, like you're thinking, Squiffy. I wanted to touch his hair. It was so clean. He was so clean all over. They had a bathroom attached to every room in Coote House. He could make me do anything just to touch that clean hair.'

Squiffy Spencer looked at Lady Coote and thought she looked like a panda. The kohl that she put on her eyes was rubbed all round her cheekbones and up into her plucked eyebrows. 'Actually, his cock was not much,' she said viciously all of a sudden. 'You haven't missed anything. But shit, I loved him. Michael has his hair, only a darker version of it. In other respects, I am glad to say, he takes after my side of the family.'

Squiffy saw his opportunity. 'Where is Michael?' he asked. But Flicker just shrugged her shoulders as she had during the weekend in the country. The whereabouts of the son and heir had always been as much of a mystery as Flicker's past. Why hadn't he stepped forward to protect his patrimony instead of letting his old man sell it off to a hypochondriac upstart like Baron Gold? The taxi stopped outside her imposing address.

'I've brought you home,' said Squiffy.

'I knew you would, darling,' she said drunkenly. 'You've got to take me in now I'm here, otherwise I'm going to fall over and frighten the servants.'

The apartment in Mayfair was covered in pictures of Aubrey and Flicker. It was as though, if no one had recorded Flicker's life in minute detail year by year, it would not have existed. There were silver-framed photographs on every available inch of space; on the mantelpiece, the grand piano. Over the fireplace there was a terracotta pastel sketch of a young boy in a smocked romper suit, and in the corner, on the marble plinth, a terracotta bust of the same boy. Michael.

After another bottle of champagne and a game of snooker, during which Flicker ripped up the blue baize table of which her husband was particularly fond, she said, 'I'll give you a blow job if you like.'

Squiffy declined. He had always been afraid of two-way mirrors. Now he had video-recorders to add to his list of traps prepared by the aristocracy for unsuspecting hangers-on. They were just some of the trappings of the way of life he studied so

Binned

assiduously but declined to join. They wouldn't have you, anyway. They had you up to a point, then, when it suited them, they always reminded you that you didn't fit in. This was exactly the sort of occasion where they would come out on top. Squiffy tried to imagine Aubrey suddenly stepping out of the bathroom, inviting him to look at a play-back of Lady Coote with his employee's cock in her mouth and asking him what he proposed to do about it. Squiffy, on his salary, could not afford that sort of behaviour.

'You can always pretend it's Aubrey attending to you,' said Flicker. 'If that is why you never married.'

Squiffy still declined. 'Go up to Aubrey,' he said. 'He'll be glad to have you home.'

'Home, where's home?' she said. 'Home is in New York or in Accron, Ohio, or wherever it is that silly ding-a-ling little bit of dinge of his flies. He follows her half-way round the United States in case she feels tempted to give anyone else a blow job in the aft toilets. Get him back for me,' she said suddenly.

Her tone of voice was so heart-rending he realized it meant she really thought she was in danger of losing her husband.

'Stay the night, Squiffy, I can't stand to be alone. I'll do anything you want. I'll give you some head or you can go to sleep. I'll tell you stories. I'll tell you gossip. You need a good column. For after the strike. First one back has to be marvellous.'

'Oh, Flicker, I can't stay.' The fabric of his whole life was always threatened by the drunken upper classes.

'I'll take the duvet, you take the coverlet,' she suggested. 'We won't do anything at all. You don't have to get in the office early. There's no paper.'

At that moment the phone rang. Squiffy Spencer saw Flicker Coote snatch if off its cradle as if her life depended on it. She said nothing, just dissolved into the most heart-rending, nerve-wracking, pitiful tears of such genuine feeling that Squiffy was completely lost. He had never felt anything remotely as much as she appeared to be feeling now. She put the receiver down and stared at it for a long while, sobbing.

153

'Who was it?' Squiffy asked after a decent interval. She didn't answer, she couldn't answer.

'What was it?' he tried.

'It was Barbados,' she said after a very long time.

'What did they want?'

'Nothing,' said Flicker. She was staring like a person who had lost all interest in life, like a person who was completely numb, like a dead person.

'You must tell me,' said Squiffy. She was feeling so much that he almost knew what it was like to feel something through her.

'It was only Aubrey,' she said. 'You don't have to worry about being here. He rang to say he won't be home tonight.'

Squiffy stayed, of course, and in the morning they were found curled up where they had passed out by Flicker's Filipino man-servant, who was employed because he did not speak enough English to betray her even if he wanted to. Squiffy was in a panic. It would be the second day he was late for work, but Flicker put in a call on her private line to show that nothing was going on there at all.

'You knew all along that the paper was on strike, didn't you?' asked Squiffy over breakfast. 'Oh, my God, what is that?' One look inside the silver dish that Manuel had laid out on the sideboard and he felt horribly sick. He put the silver cover back quickly.

'Kedgeree,' said Felicity. 'Don't be silly, darling, I don't know anything. You know I am just a dumb failed model.'

'I fancy you rotten whoever you are, even in the morning,' said Squiffy. It was what she needed to hear. 'Michael again?' he said off-handedly. On the sideboard there was a photograph of the same boy in the terracotta pastel. He was a teenager now. It was in a twin frame with the photograph of the freckle-faced man with the too-wide mouth of the provincial farm boy whom Squiffy recognized as Harry Coote.

'Yes, Michael,' said Flicker. 'Michael and his grandfather.' They were more alike than father and son. 'Oh, my head. Put some vodka on my cornflakes, darling, will you?'

'You look quite different when you talk about Michael,' said Squiffy. 'You really love Michael.'

'Of course I love Michael, he's my son, my son, conceived out of wedlock, the biggest commitment a woman can make.'

Squiffy nodded. So that was how Flicker got Aubrey to marry her. It wouldn't happen today. Today the foetus of Michael would be dismembered in some gutter and they would go on in their several selfish ways.

It was as if Flicker read his thoughts. 'I just wanted something of Aubrey's. It was Harry who wanted me to marry him,' she said, fondling the photograph like a talisman. She put her lips to it and kissed it. 'After that I was bound to. Harry always got his own way. Harry said you could have anything in the world so long as you wanted it enough. It didn't awfully matter to Harry what people wanted so long as they wanted something. Harry wanted his newspapers. I wanted Aubrey. But Aubrey never wanted anything, including me. Harry thought I could make Aubrey want something. That's why he encouraged the marriage. It was just about the only thing in the whole world Harry was ever wrong about.'

Squiffy winced. The woman sitting in front of him with a monumental hangover was just a little girl, even if she was Lady Coote. Like any little girl, she was looking for a father and a lover. It was why he shied away from women, never expecting he could be either to them, never mind both. Women expected you to be able to perform so many roles, and he could only keep one relationship going at once, the one he had with himself. I guess that's why I am a stupid diarist, a voyeur, he said to himself, a liar and aggrandizer, committed to the queer inside of me. Out loud he said: 'Harry made his bed by giving his son an odd ambiguous name like Aubrey. There's a lot to a name, Felicity. Aubrey is not the name of someone who wants to get his hands dirty down in the machine room.'

'It's the name of someone who trolls the world and never settles down,' said Flicker. 'It's the name of someone who can't resist anything that catches his eye. But he won't settle down this time with this ding-a-ling any more than he has in the past. Do you know what happens to beautiful girls, Squiffy?' she suddenly asked, wide-eyed. 'You don't know what is bound to happen to beautiful girls?' she repeated.

'What, then?'

'They become mothers,' said Flicker. She dug into the plate of cornflakes soggy with vodka. 'This is absolutely disgusting,' she said. 'Open the champagne, darling, what are you waiting for?' When she heard the pop she immediately felt better.

'Aubrey can humiliate me all he likes,' she continued. 'He thinks I am just a drunken old punch-bag who will lie down for good if he hits me hard enough, but he will never get rid of me. I can roll with the punches and what's more he will be glad I am there in the end because Aubrey's the name of someone who will always need a mother.'

Squiffy, the newspaper man, wondered how on earth she could hurt that badly. 'Well, Michael's a bold name,' he said reassuringly. 'Perhaps he will look after you.'

'Bold? Ordinary, Aubrey said. Ordinary, like me,' said Flicker. 'But I had Harry on my side over that name.'

'What's in a name?' punned Squiffy. 'Well, what did become of Michael?'

21

Second Deck

Michael Coote was reading Karl Marx in the common room of his Oxford college when the porter came to tell him there had been a call from his mother. The raw machinery and labour power of the old revolution had become the superstructure of the administration and the relations of production. Things had become bogged down over the years. Whither the revolution now? It needed the capitalist classes to rise up, the independent dreamer to fight as dirty as the opposition, but they couldn't even smooth their own paths because they didn't have the taxi money.

Michael looked out of the window at the charming quad of the college, founded in 1292. He was frozen to his extremities, inhaling the stench of wet rot, and he had twisted his ankle on the cobbles. The injury had laid him up and given him more time than usual to think. Though he was only an hour's ride from London, he was completely out of touch with what was going on in the capital. He might as well be in another galaxy, on a planet where men had green heads and toes growing out of their noses. It had been his choice to join the eggheads. He was fed up with listening to the screaming. His mother crying, his father trying to think of a way of spending the day and all his money. Harry had plotted this way out for him. When in doubt, look at the facts, boy, his grandfather had told him. Get yourself an education. He had jolly well done that.

Michael looked in the old coffee tin where he kept money for the coin-fed gas fire. The facts were he didn't even have the money to return his mother's call. Yet he knew it must be important. Of all people, Flicker had understood that he wanted to do it by himself, he wanted no part of what his family now stood for.

157

Now she had called him and he would have to call her and reverse the charges. Yet before he could do so he was called to the phone again. Flicker was sobbing at the other end. He could not understand a word she was saying. He asked whether she was drunk. She said something about a houseparty he should have been at. He never went to houseparties, she knew that. She said something about putting all her money on number seventeen and losing it all. She said something about his father. He asked where his father was. Still all she did was sob. Through her sobs he heard the name Bleidenstein. Bleidenstein was the family lawyer. When he heard that name he thought something awful must have happened.

Again he looked at the facts, and the facts were he did not even have the train fare to London. He was a graduate student trying to do the best by his country. He had turned down jobs in the United States, but what was he getting out of it? A damp bedsitter and a lot of coffee evenings with people who had given up all idea of changing the world. 'Too bloody complicated, old boy.' It was as if everybody had given up. The upper classes had just retired behind their façades while they still had them. The middle classes were trying to play at being the upper classes, and the working classes were trying to stop them. It was a society brutalized by the past and not able to wrench clear of it for the future. It was a country trapped into lethargy somewhere between the welfare office and Buckingham Palace, used to the idea that someone else would provide. Michael was trapped, too. It was a feeling he had had ever since childhood, and he hated the feeling.

He took a bus to where the ring road met the motorway and thumbed a lift from a travelling salesman in a company Granada who had a pension fund, eight weeks' holiday a year, profit-sharing and a subsidized mortgage. Michael learned that it wasn't all roses in his life either since his wife had been reading about women's liberation. When the salesman came home at night, he just wanted to put his feet up in front of television, so the last time he came home his wife had taken things into her own hands and organized a wife-swopping party. He liked it the first time he found her in bed with her girl-friend – it turned him on – but pretty soon he could not stand their chattering. The salesman thought he was doing the only sensible thing in the circumstances by going to Amsterdam with his boy-friend.

The travelling salesman let Michael off at the airport, where the heir to a theoretical fortune went to get the Piccadilly Line into town. He forgot he did not have any change. He nipped over the barrier when the West Indian ticket collector was not looking. He got off at Green Park and told them he had lost his ticket. They believed him, and that was a break at least. If he had been arrested he could just see the headlines in his own newspaper. All these years he had managed to keep away from the news-hounds.

Then he walked the last distance to his mother's house. There were grilles on the windows as if everyone was out of town. Michael knew his mother wouldn't be in Coote House – she hated the English countryside – but it occurred to him she might be in the Villa Inglese on the Riviera in the sun with the chauffeur. He had spoken to her only that morning, but he hadn't asked where she was calling from.

Now it was four in the afternoon. He stood for a while looking at the façade of the rose-red Dutch Gothic house, admiring its sense of proportion and lamenting the lack of one in the life of the inhabitants. He had long since given up carrying a door key, so he rang the bell. His mother was in after all. After a while she answered the door herself. She was still wearing a negligée. Her mascara was running all down her cheeks and there was a bottle of champagne in her hand. She didn't even bother to say hello to him. She simply threw herself into his arms, sobbing.

'Your father wants a divorce,' she was crying. 'He wants to marry his bitch dinge.'

22

Blurb

Simon Lawrence Caulfield turned the key in the lock. He had bought a little railwayman's cottage and done it up as if it were Buckingham Palace. He squeezed past Diana into the front room, which opened directly on to the street, which had been cobbled and littered with blooming window-boxes. The ceiling was so low that people felt obtrusive standing up. The situation called for Diana Cheever and Simon Lawrence Caulfield to lie down, so they did. Diana lay and looked at the ceiling. Simon lay next to her. This was a first. He had never before screwed his editor's wife. He felt in his pocket. The drugs were all there. Diana was shivering. It was pouring with rain outside. He climbed on top of her.

'What are you doing?' she said.

'Darling,' he whispered.

He was so silly, but she was united now in a pact with the enemy. To break the spell of Tony Cheever she had to belong, if only briefly, to someone else. Simon was perfect for the purpose. He could never be anything to her or she to him, but he could illustrate to her the stupidity of the physical bondage which she felt to Tony. They were only two pieces of meat, she told herself. What did it matter how they put themselves about? The proximity of two pieces of unwilling flesh would help her to understand that. If only he would get it all over with.

'How about a cup of tea?' he said instead. He got up. 'Indian or China?' she heard him say. She didn't care.

He was dismayed. He felt no stirring in his loins, only a buzzing in his brain. Suppose someone he knew had seen what happened back there in the restaurant. What a dreadful spectacle it had been. Diana Cheever had pushed over the table in her husband's favourite restaurant, knocked over a waiter carrying a trayful of snippets of sole mornay and bowled into someone who looked a lot like the Prime Minister.

At least she hadn't been sick. Instead she kept muttering something about gardening classes. She went on about whether she should have bought the gnome with the fishing rod or the one with the lantern light. Then she said she had missed her train. Simon had to put her in a taxi. Then she said she had left her pink umbrella in the restaurant. No one he knew had a pink umbrella. What would the head waiter think about a pink umbrella? How did it rate trendwise on a scale of ten? He had to get her out of there, so he had brought her home. What would Sonia think if he didn't screw her? What would Diana think? What would her husband think? He had to concede she might tell her husband he had screwed her when he had not screwed her, because she was desperate for him to screw her. All this took away any lust he might have. He felt in his pocket. Sonia said you must do it with a mirror. Do what with a mirror?

Back on the living-room floor Diana lay with her eyes tight shut. Why didn't he bloody well come and get it over with? There were men with whom you never wanted it to end and men with whom you never wanted it to begin. She looked at the time. It was half-way through the afternoon. She imagined Tony in the conference at Liverpool. It would be raining there, too. It would be cold. He would have had lunch, gone back to his room, unzipped his flies as a matter of course and whoever was with him would by now be a happy woman. Goddam it, she wanted him inside her like a baby crying for a dummy in its mouth. Tony knew it, and he only used the knowledge against her. Tony would not be having the trouble she was having now. Tony had an instant erection as long as you weren't married to him. Who was with him? she asked herself. It preyed on her mind.

Simon Lawrence Caulfield came back. He was wearing a silk spotted dressing gown. He put on a record. It was Noël Coward. Diana thought she was going to throw up, not for the first time. He threw himself on top of her. His body was limp and flaccid.

He wasn't Tony. What am I doing, she thought. This is no good. It is all very well, getting your own back, but there is no one here suffering but me. Tony is at a conference, perfectly happy, and I am unhappy because I am being unfaithful to him. She threw Simon off her. She heard him padding off into the other room. He was gone a long while. For a moment she thought she was back at home in East Grinstead. She longed to hear Tony's voice, to know that he did not suspect any of her infidelity, that she was forgiven. She called the operator to place a personal call to Liverpool. She did not want anything from Caulfield, not even a free telephone call. She would make this one and pay him back. 'Your call is on the line. Mrs Cheever is speaking from Liverpool,' said the operator.

'Mrs Cheever? But I am Mrs Cheever,' Diana said. She was, wasn't she? For a minute she wasn't sure who anyone was any more.

'I'm sure I don't know anything about that,' said the operator.

Diana lay back and took stock of the situation. The rat who called himself her husband had booked into a hotel with one of his bimbos under the pretext that he was taking care of business and registered her as Diana Cheever his wife, while here she was, Diana Cheever his real wife, having an awful time on someone else's floor. She closed her eyes while Simon made one last determined effort to take her. This time it happened. He managed to take her innocence away while scarcely entering her at all. She was innocent, that was the whole trouble, she was innocently married to a raving sex maniac. While she thought about that little glimmer of truth, Simon's limp little foreskin lolloped into her like the soft neck of a flaccid balloon in the mouth of a child and plopped right out again. He ejaculated all over her.

She thought she was going to be sick again, but she was free. There was nothing that Tony could do to her now she had defiled her own pact. He had never bothered to make one. A woman always makes the marriage pact with herself, thought Diana Cheever. It was another thing her mother had said.

The telephone rang. 'Your call to Liverpool, 75p,' she could hear the operator saying. Seventy-five pence was not much to pay for the great gift of knowledge. Diana would make Tony pay far, far more. How bitter, she thought in the bathroom as she drowned in tapwater and Floris bath oil the almond smell of semen, how bitter that the same essence could belong to two such different men. She washed the smells of sex off her body, almonds and Marmite, and they brought back memories of some of the things she had shared with Tony in bed, as well as his pleasure. There had been a time when they talked. It was in this manner that she remembered the name of Bleidenstein.

23

Crosshead

Jacob Bleidenstein was the most powerful lawyer in town. He had been the Coote family lawyer since way back when. Harry himself had taken him under his wing. He had acted for the Cootes ever since, and for Arthur Mitchell's Sunday Newspaper on many libel cases. His was one name that loomed large in Cheever's ramblings since he'd been editing the Evening. He was always being mentioned in the paper. Bleidenstein took on improbable cases and invested them with honour.

'Must get Frank Morley to give us a piece on that MP's innocence,' Tony Cheever might observe to Diana late at night. 'Stupid jerk is up for insider dealing. No one would have been any the wiser except he gave a bum steer to that loony leftie from in the House of Commons tea room.'

'How can you be sure he is innocent?' Diana would ask, wide-eyed, looking up from her magazine-offer tapestry set.

'Bleidenstein's handling the case,' was all that needed to be said.

Bleidenstein's firm also had a reputation for handling society divorces. After Diana Cheever slapped Simon Lawrence Caulfield in his silly wet decadent face, it was to Bleidenstein she turned. She wanted to be taken seriously, so she knew she must associate herself with someone who was serious. Desperation made her bold. Moreover, she had not forgotten the couple of months of investigative reporting her husband allowed her to do before the wedding in case anybody said he was marrying a typist. She stopped the taxi outside a telephone box and called the paper. She told Tony Cheever's secretary that she needed Bleidenstein's address in order to deliver Tony's manuscript on the future of

Fleet Street. What the hell, Tony was always saying he was going
to beat Arthur Mitchell into writing a book about the future of
Fleet Street which he alone could solve. She had the address
within two minutes and directed the taxi to within one hundred
yards of it.

It was a strangely altered Diana Cheever who marched into the
eau-de-Nil offices of Einstein, Epstein, Bernstein & Bleidenstein.
Einstein, Epstein and Bernstein were dead, but Bleidenstein still
rejoiced in his connection with them. Diana Cheever had a double
brandy inside her and the remnants of Simon Lawrence Caulfield's
almond sperm to remind her, if she needed any reminding, that she
hated all men. After the time spent in Simon Lawrence Caulfield's
bathroom, she had passed a profitable hour in the ladies' room in
a department store. When she emerged, she looked better than she
had done for years. On her way past an off-licence she had then
bought a miniature brandy which she had tucked into her softest
imitation-leather Sunday-supplement-offer handbag.

Though Bleidenstein was still at lunch, for he enjoyed his lunch
more than anybody, she was soon settled into his panelled anteroom with many copies of such current magazines as the
Investors' Chronicle. Tony's name held weight, she realized,
which served only to stiffen her resolve. There was another
woman in the anteroom, a dowdy thing holding a thin small
grubby child in school uniform by the wrist. She looked as if she
had dressed herself up in her Sunday best, but her Sunday best was
not good enough. Diana Cheever wondered if the woman knew
how ridiculous she appeared and continued reading her article on
Krugerrands. She was half-way through it when she realized she
was enjoying it. She would never have picked up such a thing
when she set out for lunch that morning. Now she was in a mood
to learn. By the time Jacob Bleidenstein strolled into his office
after lunch at 4 p.m., she had made up a portfolio of the money
she was about to get her hands on. The other woman was still
trying to keep the sickly child quiet.

Jacob Bleidenstein was a fine-looking man who would have
intimidated Diana Cheever on almost any other day of her life.
His name was synonymous with good living, as was his girth. He

wore a monocle round his neck and on his nose spectacles perched
rather oddly far way from his deep-set eyes like a music sheet on a
soldier bandsman's trombone. He scooped Diana up under the
black sleeve of his voluminous jacket like an overweight bat. His
liquid tongue informed her that he was delighted to make her
acquaintance and to learn, moreover, that his friend, the old
rogue, had finally something to show for the book he was always
threatening to write, and something potentially libellous, too. At
the thought of libel, Bleidenstein shot his expensive cuffs – it was
a habit of his – revealing an exquisite little watch that sat like a
ladies' timepiece on his overweight wrist. Then he spun his fat
thumbs over the buckle of his designer belt. Diana waited until his
office door shut behind him. Then she came straight to the point.

'I haven't come on my husband's behalf,' she said. 'I've come
on my own.'

'Dear lady,' said Bleidenstein as if he had absolutely no interest
at all. Such a blank-wall approach always made his clients lapse
into nervous talk, and talking give away their secrets. 'Tea,
coffee, or something stronger?'

'Nothing,' she said.

Bleidenstein heaved himself backwards in his leather chair. 'So
you have written a book, too,' he observed. 'There's no stopping
you ladies these days.'

Diana was puzzled. What did he mean?

'Or are you in some other business?' he asked.

'I am now,' she said. 'I am in the business of suing my husband
for divorce. I want to be sure of powerful representation, so I
want you to act for me,' she said. She was surprised at herself. She
had not found it difficult to make her speech at all.

Bleidenstein said nothing. Instead he rang a little silver bell he
kept on his desk and ordered tea from a secretary.

'Are you sure you won't join me, dear lady?' he asked.

He was enormous, but not unattractive. He was fascinating
and alien in his starched shirt, like an enormous white-bellied fish
who inhabited a different environment. Diana could not dislike
him, but she realized she would have to get him to like her.

'Divorce is an ugly business, Mrs Cheever,' Bleidenstein said

166

when the girl had left the room. 'And rarely very rewarding on any level. I try not to get involved with it and I try to advise my clients the same. Especially if they are women.'

'This will be a very simple divorce, Mr Bleidenstein,' she said. 'Very little advice will be needed. I wouldn't have come to you if I had wanted a marriage counsellor. I don't want you to advise me at all. I want you to tell me what is my right in law and I want you to get it for me. More if possible. I think this is something you can do.'

Bleidenstein preened himself. He was a vain man who could not resist a challenge. 'Thank you, Mrs Cheever,' he said.

This time he pressed a bell under his desk and a young man entered the room, staggering under the weight of a large legal volume. 'This is my pupil,' Bleidenstein explained. 'He will tell us all we need to know about divorce.' The pupil left the room and came back carrying another huge volume.

While this was happening, Bleidenstein said to Diana: 'The law is not black and white, you know, Mrs Cheever. If it were there would be no need for lawyers. There are still a lot of grey areas.' He leaned back in his chair. 'I specialize in the grey areas.' He paused and folded his hands like flippers over his stomach. 'It might be possible to get you a great deal of money. On the other hand, Mrs Cheever, your husband is a working man. There may not be an awful lot in it for you. When you have divided up the house and the contents you will probably find it more worth while to make up your differences.'

'I don't want to divide anything up, Mr Bleidenstein,' she found herself saying. 'My husband scarcely ever comes near the house. I don't think he will remember what's in it. I want the house and the contents and I want the money to live as well as he does. I want an old-fashioned divorce, Mr Bleidenstein, because I am an old-fashioned woman. I don't expect my husband to go screwing around in the afternoon when he has a job to do, or to humiliate me in front of impressionable members of his staff by passing off his mistresses as his wife.'

'I see,' said Bleidenstein. 'And who will pay for this divorce?'

'Tony will, of course,' she said. 'It's his fault, so he will pay for it.' She was not going to be put off.

'Grounds for divorce?' Bleidenstein intoned at his pupil. The boy spluttered. 'Oh, come on, for God's sake,' said Bleidenstein. 'I could pick myself anyone off the street to answer that question in this day and age. This is the age of do-it-yourself divorces.'

'Incompatibility?' spluttered the boy.

'Incompatibility,' intoned Bleidenstein. 'Does that fit the bill, Mrs Cheever?'

'Of course we are incompatible,' said Diana irritably. 'Why else would we bother to get divorced? We are more than incompatible.'

'More than incompatibility,' Bleidenstein said to the boy, who fell upon the pages, turning them noisily.

'Adultery?' wavered the pupil. 'Cruelty, mental cruelty . . .?'

'Adultery? Cruelty? How about mental cruelty, my dear?'

'All of those,' said Diana. 'That's just for starters.'

She had Bleidenstein's interest now all right. He had to admit he saw a woman sitting opposite who was quite unusually firm in her resolve. There were none of those wet tears in her eyes that made him feel inadequate in common with the rest of his gender, only an absolutely steely glint that refused to be denied. Bleidenstein thought it was frightening what men could do to women. They could make them into men.

'What has your husband done to you that you want this divorce so badly, Mrs Cheever?' he asked. He leaned forward over his desk and his pupil leaned forward over his book to catch whatever she had to say.

'My husband has committed the ultimate sin, Mr Bleidenstein,' said Diana.

'And what might that be, dear lady?' asked Bleidenstein. Yes, he was intrigued.

'Disappointment I guess is par for the course in any marriage,' said Diana reflectively. 'But the ultimate sin is boredom. My husband has bored me to death. He has bored me to death for years and he has made it impossible for me to do anything about it. He has not allowed me to live my own life, but has kept me a prisoner of his promises. "We'll do this, we'll do that." None of it ever happens, Mr Bleidenstein. I don't mind waiting, but he just strings me along with lies. I am better than that. I could take the truth.'

Bleidenstein wrung his hands. 'What is the truth, Mrs Cheever?' he said.

He had never known anyone answer that question, but Diana did. She was in no mood for subtle philosophy. 'The truth is he makes his life interesting by living his pack of lies. His life is full of stories, and not just newspaper ones. No wonder he keeps forgetting the plot. There are so many. Well, he's forgotten well and truly this time. My husband's been seducing some bimbo in the afternoons.'

'A bimbo?' said Bleidenstein. He looked at his pupil and shrugged his shoulders. 'What is a bimbo?'

The pupil giggled. Diana could not believe the lawyer did not know. The man was beginning to unnerve her. Bleidenstein looked from her to the pupil and back again.

'A chick,' the boy said. 'A bimbo is a chick.' Still Bleidenstein kept the blank, baffled look on his face. 'A slag,' the boy tried again. Bleidenstein raised his eyebrows. 'A ding-a-ling, a skirt,' the boy said. 'A doll, a moll, a whore, a girl.'

'Thank you,' said Bleidenstein. 'We'll need proof about this bimbo.'

Something was wrong, thought Diana. The lawyer did not believe her.

'Not strictly to achieve a separation, but it might improve a settlement,' expanded Bleidenstein. 'Judges are still swayed by sympathy.'

'I'll get proof,' she said. 'What do you want?'

'It would make a lot of difference if you could get a photograph. If you could get a picture of your old man on the job with someone else, preferably someone of immature years, then I think I could get you the house.'

He rubbed his palms together salaciously, but the woman was still determined. She did not flinch one bit.

'OK, I'll get one,' said Diana.

'I am curious to know why it was me you came to see, Mrs

Cheever,' he said. Suddenly he was alarmed to notice that she looked like a little girl.

'I came here because I thought you would know what to do,' she said. 'It was you, wasn't it, who witnessed my husband's contract with the paper on behalf of Sir Aubrey Coote? It is a simple matter of referring to your records to find out what salary he has and to ask for my rights. If it is not enough, he can bloody well go and ask Aubrey Coote for more. I want to put him in the supplicant position for once because I have had enough of it.'

The internal buzzer rang.

'Yes, yes,' said Bleidenstein irritably. 'I have another client to see, Mrs Cheever. Obviously these are interesting times in the newspaper business. Tomorrow I am lunching with your proprietor's son, Michael Coote,' he said. Then he spoke into the buzzer: 'Tell Mrs Arthur Mitchell I will be with her directly.'

Coote, Mitchell, suddenly Diana realized who it was who had been waiting with her in the anteroom with the sickly-looking child. It was Arthur Mitchell's wife.

'One thing before you go,' said Bleidenstein. 'It could be that we have an ethical impasse here. A conflict of interests. It is true that I am not strictly Tony's personal lawyer. All the same, I have a good many dealings with him. I'll have to give some thought to the possibility of representing you. Is there somewhere I can contact you?'

Diana stared at the man. He had listened to her story and he was not going to represent her. He had never meant to represent her. Surely her grievances were as good as anyone else's under the law? Surely her money was as good as Tony's, even if it was strictly Tony's money?

Bleidenstein rose and held out a hand. 'I'll be in touch, then. Good luck, my dear.'

She bit her lip and threw her shoulders back as she left the room so that Nora Mitchell should not see another woman in distress.

'So I'll get you a picture,' she said out loud. 'This is one for Rizzi.'

She would call the *paparazzo* photographer. They had had good times when they worked together. But there was no one to hear her determined tones because the waiting room was empty.

*

After Arthur had left his office for Dallas Nora had gone to the airport to see him off. She had thought it was not right that anyone should have to work as hard as he did. He had been so looking forward to taking Laurie on his outing to the Tower of London. After he put the phone down to her, she tried to call back. She was going to suggest she bring Laurie up to Fleet Street instead. Laurie could have his name set in type by one of the operators and they could grab a sandwich with Arthur in the office if necessary. But there was no answer. Poor Arthur had gone to work already.

She heard the sound of tyres on the road outside. It was the special school bus depositing her son. She rushed to meet him. He bounded up the crazy-paving path stumbled and nearly fell. She quickened her pace and threw herself on the path beneath him. My God, don't let him fall now, she prayed. He didn't. He laughed and picked her up. 'You idiot, Mum,' he said. He looked healthier than she did these days. They were obviously treating him right in the country. It had been a good idea of Arthur's to send him away after all.

The idea came upon her gradually during the day. Arthur had called four times. Twice he had to hang up quickly. 'The new boss,' he had explained. 'Americans.' It was the word America that gave her the idea. It could work, she thought. She laid her plans carefully. First she looked in the fridge. The bottles were laid out in a row in case of emergency. Bottles of pure Factor VIII. She counted them. There were enough for one incident every day for a week. It would be more than enough. Besides which, in America they had the answer to everything. It wasn't as if she was going somewhere where they did not know about these things. She ought to telephone the insurance company and put them on notice of her intentions. She looked in the linen cupboard. She had enough clean clothes to last as well. She was a good housekeeper. Arthur had always told her that. Then she thought of something else. She ought to make a reservation for herself and

Laurie on the plane. Which airline was he flying? He had said the American one. She would make two reservations on that plane, and when they met up at the airport there would be no obstacle to Arthur asking them to fly with him.

She imagined his face when he saw them, the slow look of growing pleasure, the congratulations implicit in the look. Though he might not say it in words, he would be thanking her for having the imagination to cut through their problems. She figured it was only for want of organization that your private life never had time to catch up with your career as it advanced. Well, she would take care of all that. She was not just Laurie's mother and Arthur's housekeeper but a woman who could contribute to his famous career.

If Nora had looked in the mirror when she arrived at the airport she would have seen a woman laden down with unfashionable hand-baggage, dragging a small boy behind her. She would never have concluded that this woman was a famous editor's wife. By now, however, she was obsessed with the new role she had found, a role that brooked no opposition, not even the existence of a handicapped child. She had dressed Laurie in his school uniform and thought he looked a credit to both of them. The boy had started to behave differently the minute she told him they would be joining his father. He had acquired dignity, vision, purpose, as had she. Nora knew that the only problem in life was that it did not give people a chance.

She tried not to think it was Arthur who had not given her a chance. He had planted her outside town and left her to her own devices. He had insisted on sending her children away to school, thus making her completely redundant. She tried not to think that Arthur might have done these things to make life easier for himself. She argued he had done it for them both. Now she would repay him by showing him what she could do for all of them. The American plane took off for Dallas in under two hours, and she would be on it, taking her rightful place next to her brilliant husband. She looked around for him but could not see him yet. She stood in line at the check-in desk with a trolley piled high with all the things she calculated they would need. She did not quite know what she would do if Arthur did not turn up by the time it was her turn to check in. He didn't. 'I am Mrs Arthur Mitchell,' she said proudly. 'I have a reservation in first class.'

The girl punched up the name on the screen. 'Do you want to downgrade?' she asked. 'Your husband's travelling economy.'

'Economy?' faltered Nora.

She looked around for Arthur. The booking clerk looked round, too. 'There he is,' Nora said.

They all looked. The entire queue looked. Laurie looked.

'Dad!' shouted Laurie.

It was just instinct that made her hold on to him. She saw the marble floor, the way he could slip and gash his face open and they would all end up in hospital again while he fought for his life.

'Wait with me,' she said. 'Your father is with his new American proprietor.'

She looked for a man in jeans wearing ostrich-skin boots and a fringed suede jacket. But Arthur had his arm round a blonde girl with an ostentatious figure. He hadn't said anything about his new proprietor being a woman. Arthur was too involved with the blonde woman to notice his wife looking at him. As Nora watched, he gave the voluptuous woman a little peck on the cheek, then his lips slid down her face till they found her lips.

'Separate planes, then. See you at the other end,' Nora heard Arthur say.

'Oh well, in that case I'll just have to find someone else to conduct my little experiment then,' the blonde woman answered.

'What little experiment?' asked Arthur.

'They say that if you come at 35,000 feet it makes your nose bleed,' the blonde woman answered.

'Come with me, Laurie!' Nora cried.

She forgot her son's disability. She dragged him across the marble floor. He fell on his knees. She did not notice in time to save him. They were both bruised. He was screaming. No one did anything. They looked at her as if she were a child molester. Even that was an improvement, she thought. Only the night before she had been a housewife. Nothing had happened to her since she had

had her family. Nothing would ever happen to her again. She was completely powerless. Now she looked at herself in the mirror in the ladies' room. To make matters worse, she was not the most beautiful girl in the world. She said it out loud. Even Laurie stopped crying as if he realized a momentous moment had happened.

'You are, Mother, you are,' he said.

She looked at him. He was a mess and it was all her fault. Now she would have to do something about that.

'Don't you lie to me, too,' she snapped.

She had seen the other woman and she had blamed herself. She had no taste for this sort of confrontation. She had a sick child and she wanted her husband back.

*

Bleidenstein shot his cuffs, went back into his office, leaned back in his leather chair and laughed. There were still a lot of foolish people out there after all, and things were hotting up just the way he liked them. He liked to give people a piece of rope and then see whether they hanged themselves with it. Usually they did. Perhaps he would call Tony Cheever and warn him his wife was on the warpath. But first he would wait to see what Michael Coote had to say tomorrow.

24

Viewing Figures

Crumm had agreed to be on *Newsnight*. It made his heart beat very fast. He should have preferred the *Terry Wogan Show*, but the way he saw it it was good to get in some practice before he went on the big one with all his friends watching.

The girl who had talked to him on the telephone seemed nice enough, and there was going to be some girl interviewing him, too. Well, he knew the female of the species did not have a full set of brains to pass round, so he thought he would be able to handle that or he wasn't the man he thought he was. When they sent a car to pick him up from his own front door, he felt like a proper hero.

Funny life, he said to himself. One minute you were making Horlicks and cleaning out the budgerigar, the next you were on the box. A famous person whose services were required to entertain and instruct the nation. It struck him as peculiar that he should owe his patch of fame to the weaker sex. Miss Sonia Fraser! The Honourable, no less. There was nothing honourable about her or the rest of her class. Bloody nymphomaniacs in bloody cocktail frocks. Poor Mike Green had had a narrow escape, picking her up in Fulham. Lucky he was not devoured. Like a Venus fly-trap, women were. Part sweet, part man-eating. They certainly wanted it both ways, you could say that again. They wanted to get you at it and now they wanted to boss you around, too. Well, now they would see who was boss. It took a real man to rise to this sort of challenge and to spot the exploitation they had in mind.

At the television centre, Crumm was greeted by a receptionist in a blue kaftan who was eating a doughnut.

'You Charlie Crumm?' she asked. 'I'm Maggie. I'm taking you to make-up.'

'Make-up what?' asked Crumm. He knew that as a printing term. He had not expected to be asked to work.

'Whatever you like, dear,' said Maggie. 'Most people choose the face.' She pushed past him into the lift and looked at herself in the mirror that lined it. 'I can't believe myself,' she said. 'I am so overweight I look like Andrea Dworkin.'

Crumm did not know who that was so he said nothing.

'Look at me.' She put her thumb and fingers together like a pair of callipers and grabbed hold of a whole lump of leg through her kaftan. 'I should not be allowed out of the house with thighs like this. I am gross.' She took another bite out of her doughnut. 'I'm going to do something about it in the summer. You going away?' she asked Crumm.

'Away where?' asked Crumm. This young lady was extremely familiar. Next thing she would be asking him to join her.

'I'm going to Gib,' said Maggie. 'We did Rosarias last year and the year before that we did Torremolinos. I wanted to try the Greek islands but my boy-friend says the beer's rotten and the women are ugly. You're not shaking, are you?' she said. 'Your first time on, is it?'

'Yes,' admitted Crumm.

'Never mind, you'll soon feel better when we get to hospitality.'

'Hospitality?' asked Crumm.

'That's where they get you drunk before you go on.'

'Really?'

'Sure. Everyone's tongue-tied when they first try. They wouldn't open their mouths but for a bit of liquid libation. We'll soon have you gassing your head off when we get to hospitality. Here we are.'

They got out of the lift and Crumm thought he recognized someone standing waiting for it. He was someone who brushed with other famous people now. They went into make-up.

'Over to you,' said Maggie to another young woman wearing a kaftan and carrying a tool-box this time.

Crumm thought she must be an electrician. These women,

Sonia Fraser was one of them, thought they could do anything these days, but all they were really doing was taking the bread out of a man's mouth. The electrician told him to sit down in a chair. He felt momentarily as if he was going to be executed.

'I'm Sharon,' she said. Then she ran her fingers through his hair.

'Ger off,' he said. He was not accustomed to being touched up by strange women.

'Sorry, didn't mean to offend,' Sharon said. 'I coulda swore it was real.'

'Cheeky devil,' he said.

'Come on, I'm supposed to make you look good,' said Sharon. 'And we haven't got all night to do it.'

Crumm looked at her. Her hair was braided into tiny little pigtails all over her head. It was green except where it was pink. She looked a bloody mess. How did she think she was going to make him look good? She should start on herself before she tried to make anyone else look good.

'Would you like it off your face? Or shall we keep the quiff?'

'I'll keep it as it is, thank you,' Crumm said coldly.

'Please yourself,' she said.

Sharon walked over to the door and opened it. 'Grandpa's ready now,' she yelled.

A young boy appeared. His hair was white blond except where it was patent black. It was cut short up the back as if he had just come out of the army. He stood and stared at Crumm in the mirror surrounded by light-bulbs. 'You've got nice cheekbones,' was what he said.

Crumm sat on his hands. If he did not he felt he might slap the young man.

'Some blue on the lids for the blue eyes?'

'No thank you,' he said.

'OK, darling, as you like,' said the young man. 'We'll just take the shine off then.' He dipped a brush into a pot of powder and waved it at Crumm's nose.

'Stop that!' said Crumm, flailing one arm.

'Oh, be like that, then,' said the boy.

In the mirror, Crumm could see Sharon and Maggie standing behind him, holding their sides with laughter. If one thing made Crumm mad it was to be laughed at by a woman.

'He's a raver. Get him off me,' he shouted and caught the boy with his flailing arm somewhere on the nose.

'You fucking animal,' the boy screamed. 'I'll have you for assault and battery. I know my rights. My God, you've drawn blood.'

Crumm paled. The fellow was a flaming pansy and now he was bleeding all over him. If this was showbusiness he had had enough of it already. His first time at the BBC and already he needed an AIDS test.

'Serves you right, you silly queen,' said Sharon, coming to Crumm's rescue. 'Not everyone wants to look like Michael Jackson,' she said. 'Oh, do stop snivelling, Gary.'

'What you need is a drink,' said Maggie to Crumm. She steered him into hospitality. 'Wine?' she asked.

'I'll have a beer,' said Crumm.

And then he was on. The hot lights seemed to melt him and his mind went blank for a minute. Then a photograph of Sonia Fraser flashed on to the screen, bringing back all his anger and insecurity. Sonia Fraser? What were they doing, flashing life-size pictures of her all over the nation? Crumm felt the injury to his ego. This was his strike, not hers. Bloody woman seizing centre stage. Bloody titled woman. As Crumm sat waiting to be asked to speak, he knew what he had to do. It was up to him to defend basic British manhood. When they asked him about Sonia Fraser, he would let them have it. And so it was. The words poured out of his mouth. He talked about the glorious past of the trade-union movement, about how men with women to keep and families to feed had put their heads together and come up with formulas that put the country where it was now with its high standard of expectations.

Crumm explained that the Crumm Amendment was his gift to the British nation. All he wanted was justice for British men in a world governed by Japanese microchips and German gearshifts and American politics. Even that Russian had seized the star position for himself, flaunting his friendly little face all over televison when everyone knew they were killers. Meanwhile the British just looked on. They had become a nation of voyeurs. Let each Britisher be his own guardian, he said, and guardian to his own little family, and then they would not let themselves be ripped off. 'I'll never forgive the Japanese for what they did to our chaps on the Burma Road,' he said. 'We should be shoving their bloody microchips up their bloody fingernails. That's a language they understand. That'll put an end to their nonsense once and for all. And the bloody Hun,' he said. 'Don't tell me you've forgotten that already. And now we have Yanks in Fleet Street. Well, the best thing we can say about Yanks is they can't even spell properly.'

The interviewer could not stop him. The more Crumm said, the more resentment came to the fore. He thought of arguments he never knew he had. Everything that had festered inside him for ever came out. He found an almost religious fervour which worked brilliantly on television. He stared straight into the camera and told the nation what they wanted to hear. You could not sit around expecting your dues, he said, you had to demand them. That was all he was doing. That was the meaning of the Crumm Amendment.

The Crumm Amendment was about the rights of the British working man. It was about his ability to run his own life and not submit to any form of oppression. Men submitted to oppression because they wanted an easy life. The time had come to throw away the old ways and to think things out anew.

Oppression came in many guises, explained Crumm, and this little dispute at the paper comprised most of the guises. Like most other people, he had been tempted to see everything as a great accident, but it had been given to him to understand that there were no accidents, only conspiracies. If he had still been thinking the way he used to think, he might not have seen the significance of Fraser's daughter hitching a lift that day. But once you had seen the significance, there was no denying that this was part of the gigantic conspiracy that had the nation in its clutches. He had been sent to unravel this conspiracy. He, Crumm, was a man of destiny. The solution was his Amendment. That was the beauty of it all.

Outside the studio, Maggie was waiting for him. She was sitting on a chair with a bottle of white wine beside her. When she saw him coming, she stood up, but the wine went to her head and she fell down. He picked her up. He was back in control. She was all right really, and so was he. Crumm was more than all right. He had nothing personal against women, it was just they needed to realize who they were.

'It really is the most fantastic story,' the producer said, shaking his head seriously from side to side. 'You were fantastic, Charles. Everything about this dispute is a little metaphor of the times. A real clash between the old order and the new. It has absolutely everything going for it. All the isms, isn't that right, Dorcas?' He turned to his girl assistant. 'Sexism, classism, egalitarianism. Damn it, what a pity there's only one thing missing.'

'What's that, Brian?' asked Dorcas.

'Racism, dammit,' said the producer. 'It is a real tragedy Charlie Crumm isn't black.'

25

Union

When Crumm thought about what he had done, his heart nearly stopped, so he didn't think. There were men over at his union headquarters who had no fear at all from lack of thinking. Crumm decided to take it to them so he could be sure of the support of all the combined chapels of all the newspapers. Under such circumstances, he was sure he could not fail. The TV producer had said his story was a real metaphor for the times, TV was the oracle of modern living, and his experience only served to prove the fact. Ever since the word had been spread around about his performance on the television, everyone was focused on the future of Fleet Street, where newspapers were printed and he helped to distribute them, as if it was the future of the entire nation. Crumm was as chuffed as could be to realize everyone knew all about him even before he told them himself. It all went to prove that destiny was still in no mood to let him down. Everyone knew Crumm's time had come.

For even while Crumm had been building on his own machinations at the Evening Paper, the strike over at Fisher's newly amalgamated Weekly had not resolved itself either. At first it was just a little matter of the secretaries and the researchers, but gradually, as they tried to get their woes down on paper to submit them to the new proprietor, everyone had discovered they were feminists no matter which sex they were. All the men had wives or mistresses and their sex-life was seriously threatened if they did not take the women's part.

Some of the more macho had put up a bit of resistance at first, but then they quickly realized that, if they just gave in to the situation, went along with the spirit of the times, they were free.

They could go off to the pub or play a game of golf, or snooze around in bed all day or put up all those bookshelves they always intended to put up, or go out and buy a new hi-fi or even find a girl-friend on the side who was not taken in by the feminist movement.

All over London, the sound was heard of nest-making by New Men in their kimonos while the girls huddled together in their dungarees rehearsing their union arguments. An almost total role reversal had been achieved which brought pretty well everything to a standstill. For whereas both sexes innately understood all the peripheral activities of the other, particularly the more glamorous ones, neither fully appreciated what dull repetitive tasks were needed to keep the ball really rolling. The men were fantastic at fixing the decibels, but every one of them had forgotten how to unblock a sink. The women, who knew so well what a newspaper ought in theory to contain, found it quite a different matter when it came to putting it out as a daily exercise. They all seemed to glory in each other's inertia and there was much saying, 'I told you so.' While they loudly deplored the entire state of affairs, for which they blamed Fisher and Gold and Aubrey but still drew their pay-cheques, the inertia was a pleasant enough way of passing time.

Yet there was one person with whom, for once in his life, inertia rankled. Crumm. He scented the danger the minute he saw how the union boys were starting to plan a total shutdown. Crumm liked a good shutdown as well as the next man, especially now he had got the bit between his teeth over the sweet peas. Yet there was a problem about a shutdown.

Once Crumm had had a taste of the limelight, it had become like a fix to him, and he was damned if he was going to do without it. He spent all his waking hours thinking about how to ensure a supply of the stuff. He needed a masterstroke, a new trick to keep those calls from the television studios coming. Herein lay the problem. It was Grant who had first warned he was in danger of killing the goose which laid the golden eggs. But the goose was not Grant, it was publicity, exposure. So sympathetic had those TV boys found Crumm's cause, so right for the times, that they all wanted to join the strike. Crumm could see as plain as the nose on his face that this would not do at all. In the end, it would mean a total blackout of the screens just as he started to appear on them. The long and the short of it was he did not want the television people out. But it was more than that.

It was when Sparks and Spratling were leaning on their brooms, congratulating themselves on the efficacy of the strike so far, that Crumm's next brainwave came upon him. So far his experience as a leader of men had taught him not to tell the underdog what he had in mind, just to go ahead and do it anyway. He would lay a smoke-trail, just like those people upstairs. He would tell them when the time was right.

And so one day: 'When is a strike not a strike?' he asked, looking up from his football pools.

'Give up,' said Spratling.

'When it is not an all-out strike,' said Crumm triumphantly. Spratling and Sparks looked bemused, so Crumm continued. 'So far there is no problem with this strike,' he said. 'But, mark my words, I can see a problem on the horizon and I will tell you what the problem is. The problem is that this whole business is going to be taken right out of our hands if we are not very careful. For starters, we are going to have to be very wary of those chaps over at headquarters. I saw the glint in the eye all right when they clocked the possibilities of this little situation. I saw them rubbing their hands together – metaphorically speaking, that is – the way they wanted the print to follow the distribution, type to follow print. I saw the way they wanted the whole lot out. They could see a general strike on the horizon, the fall of the government, the election of a leader of the people. But I saw a damn great snag, too, lads, if we go along that route. Do you want to know what the damn great snag is?'

'Yes, Charlie,' said Sparks and Spratling in unison.

'The snag is that that sort of thing is not ultimately going to cost management, with their little nest eggs against all eventualities. It is going to cost us. Once they've got us out, they'll find a way of doing without us. They'll have us all laid off, and that is what they have been waiting for. Mark my words, too much striking and they will have us all playing right into their greedy little hands. Let them do what they like over at Fisher's place, but we at the Evening Newspaper do not want it done that way, do we?'

'No,' they all cheered in unison.

'Not after we have been fighting for our place in history all this while.'

'No,' they cheered.

'We don't want that at all. We want to do it our way.'

'Yes,' they intoned.

'In order to get out of them what we want to get out of them, we have got to bleed the buggers dry. We've got to have them down on their knees, begging us for mercy rather than the other way round. What do you say?'

'Yes, yes, yes,' they said.

They liked the way he was thinking. This was the alfalfa sprout, the little germ that germinated when Tibbet likened the print to an obsolete thing. At that time Crumm had not been able to put his finger on it. Now he had been to the TV studios he had it. He had seen how the TV people conjured up images out of nowhere. There one minute, gone the next. That is what had set him thinking.

Crumm knew now what it was that newspapers had which television did not. It was a tangible product. You could beam any amount of TV stuff into the ether and it just consumed itself up. It was there only for a split second, and once it was gone it was gone without trace. Crumm's world, on the other hand, had product, and Crumm's great weapon was this very product. The product was not what was in the newspaper, as most people thought, the product was the newspaper itself. What was written in it was old hat as soon as it was written. It was a vanity. It was trivia fit only for lighting fires with. It was hot air, here today, gone tomorrow, just like the intangible pictures on TV. And there you had it.

The down-home, nitty-gritty, real-life nub of the issue was the paper the newspaper was written on. That was the product, and the beauty of it was it was also waste product. Crumm was sitting on the greatest waste-paper basket in the world, the wonderful white wedding-cake building. Now he knew exactly what he had to do in order to make himself the long-awaited leader of the people. He had to keep those editions coming as they were coming, not shut the whole place down. His strike for the introduction of the Crumm Amendment was a little particular van drivers' strike, not a great big national bean feast. He must make it plain to the union that the other trades at the Evening Newspaper must not join the strike. This, not complete inertia, was in their best interests. The writers should carry on writing and posturing and entertaining themselves, and the typesetters should set the mass of words in type. The printers should stand by the presses a few weeks more, waving their oily rags impotently at the machines, watching the stuff come off the endless roll like giant-size toilet paper. In all this, the process would be the same as always. The difference was that the van drivers would not distribute the newspaper. They should tear it off, stack it up and wrap it right round the goddam building till the whole place drowned in it and strangled itself to death.

Crumm could just see all the arguments now, and how he would benefit from them. The writers would be up in arms about the ecology problems this strike highlighted. All the trees coming down uselessly and landing as tonnes of paper on Fleet Street to suffocate it. Forests denuded, the earth's atmosphere threatened, the ozone layer gaping, carcinogenic rays leaping through the gap. The end of the world was at hand. Crumm rubbed his hands together. His was truly the destiny of a visionary. While they railed on about it and wrote pieces in their paper, he would make certain the paper had no readers to share their sense of apocalyptic injustice. They would soon beg the management on behalf of the human race to incorporate the Crumm Amendment into the new economy of things.

And that, of course, is pretty well how it all happened. The writers wrote and the presses printed, the folding machines folded, the stackers stacked, but the van drivers did not deliver. Crumm and his lads drank beer and played cards. If ever it was his misfortune to bump into a representative of management now, he no longer called him sir but dickhead, and definitively added he could shove his newspaper up his arse. Grant stood helplessly by and enjoyed his weekends in Little Nelling more and more. Frank Morley replaced all his furniture with the editor's own, so that anyone making a comparison against the list of what was allowed at what level of management would assume he had in reality become editor of the paper. Tony Cheever, who might have taken a more authoritative stance, quite simply never came back from the conference on the new technology, but holed up in his room at the hotel at Bleidenstein's behest. He was, in turn, besieged by Rizzi the *paparazzo* photographer in the pay of Cheever's determined wife, and by Arthur Mitchell's reporter looking for a story.

Crumm was asked back on television and achieved a popularity he never dared to imagine, for his imagination did not take him far enough. What he did not foresee was how all his viewers, no matter what trade or profession they pursued themselves, wanted to play a role in incorporating the Crumm Amendment into the constitution of Coote Newspapers. He filled a great void in the national psyche and learned to believe his leadership role was sealed.

At first the people were just curious. They were drawn to Fleet Street by this curiosity during the evenings and the weekends. Soon they started to take time off during working hours to hang around the place and see how the strike would progress or be resolved. A permanent camera team was installed opposite the wonderful white wedding-cake building to record every incident as it happened. Scheduled programmes were interrupted by newsflashes of scuffles and impromptu speeches. Fleet Street, robbed of the written word, became the cradle of a new sort of demagogy which, in turn, attracted even more attention.

The throng of the curious grew so large that it became impossible for the van drivers to control the people all by themselves. There were not enough of them. Pickets were needed to make sure certain copies of the newspaper which were still being printed were not stolen by members of the public. Crumm toured the country, explaining his strategy to crowds of well-wishers. Whole trades quite unrelated to the production of newspapers went on sympathy strike to provide pickets to ring the wonderful white wedding-cake building.

26

Quire

When Michael contacted Bleidenstein it annoyed him that the family lawyer seemed to be enjoying the family misfortunes. Michael himself could not rid his memory of the sight of Flicker Coote with her bottle of champagne, standing in front of the shuttered house in Mayfair. Bleidenstein asked him to lunch, for Bleidenstein always preferred to do business over lunch.

The lawyer was indeed thrilled that finally something was happening on the Coote front. He liked movement, scandal, the manoeuvrings of larger-than-life figures, but ever since Harry died the Coote dynasty had provided him with little amusement. It was like an hour-glass in which the sand was draining out. However, in the last few days his client Aubrey had asked him to make overtures to his wife Flicker to ascertain what she would consider a suitable pay-off in a divorce. Bleidenstein felt as if he had been watching the final grains of sand suck themselves downwards. Then Flicker, the old Page Three girl, had proved there was some life in her yet. She had replied through her solicitor that she wanted the newspaper. The thought of a good squabble was like an intravenous shot to Bleidenstein. He put it to Aubrey that he should not let his wife have it, then delighted in conveying Aubrey's intransigence on the matter to Flicker. Flicker had then said, 'Michael will know what to do. He's brainy. He'll get it for me.'

Bleidenstein went through four courses before he laid this scenario out before Michael over lunch. 'Real life should never be allowed to interfere with the inner man,' he said, wiping his mouth finally and replacing his napkin on his large lap.

Michael wondered how long he could endure this charade and

what, in reality, he could do about any of it. Throughout the meal
he looked as if he wished himself on another planet. Still, the
lawyer was confident that what he had to say would bring him
down to earth soon enough.

'Your mother seems to have made some sort of deal with her
father-in-law Harry,' Bleidenstein now told Michael Coote.
'She's quite implacable on the subject. She will not give up the
newspaper, not to Aubrey, not to anyone. I gave her to understand
that if she co-operated there would be quite enough for her to buy
a yacht and take the chauffeur to the sun for ever and ever.'

At this insult to his mother, Michael finally felt himself
reacting, but Bleidenstein gave him to understand it was a bit late
for mere pique. The lawyer eased his enormous bulk back on the
banquette in the restaurant where they were lunching, squeezing
Michael into a corner in more senses than one. 'As things stand in
law at this moment, there is nothing that can stop your parents
doing what they want with the newspaper,' he said. 'I imagine
sooner or later there will be a divorce, and as with most divorces
the family silver will be sold to finance it. But it could have been
very different. Read this,' he said.

Bleidenstein drew a large document out of his inside breast
pocket. It was a document of such dimensions that it could only
have fitted in the inside breast pocket of someone of Bleidenstein's
size. Bleidenstein spread the document on the table in front of the
two of them.

'This is Harry Coote's will,' the lawyer explained. 'Your
grandfather lodged it with my firm before your father Aubrey
married your mother Flicker. Of course, this will is public
knowledge now for those who can be bothered to take the time to
research it. I don't think that has ever included you, with your
scholarship life at Oxford, Michael, but I do think you will find it
very interesting,' he said. 'Read it. Read it now. If there is
anything you don't understand, I'll translate it for you.'

Michael read. He pushed the *petits fours* away and spread the
document out on the tablecloth. The legalese went round and
round. He read it once, then he read it again. He could not take it
all in, but he certainly understood the gist of it. He sat back on the

banquette. He had known Bleidenstein since he was a child. He had sat on his lap and been smothered by his paunch. Why had no one told him these things until now?

'You didn't seem frightfully interested, Michael. You wanted to do it your way,' the lawyer answered.

Michael understood from his reading of the will that the finger was pointed firmly at him. There was a sense in which he, just as much as Aubrey, had let them all down.

'That's the score, I am afraid,' said Bleidenstein. 'I told your mother it was up to you. I don't suppose she understood completely, but now you have seen it in print, you can try to explain it to her again.'

He ordered a port. Michael declined one. He had completely lost his appetite.

'It was all your grandfather's idea,' Bleidenstein was saying. 'Harry thought Aubrey would come to heel once he was married and he had always liked Flicker so he devised a trust that he didn't think could go wrong and would benefit her meanwhile.

'It was supposed to benefit you, too, you see. You went along with the first conditions soon enough. I think you were born rather sooner than is customary after your parents were married, weren't you, Michael? Since then you haven't fulfilled the terms at all. Your mother refused to put any pressure on you. She said she had never had her freedom and she had done things that way so you could have yours. She said you knew what you were doing. That may be, but unless you pull your finger out, you are going to end up your life a poor man.'

Michael looked miserable. It wan't the money. It was because he felt cornered. All his life he had tried to avoid that situation, and now here it was.

'Can I take a copy of the document?' he asked Bleidenstein.

'I don't see why not. You might as well have this one.' The lawyer pushed it across the table at Michael. 'But I think you have got the drift already,' said Bleidenstein. 'You will see from the text, when you study it at your leisure, that there is one obvious way out. One very simple and legitimate way in which you can influence the future of the family.'

Michael had no doubt as to what he was saying. On his quick reading to date, Bleidenstein's meaning seemed obvious. There was one relatively easy way in which he, Michael Coote, could take control of the family fortunes, and it would not take all that long. It was such a traditional way that the very thought panicked him. Michael Coote hated the inevitable. He wanted to get out of the restaurant and back to his own unique life. He slid the will back into its foolscap envelope.

'I can see you don't like such a domestic solution,' the lawyer conceded. 'Chip off the old block, you're Aubrey's son after all.' He ate Michael's *petits fours*. 'Of course, there might be another way out. This one might appeal to you more. If you could prove you had a serious interest in the business, you might persuade the other trustees to buy your father out. You would have to get some proper advisers, of course, but it could be done and you would certainly not be worse off. At the moment, you only stand to benefit from the dwindling income from the newspaper under your father and mother's regime. It is at the discretion of the trustees whether they advance any of the capital to you, and as things stand that is unlikely. So far you haven't really shown much interest in anything practical, Michael. So, the trustees are looking for a buyer to safeguard what remaining income you have for the rest of your days. It's not much consolation, is it, for someone who once had £450 million in his sights?

'In a nutshell,' recapped Bleidenstein, 'the problem is your father doesn't want the newspaper but he doesn't want your mother to have it either. So he is determined to sell it, which suits everyone nicely, and as things stand, unless you do something about it fast, it is his to sell. You now know the choices.

'If he does sell it, he had better do so fast or there won't be a hell of a lot left over to share between the three of you. You know as well as I do that ever since Aubrey got his hands on the money, he has spent it and has gone on spending it.' He shot his cuffs, which was something he always did to emphasize his self-importance. 'My God,' said Bleidenstein, 'your grandfather Harry must be turning in his grave. He did not think his plan could go wrong. In his generation, young Staffordshire men did not spend the best years of their lives sitting on the bank of the Isis watching the world go by.

'OK, Michael, so you know everything there is to know about what happened in history. You have several degrees in the subject, but what are you going to do about the present day? What are you going to do about tomorrow? Who the hell is going to look after your mother now? Aubrey has already sold the Daily Newspaper he inherited from your grandfather, and the Sunday went long ago, as you know. The trustees were won over by his talk of foreign investments. That went wrong and now he's parted with half the Evening. You sat by and let it happen. I'll do it my way, you said. When are you going to get round to it?

'Frankly, the trustees thought Gold might boost the profits a bit and there would be more in it for all of you. But the rumour is Gold wants out. He is a sick man, Michael. He hasn't been seen in *schul* for weeks. You could buy his share back if you were smart, but now I hear there's another contender for both your interests: Frederick Fisher. He is likely to step right in over your head. Fisher is making a real bid to clean up.'

'Fisher?' It was the first time Michael had heard the name.

'American chap,' mused Bleidenstein. 'Owner of a whole string of newspapers and a whole lot of *chutzpah* to go with them. I can't tell you anything more. But I can tell you that at this point, Michael, if you don't take an interest in your own life, no one else can help you. This Fisher who is after your paper is used to getting his own way.'

'Where is my father?' asked Michael.

'I am sure I don't know,' said Bleidenstein, and sank his teeth into a pink fondant, which he washed down with port.

So that was that. Bleidenstein told the heir to a theoretical fortune that his father, Aubrey Coote, rang in from time to time to insult his wife or to instruct his lawyer, but he never left a number and he never even said which country he was ringing from. Michael could not consult with him. He would have to make up his own mind what he was going to do.

'Damned unfair, really,' said Bleidenstein. 'Will you have a brandy now? There's many a less fine man who has been given a better break in life.' He pushed the bill across the table to Michael.

'Oh dear, I can't actually,' said Michael, feeling in his pockets. 'Don't worry. I'll put it on the family bill,' said Bleidenstein. 'To consultation,' he said.

Michael watched the lawyer hail a cab right outside the restaurant. It would make one turn round the square, not quite that even, and deposit him less than half a mile away. That was how Bleidenstein kept up his fuller figure. Michael clutched the will to himself under his jacket and walked idly down Greek Street. There was a gay black man in a pink tutu sitting in a restaurant window open on to the street. He had a cardboard sign around his neck asking for money for research to find a miracle cure for a modern plague. 'I am the magic AIDs fairy,' it read. 'Put a fistful in my slot.'

Michael needed a miracle cure for his own problem, but he didn't have a fistful. He did not have as much as the money for a taxi back to Flicker. He would have to walk, and he would use the walk to think. Instead, without intending it at all, his steps took him in another direction.

First Michael walked down to Piccadilly. He tried to buy a copy of the Evening Paper. It was the first time he had done so for about ten years. But he could not buy one because the stands where the paper was sold were all shut and bolted. Someone told him the newspaper was on strike. At first he was very annoyed. He had taken Bleidenstein's point about the family fortunes, which must be further dwindling because of the strike. Then he started to find the proposition interesting. He was beginning to realize just how interesting he had found everything about the last twenty-four hours. He had even found Flicker interesting, wanting to solve her predicament rather than shy away from it. It was as if, before her telephone call to the common room, he had been wrapped in a cocoon, his senses all cushioned from reality while his mind had been constructing a theoretical universe which was nevertheless a dull thing, totally lacking in inspiration. The real universe was a much more interesting place. Now every minute seemed to be part of some new learning process.

Michael was beginning to feel alive, and more than that, to acquire a sense of purpose. His steps quickened as he walked. Other people, too, started to notice the seed that was growing within him and started to look at him. For the first time he felt some curiosity about this mismanagement of his mother's future, though he had to concede he might have felt it any time had he only allowed himself to be receptive to the feeling.

The streets of London were filthy. Michael shuffled through slogans and cigarette cartons, old bus tickets and ice-cream wrappers as he turned his feet to Fleet Street. On the threshold of the street itself, he felt his pace quickening all the more. He had to have a look at the source of his family business before he put all this débâcle behind him and hitched a lift back to Oxford. From what he could see of the capital, it was no very pleasant place to linger, which was what he had always felt. On the other hand, what would he find when he got back to his medieval cell? Would the quality of life really be very much improved, and what good was he doing to anyone there? He could sit in Oxford watching little stone bits fall off the dreaming spires till he just dropped off the planet, too.

Then he walked down Fleet Street. The whole of London seemed overcrowded to him, but here he could hardly find his way through the throng of people. He clutched the will tighter to his body, afraid it might be snatched away and with it his renewed interest in the things going on around him. The people in the streets seemed to be waiting for something to happen, but he couldn't see what it was. From time to time he asked someone in the crowd what they were waiting for, but no one seemed to know. They were walking by common consent towards the unknown goal. He walked further, elbowing his way through the people, stepping off into the street when he could not get through on the pavement. The tide was moving slowly eastwards and he was carried relentlessly along with it till he reached the far end of the Street.

Now he stood opposite the wonderful white wedding-cake building that had been his grandfather Harry Coote's pride and joy. As he looked at it again, Michael remembered that much. He remembered Harry telling him about the opening ceremony when the Princess Royal cut the tape. Harry Coote had had yards and yards of typewriter ribbon tied right round the building and tickertape thrown out of the windows on the top tier. Pictures of the opening were on the front pages of all the rival newspapers and readers could quite clearly read the slogan streaming out of the beak of the pigeon he released from the pinnacle, which was to find its way back to the dovecote in Coote in Staffordshire. The slogan wrapped its way round the stucco top of the building: 'Coote, the name for news.' The pigeon soared and let go and the slogan was left behind. Michael remembered very well how pleased his grandfather was about that. He wondered how he could have forgotten this scene in the years in between. He could remember exactly how the building looked in the pictures Harry had shown him, lovingly stuck into the scrapbooks of his career, with each year embossed in gold leaf on the outside. He remembered how he had realized, as a small boy, that the building had his name on it as well as Harry's.

But now that Michael was standing in front of the real thing, he could scarcely see the building for people, and for something else as well. He could not see it for newspapers. There were quires of papers everywhere, stacked right up its rococo façade, towering way above the great arch of the doorway that led into the offices. Here and there were gaps in the piles where some people had resorted to private enterprise, perhaps stolen a quire or two and sold them on the motorway for pocket money. Around the piles they had tied some white ribbon to show it was a no-go area, and the whole lot was guarded by uniformed men.

From time to time someone came out of the back of the building and dumped another bundle of newspapers, hot from the presses, on top of the last. The newspapers kept coming. It was as if the wedding-cake building was standing in its own white and black life-blood, bleeding to death. Someone had scrawled graffiti in red paint on the white façade. The three colours of Fleet Street: white for the blank page of history, black for the folly of men written on it, red for the logos, the slogans, the hype. Michael picked up one of the newspapers. He had enough time to see it was not a new one at all; it was dated a week or so back. But as soon as he had seen this it was knocked out of his hands by a man with menace written in all his muscles.

'Don't touch that,' the man said. 'That's not yours to touch.'

Looking back on that day, it was the moment Michael would remember, the moment when the man told him his newspaper was not his newspaper.

27

Banging Out

'There's a girl on line two,' Charlene said.

He took the call. 'Yes,' he said.

'I wondered if you would like to say goodbye,' she said.

The English voice; he knew who it was. 'We didn't say hello yet,' he said.

'Hello, goodbye,' she said.

'You didn't go home with Arthur?'

Sonia had not gone home with Arthur. She had told Arthur that, since she had not flown in with him, she was not planning to fly out with him either. Arthur was a pain in the neck, but she did not tell Fisher so. She did not tell Fisher she was damned if she was going to spend ten hours trapped with his editor on an aeroplane while he agonized about what he was going to do about the strike, his job, his contract, his child, his wife. She certainly did not tell Fisher that her lover was terrified his wife would meet him at the airport and discover his guilty secret. It did not give her any more dignity than it gave Nora.

She told Fisher she had stayed behind on a story. 'I am a writer,' she said brightly to disguise her annoyance.

Arthur had said he would make her his new features editor, but Arthur was always chopping and changing. She didn't trust Arthur. She wanted to trust a man one day.

'How do you say goodbye?' Fisher asked.

'You say it face to face,' she said. 'Over dinner preferably.'

He was disconcerted to find he was momentarily thrown. He looked out at the wide flat landscape that he loved below his office. 'I can't make dinner,' he said.

'Too bad,' she said. 'I'm on the plane tomorrow.'

He was curious. It was a long time since he had had dinner with a woman who had a mind of her own. He picked her up at her hotel. He had no difficulty identifying her in the lobby. She was all in black. It was not a colour Southern women often wore. He certainly found her attractive. She was built, she made no attempt to hide that fact, or that she was geared, as they say in the state of Texas. Geared for sex.

'So you are Frederick Fisher,' she said.

'You can call me F.J.'

'I don't know you nearly well enough yet,' she said.

'Where do you want to go?' he asked.

'You're in the driving seat,' she said. 'You're driving that?' As usual he had brought the pick-up truck.

He was not at ease in the fancy restaurant where he took her. He was too big. He did not know how to arrange his legs under the table. He did not seem to be hungry. He could not sit still. He sipped his water and rattled the ice in the glass. He seemed to want to stretch all his limbs. He was like a kid, she thought, going through the motions with the grown-ups but stir-crazy and anxious to get out to play.

'Relax. Have a drink, Freddy,' she said.

'I don't drink,' he answered.

'What *do* you do?'

'I work,' he said. 'All I like is working.'

'There must be something else you like?'

'What do you want from me, Sonia?' he asked.

'I want to work for you,' she said impulsively.

'What would you like to do for me?' A little smile came over his face. She smiled too. She had a mouth. 'What can you do?'

'What do you want me to do?' she asked.

Would he never get to the point? Other men always propositioned her. Not him. He would not do it. He looked at her appraisingly. He was by turns polite and vulgar. The excitement shot off him. She could feel it over the table. It was feeding her excitement, but it never got the better of him. He did not seem to want anything from her. It drove her crazy.

'Oh hell, Freddy,' she said. 'Let's fuck.'

198

He did not answer immediately, and his silence made her horribly afraid. Surely he was not going to say no. She had never seriously been refused anything in her whole life before.

'Sonia Fraser.' He said her name slowly as if he was trying to get used to it, and he smiled gently at her. 'Are you sure you can handle it?' he asked. On the whole he thought a girl should wait to be asked, even if it was the late twentieth century.

It was the last reaction she expected. To answer it made her into a virgin or a whore. It thrilled her hopelessly. She was used to men who would enter into a bargain with her. Frederick Fisher did not want to enter into a bargain with anyone ever again. She could tell he was interested. He was looking at her steadily. She had the breasts he liked and the hair he liked to hold. He would like to gather her hair up behind the nape of her neck and pull her head back and bend to kiss her and see the anticipation in her eyes. He would like to screw her.

He had not had a girl lately, he thought to himself. He was so goddam busy. Time was when he had one a day. He would slip off on his way home. He knew where to go. He had a list of them lined up for the purpose. It only took ten minutes and it always put him in a good mood. No matter what had happened during the day, just to put his hand up a girl's skirt made him feel younger again.

He imagined doing it now; still he made no move. He let his imagination work on the situation instead. He looked at her mouth across the table. He liked her smile. He imagined his prick in Sonia Fraser's mouth. In his imagination, he held it in his hand and traced with his erection the outline of her smile. He imagined her tongue licking him. He looked at her and wondered whether she was thinking the same thing. She was. She was thinking how she would take her tongue and press it against his soft hard thing and commit every vein of him to memory through the rough sensitive cells of her tongue. She was thinking how he would look when she did that to him. She was thinking how he would become vulnerable. She was thinking how the years would fall off him when he came, so that she would be left holding a child in her arms. She looked at his hand resting on the table. It was small for so big a man. All of a sudden she thought how precious that child could become.

He was thinking he was sure she knew what to do with her tongue. But he was thinking that he would not let her finish the job. He would not put himself in her hands. He knew exactly what he would do to take control instead. He looked her in the eyes across the table and imagined the thing between her legs. What would it be like? Would it be dark and smooth, would it be soft and pale, would he be able to see the flesh beneath her hair? He imagined the hair wet and trimmed into a strip between two cushions of flesh. He imagined the smell of her, and the thought made him inhale deeply so he could almost smell her in reality. He smiled a secret smile.

He imagined how he would make her undress for him, very very slowly, and how he would make her embarrassed, and how he would stare for a long time, concentrating on the area between her thighs, holding it in his memory. As soon as he thought he would remember it properly with his eyes for all time, so he could conjure up the vision when he was alone at night, he would put himself into her.

He would put himself into her quickly, he would not wait. She was small, he was sure, and he would hurt her and something deep in him would enjoy hurting her just as something in her would enjoy being hurt. 'Like an oyster in a slot machine,' he said below his breath.

'What?' she asked, but he did not answer, just smiled that long secret smile and kept on with his imaginings. He was thinking about how he would kneel on the bed, his long legs up under him, and how he would open up her legs on either side of his thighs. He was thinking that he was inside her now and she was opened right up against his stomach. He was holding her buttocks in his hands underneath her and he was gyrating her body on his. He would not let her move herself. It drove them crazy.

He was thinking that he knew exactly what he was going to do next. When he could feel her straining for the feeling, when he knew she wanted to feel more and more, he would withdraw from her. He would not let her have her satisfaction. Instead, he would get down on his knees at the side of the bed and pull her legs over his shoulders and spread them wide till his mouth rested against her crotch. Very gently he would run his tongue round and round, slowly at first and then faster and faster. He would take all of her in his mouth bit by bit and let it slip out again, then he would put his tongue right inside her, and when she started moaning he would take his tongue away.

Then he would sit on the edge of the bed and masturbate himself. He would not let her touch, only watch. When he came, he would do so noiselessly as if he were experiencing nothing, as if he were not there at all but just a spectator at the scene. He had never said anything in bed, never made the slightest sound for many years, he had always been completely in control.

'Waiter, the check,' he said.

She smiled. It was going to be all right after all.

'Excuse me,' he said. He left the table. He was gone about five minutes.

While he was away, the waiter brought the bill and left it in the empty space in front of his seat. He brought a pot of coffee, too. 'All for you,' he said. 'F.J. won't have any.' Then he said something she found enigmatic. 'He's a good man. Look after him.'

Then Fisher came back. He didn't bother to explain his absence at all. He sat down, his legs stretched out to the side while he signed the bill. 'You shouldn't drink that stuff,' he said. 'Coffee's poison. You won't sleep.'

'I'm not planning to sleep,' she answered.

'You don't want fucking, Sonia,' he said suddenly. 'And I'm not going to fuck you.' Sonia sat straight up, shocked. Was he a load of talk, why did he not take up the challenge?

As with everyone else, it was as if he read her thoughts. 'Oh, I'm into pussy all right,' he said. 'Make no mistake about that, Sonia, I love it. But you're into something else,' he said. 'You're into power. I recognize it when I see it because I am into power, too. Power can be complicated in a woman. Why are you into power?'

'You tell me,' she said. 'You seem to know everything about me.'

'I guess it's because you come from a powerful family,' he said. What did he know about her family?

'What do you know about my family?' she asked.

'Personally I don't give a shit about politics,' he said. 'The way I see it, there are more crooks on Capitol Hill than there ever were in the nation's gaols. It could be different in England, but I doubt it.'

'It isn't different in England,' she said gloomily. 'It's worse. In England everything depends on context.' She was furious with him, with herself. Why was she colluding with this man by explaining anything to him?

'Then it can't really be all that bad being the Home Secretary's daughter,' said Frederick Fisher. 'In this life you got to use everything you got, Sonia, the only trick is knowing what to use it for.'

He stopped her in her tracks. He did know who she was and he was confronting her with it. He was saying it was OK. He was telling her it was not enough. He was telling her to get on with it. What was he saying? What did he know about her?

'I like you, Sonia,' he said. 'But you are all over the place at the moment. You don't know what you want, where you are going or who you are.'

'That's not true,' she said angrily. 'I just don't plan to wait around all my life for you fellows to get your act together, that's all. I'm me, Frederick Fisher, and I don't want anybody else telling me who that is, including you. This may come as news to you, but I want to do it my way, just like you do.'

'If you want to do it like me, you must first learn how to be happy, Sonia. It's an inalienable right,' he grinned. 'If you want to listen to me I'll tell you. If you don't it's all the same to me. Believe me, I don't help everyone. I don't help anyone if I can help it. I don't like people.'

'Shit, I guess the feeling's mutual,' she retorted.

'Now listen to me good, Sonia,' he said. 'First I will tell you how to get what you really want. After that my driver will take you back to your hotel and tomorrow I have arranged for him to take you straight to the airport.'

Sonia dug her nails into her palms. She had never felt so angry or insulted before. Nobody had ever told her what to do and thereby struck any sort of truth in her. She wanted to storm out of the restaurant. She tried to push her chair back from the table, but he held up the palm of his hand to stop her.

'You have the misfortune to be a woman, Sonia,' he said. 'You had better be kind to yourself.'

'Oh boy, are you old-fashioned, Frederick Fisher,' she said angrily. 'What the hell are you so afraid of?'

28

Bold

Michael Coote took a plane to Dallas and hired a car at the airport. He drove out through the flat streets and asked directions at a gas station.

He drove for about half an hour. The concrete quickly gave way to flat countryside. There were dead skunks lying by the roadside where they had been hit by cars. It was not a beautiful place, but the inhabitants had certainly done their best with it. Each little green patch of lawn in the front of each house was perfectly trimmed and sprinkled. The houses were in the shuttered ante-bellum style and they seemed to have been bought from the interior decorator by the yard. The drives were perfectly raked as if no one ever used them. Yet each garage had a couple of cars parked outside.

Everything looked so perfect it might have been painted on canvas. Each perfect patch was topped with the American flag, and next to it, flying at the same height, the Texan state flag with its lone-star moniker. Michael felt embarrassed at such a show of patriotism: not for America, but for the country he had left behind where they made tea-towels out of the flag and underpants out of the escutcheons of his Oxford college. He did not know yet exactly how he was going to do it, but he knew for certain he was not going to let Frederick Fisher have his Coote birthright.

He was in wild country all right. Hawks followed his car as seagulls might at sea. At times it seemed as if they might swoop down through the open window and peck at his eyes for moisture in the relentless heat. More than once the tyres of the car surprised a rattler basking on the hot tarmac of the open road and Michael swerved to avoid it. It put him on his mettle to see how slender a hold human beings had on this part of the planet. It was as if men and their fancies had only lightly brushed the earth's cheek at this point. There was the tangle of trees and grass, and apart from that there was nothing there except what had been put there by the people themselves. They had inherited nothing but the dirt. The very people who lived here now had built their own homes brick by brick with their bare hands. They had laid their own concrete, and even as they smoothed it over, animals had come and trampled on it with their paws and taken the smoothness away. Nature screamed her determination to have her own way, and Michael saw her poised with a twister, a snowstorm, a heatwave, a wild beast to wipe out the imprints of human beings even as they put them down.

He thought he must have overshot the ranch because he had left the houses far behind, so he stopped at another gas station to ask directions. The attendant in baseball cap and sneakers was impressed when he told him where he was going.

'The Alamo Ranch?' he said. 'Ain't no one from round here ever gotten an invitation to see inside that place. Alamo belongs to F.J. Fisher,' he said. 'Fishers are tough and F.J.'s toughest of the lot.'

Michael started to take stock of what he had done back in London. He had had a drunken lunch with a divorce lawyer, he had found his mother crying into her champagne again. She was blubbing something about another telephone call from Aubrey. Her husband had phoned from some credit-card phone on an airliner overflying the Grand Canyon. When he could not make an international call from the plane, he had called his lawyer in New York and had him dial Flicker in London and put the connections together. He was so determined to speak to Flicker at that moment in time that she was obsessed with the idea that he was fucking his airstewardess in the plane even as he was talking to his wife. 'This is the moment you have been waiting for,' he had said. 'You're free to do what you want to do from now on, and that includes the chauffeur. I've had an offer from Fisher.'

'Michael!' Flicker blubbed. 'Your father's a fool. He's going to sell our last newspaper. He's going to sell it to Frederick Fisher.

He's going to settle for nothing from Fisher just because he is obsessed with this bimbo he's screwing. You've got to do something. The real estate alone is worth £20 million.'

Michael had tried to find out about this man Fisher who was hanging over their future, but he had no luck beyond discovering just what everyone else knew. Once again, just as it had been when he picked up his newspaper and was told it was not his newspaper, he was assailed by the lack of logic in the situation. He was heir to a news fortune, even though it was a diminishing one, and he could not find out a thing about the news. He could not even ring his own library in the wedding-cake building because they would refuse the call.

Fisher's switchboard was not even answering. Beyond what everyone else knew about Fisher, Michael could find out nothing. He knew that the oldest newspapers in England had fallen into his hands after their old proprietor died, that Fisher had immediately fired the editor of the Daily Newspaper, found himself with a strike on his hands because he had inadvertently crossed some feminist, and had then gone back home to Dallas. That was all Michael knew. The people at his Sunday Newspaper were under the impression they had seen him off. Michael's mother thought something quite else. 'I know Fisher's reputation,' was what she said. 'You don't fuck with Fisher. He always gets what he wants. This time he wants my Evening Newspaper.'

Michael had then gone to bed in the house in Mayfair, but he had not been able to sleep. One thing was worrying him. Everyone was speculating about Fisher trying to add Aubrey's Evening Paper to his hand, but Fisher wasn't asking anyone in London for anything. Though he had problems in London, he was not in London, and that he had in common with Aubrey. Michael imagined the two of them together, doing a deal over the sale on the other side of the Atlantic. In his sleeplessness, Michael had opened a magazine, and the first thing his eyes rested on was an advertisement in bold type for the airline which flew to Texas. He had taken it as an omen.

In the morning, he had done something he never would have thought he had it in him to do. He had picked up the phone to

Bleidenstein and asked him to arrange a loan from the family trust. Then he went straight to the airport and he bought a ticket for the plane. It was only when he landed at Dallas-Fort Worth that he realized he could not call Fisher. The man's house was not listed in the telephone directory and he was not at his office at Fisher Ink. Michael put the phone down and wondered what he should do next. So far he had been buoyed up by the momentum of a situation which was very new to him. He knew he had to keep the momentum going, so he had taken a car and determined to find the ranch. It could not be difficult in a place where everyone knew the name of Fisher as if it was their own middle name.

Twelve hours after leaving London, here he was in a part of the earth where he had never been before, but the curious thing was that the compelling feeling that he was doing right had still not left him. It was nearly midnight back at home, but he was nowhere near getting tired. On the garage wall where he stopped for directions there was a poster for a local rodeo. It reminded him again that he was in pioneer country, and even on the garage forecourt there was only a thin veneer of concrete over the wild earth. The concrete was cracked like baked meringue and the parched grass was thrusting up through it. Michael was about to go in the ring in a rodeo and he was supposed to take the bucking steer by the horns. The steer would buck all right. He would buck as if he had elastic round his balls. Now the combat was close, Michael wondered if it was such a good idea after all. If he looked towards the city, he could see the great glass towers thrusting up out of the plain like the welcoming gates of a fort in the desert in the days of the Indian traders. They beckoned the traveller to come in out of the flatlands like friendly beacons, but Michael was going away from them, not towards.

The attendant gave him directions, and he set off once more in his small rented car. Modern Oxford had not given him any of the extravagances of his father, neither did he think he ever would have them. If he had something to do, he did it in the simplest way possible. That much was true even of his jaunt today. He never employed any of the devices other people used to kill time or beat around the bush.

This time he found the Alamo. There was a small white unmarked gate leading into a narrow drive demarcated by white fencing. He drove through the gate, over a cattle grid and into two deep furrows which must have been ploughed by a four-wheel drive. It was a bumpy road, and the chassis of his small car kept grinding on the baked mud thrown into the centre of the tracks by all the vehicles which had gone before. From time to time he found himself wallowing in a fresh puddle, then the road would be baked dry again as if rain never fell.

It was lucky that the way was difficult to negotiate. Michael had to concentrate so hard to miss the furrows that the effort took away any remaining fears about the confrontation he was about to engineer. In the briefcase on the seat beside him he had the copy of his grandfather's will. He put his hand out to make sure it was there. He threw the little car backwards and forwards on the high ground of the drive so as not to get stuck in the tracks, and it was only when he saw the ranch-house in front of him that he realized he must have driven like this for about two miles.

It was as if the house had been dropped from the sky right into the middle of nowhere. Even in this tiny corner of it you could see you were in a big country. In front of the house was a green field, and in the field a girl with straight auburn hair was exercising a horse. She was a girl about twenty years old. Her hair shone red in the sunlight and the horse shone jet-black.

At the door of the ranch-house stood a man who must have been Fisher. He was well over six feet tall. At the sight of him, Michael felt his heart beating unevenly. He swung the car on to a gravel drive. For a brief second he wondered whether Fisher was armed, whether the house was garrisoned. He had heard that this was the land of private armies and trigger-happy nuts.

Fisher did nothing to reassure him. He was standing there wearing black velour exercise clothes. There was something about him that bristled like an untamed animal as if all his senses were roused to take care of whatever might happen next. He did nothing threatening, but Michael noticed he never quite stood still on the spot. He seemed to be looking around him all the time as if he expected to be surrounded by a bunch of Indians armed with bows and arrows.

Michael parked his car more neatly than was necessary in order to give himself time to think. Even if this was a bad idea, he had to go ahead with it now. He reached for his briefcase with the will inside it. Then he got out of the car, tucked the briefcase under his arm and walked towards Fisher with his right hand outstretched. 'I'm Michael Coote,' he said.

Fisher did not move. He did not take the visitor's hand. His eyes did not move from the intruder. He nodded slowly and looked him up and down. 'I know that,' he said after a long while. What does he want, he thought, but he said nothing more.

'I'm Aubrey's son,' Michael explained.

'Yup,' said Fisher this time, 'I guess you are.'

'I've come from London,' said Michael.

'That's a long way,' said Fisher. He was playing for time. He stood there, studying the man who had driven uninvited up his drive. No one had ever done anything like this before, and he did not like it because he could not read the signs right. What would make a person take a plane 5,000 miles, he asked himself. He came up with the answer, too. Money.

He looked the kid up and down. He was handsome enough. He had a full head of dark hair and a slightly tawny complexion. He was thin. There was not an ounce of fat on him. He had looked after himself. He thought perhaps he could be a mean fighter. Fisher took a step back. The kid was wearing clean clothes, though not formal ones. He had on a tweed sports jacket and slacks. They were the wrong clothes for the place and he was sweating slightly, unused to the heat.

Michael looked past Fisher into the green field. It seemed to be covered with lilac poppies. The girl had come down off the horse and hitched it to the white paling fence. Michael saw that she was wearing a gingham blouse with old-fashioned fringed riding chaps over blue jeans. When she moved, she danced a bit. She was watching the two men very carefully, but she did not come any closer. It was as if she was waiting for some sign which she did not get.

'OK,' said Fisher finally to Michael. 'We can talk if that's what you want.'

Instead of going into the house, Fisher stepped off the porch into the heat and started walking very slowly away from the door and away from the girl. Michael followed him. There did not seem anything else to do. He looked back, but the girl was making no move to join them. Fisher walked very slowly, his hands clasped behind his back. He started walking round the house and still his uninvited guest followed him. Still Fisher said nothing. They went on walking round the house. It was a white clapboard house, something from a Wyeth picture, a traditional house but absolutely clean as if it had just been built. Even the nails that held it together were shiny and rust-free, and the flowerbeds dug out against the walls were empty, raked clean as if they were waiting for something to be planted in them. The place had an air of waiting for something to happen. It was as if the house were fast asleep in the great heat. The only sign of life was Fisher himself, who was wired up with energy, and the big insects, which would dive from time to time out of a clear sky. It seemed too hot for anything more friendly.

'I got to figure out a way of keeping these goddam bugs away,' Fisher said. It was the first time he had said anything, and just as quickly he was silent again.

He walked on, watching Michael surreptitiously. Michael could not work out how to begin to say the things he had come to say. For the time being it seemed better to say nothing at all or to stick to words soothing and vague. 'It's a nice part of the country,' he said.

Fisher ignored him. 'Hot enough for you?' he said after a while.

'I don't mind the heat, sir,' Michael said.

Fisher shot him a look. Again he went silent. 'Fence needs painting,' he said. 'Again.' To Michael the fence seemed absolutely perfect. It was as white as if it had just been put up. Someone had sandpapered it as if it were a work of art, and finished it off with a high gloss, which shone in the sun.

'I know what you mean,' Michael said. 'The Coote House is like the Forth Bridge.'

Fisher raised an eyebrow, and for the first time since he arrived he looked his visitor full in the eyes as if he had been waiting for this opportunity to do so. 'A house like a bridge?' he said with barely an inflection.

'English expression,' explained Michael. 'As soon as you've finished doing it up, you have to start all over again.'

'Well, that's true of most things in life,' said Fisher.

He did not say anything else, so Michael went on. 'Coote's the family seat,' he explained further. 'My grandfather must have thought he was doing us all a favour when he built it. Sometimes I wonder. The wedding-cake building in Fleet Street, Coote in Staffordshire, the Villa Inglese in the South of France – the old man collected a herd of white elephants for himself and we have to keep them up. White elephants eat a lot of money.'

At the mention of money, Fisher bristled. 'There should be no such thing as inherited money,' was all he said, and he carried on walking. 'In this town we spend what we earn. We have a saying: Go first class. Your heirs will.'

They had come to a courtyard behind the house, laid out Spanish-style with several fountains and a swimming pool in the middle.

'Pool,' said Fisher unnecessarily. 'Stables,' he waved his hand towards another block behind the main house. 'Ain't no one gonna bother to keep all this up when I'm gone. I got no illusions.'

Michael was fascinated. The Alamo was no San Simeon. It was plain, sheer, functional. Fisher did not seem to be a collector of things. Most people kidded themselves about immortality. Fisher talked about death. It made him seem almost invulnerable, as if there was nothing at all he expected from the universe but what it was surely going to give him one day, a nameless grave.

By now they had walked right round the house, mostly in silence, and had come back to the front door. The auburn-haired girl had disappeared, and with her the horse she had been riding. Then Michael heard the crunch of gravel underfoot and she appeared around the corner of the house from the stables, her chaps swinging as she moved from the hip. She moved part gracefully, part awkwardly, like a young puppy who had not quite learned its best points. She stopped, then loitered in her tracks when she saw the two men. Fisher looked at her, his hand on his velour hip, then, when he was ready, beckoned her. She ran up to Fisher, jumped up and kissed his cheek, and he put his arm round her waist and swung her round beside him.

'We have a visitor,' he said. Suddenly he became very formal. 'This is Michael Coote,' he said. 'This is my daughter Melanie.'

Michael held out his hand. The girl took it and their eyes met. For God's sake, she did a sort of curtsey to him as well. She was flushed from her exercise, but despite the heat her skin was quite dry. Michael was thrilled by her auburn hair. It was so sleek he had to stop himself putting out his hand to touch it.

'I have to have a drink,' Melanie said. 'You coming in?'

Michael was immensely grateful to her. All of a sudden he was very tired. It was late at night where he had come from, and Fisher was playing on his nerves like a virtuoso. Now the girl had come to his rescue, whether she knew it or not. It was as if she sensed, with her female intuition, that the two men were at an impasse and knew just what to do about it. Fisher pushed Melanie through the screen door into the darkness of the house, and Michael followed them blindly. He could not see anything but he could feel the cold air flooding all over him like water.

'Make sure the screen's good and shut,' said Fisher. 'We got bugs the size of footballs. You can't match that in England.'

Michael followed Fisher and his daughter down a long corridor, his eyes gradually adjusting to the darkness. As they passed by a sitting room, he could see glass table-tops and oriental statues. There was a large zebra skin on the floor, its dark stripes criss-crossed again with the stripes of light coming in through the shuttered windows. A pair of lynx statues were camouflaged in another patch of stripes. It was a sitting room, but it looked as if nobody ever sat in it. The cream upholstery was drawn tight on the cushions as if no weight had ever rumpled it. There was no scuff mark on the wooden floor, no shadow on the glass. Again it was a room in waiting, just like the house.

Fisher did not turn into the room. Instead he led Michael

straight to the kitchen and opened a huge refrigerator door. He stood in the cool air, then he picked up a paper cup and filled it for himself without offering it to the uninvited guest.

'Want some?' asked Melanie.

'Sure, I'll have some,' Michael said.

'It's Kool-Ade,' Melanie laughed and pirouetted round in her blue jeans. 'It's for kids. My dad always drinks it. You probably want some gin in it? You're British.'

Fisher said nothing at all. The fan whirred in the middle of the ceiling. The refrigerator changed the note in its cycle. There was only the sound of machinery. It was soporific in the heat. The heat itself seemed to have a sound. A sound of white light, of solid, almost visible particles filling the air and whispering up against each other. Michael found it soothing, so that this place in which he should by rights have felt an intruder was a sort of home. He was bewildered by the intense feeling of misplaced well-being. Michael looked out of the window. It looked out on to the swimming pool, which was filled with dazzling blue water and decorated with Hispanic tiles. There was another machine in the pool. It walked lazily up and down, cleaning it as it went.

'Too bright for you?' said Melanie.

She pressed a button by the refrigerator and the blinds came down over the window. Everything was automated. She went to the cupboard and took out a bottle of gin.

'Wow, that's enough,' said Michael. He was talking about the gin.

Melanie was laughing. She had tipped nearly a whole half-bottle of gin into the glass she was holding for Michael. He did not know whether she was playing with him or whether she was a complete innocent. He put the cup down on the draining board and opened the door into the yard.

'Shut that,' ordered Fisher. 'It's hotter 'n a pistol out there. Come on in and tell me what it is you want.'

Fisher sat down at the kitchen table. He leaned back and put his long legs on the table top. He was wearing ostrich-skin boots over the velour exercise pants. 'You can say anything you have to say in front of my daughter,' he said.

213

He pointed to one of the chairs along the side. Michael pulled it up and arranged himself neatly at the table, his two hands resting on the top, nervously playing with his fingers as if he was about to take a boardroom meeting. He took a deep breath. He was relieved and amazed to realize that the plan he had plotted on the long journey had entered quite involuntarily into his brain. He was relieved, too, to find it sounded quite plausible in the circumstances in which he now found himself. There was nothing for it now but to seize the moment. He could not postpone it any longer. He laid the briefcase down on the table in front of him and slowly opened it. Equally slowly he drew out the copy of Harry's will. He watched Fisher to see if he was watching him. It crossed his mind that it was like drawing a card out of a deck at a poker game, and he was sure poker was Fisher's game.

'It's like this, sir,' Michael said. 'I understand you are interested in buying our family interest in the Evening Newspaper.'

Fisher remained absolutely still.

'If so, it is no use you thinking you can do a deal with my father Aubrey.'

Still Fisher did not move. He did not move as much as those eloquent eyebrows. He noticed everything, even though he did not seem to be focusing directly on anything, not on the will or the boy but somewhere in his own imagination.

Michael continued. He was getting into his stride and he sounded more confident now. 'The paper is not my father's to sell,' he said.

Still Fisher did not react. There was only the whirring of the fan on the ceiling to encourage the speaker. Outside it was dark already. The night had dropped on to the earth like a cloth over a parrot cage. Sometimes the bugs thudded into the windows looking for light. Their shiny plastic wing-cases splattered on the glass. If Michael was playing a poker game, and he was, what would Fisher's next card be? But Fisher was not playing any cards. Michael was still being asked to draw from his own hand.

'This is my grandfather's will,' said Michael. 'He died in 1970. He was a friend of mine.'

At the word 'friend' Fisher reacted very slightly. It was an unusual word to use about a grandfather. He liked it.

'The will sets out exactly what can be done with the newspaper and what cannot,' Michael said. As with all good lies, there was an element of truth in the one he was about to tell. He took a deep breath. 'Under the terms of this will, which my father accepted when he inherited, the newspaper belongs to the son and heir of the Coote family. I am the son and heir, Mr Fisher. There is no one else but me. If you have any proposals about buying anything that is mine, it is me to whom you should address them. The paper belongs to me.'

Michael wondered what Fisher would do. The man was looking at the will now, but he made no move to ask to see it more closely. Michael left it on the table between them for the time being, like an invitation to take what he had said seriously. Soon he would slide it back into the briefcase and take his leave. After that, if Fisher researched the will, as he could at the Register Office in London, Michael calculated it would stop him in his tracks while he grasped the complexities of it. He would have to employ an English lawyer, and he would have to find the right one. The family trust was not a simple thing. He would grasp it sooner rather than later, of course, but all Michael needed was a little time to get his own act together, to go back to Bleidenstein and work out a plan of campaign. To get time, he had to stop Fisher negotiating with his father, who was in a mood to do anything to ease his cash-flow.

Time was what Michael had none of, he realized now, and he prayed he had not realized it too late. He had spent the last ten years in a classroom at Oxford, thinking he had it all before him. Experience was the other thing he had too little of, so he prayed for a second chance. He thought it might be granted to him because he had discovered one significant thing about himself when he boarded that aeroplane to Dallas. He had discovered something real that meant something to him at last. He had discovered he had a passion.

Michael wanted Fisher to withdraw any offer to his father Aubrey for long enough so he could tell the trustees what he had in mind to bring the company into the future and persuade them he could improve the performance of the Evening Paper. He would work together with Gold, if necessary, or buy him out if he could. That was the next step. His undertaking, combined with the natural suspicion that would surround another Fleet Street takeover bid from the American, should give him the chance he needed to get on to that step. After that it was up to him. He did not know whether he could do it, but he would have a damn good try. And the bottom line was that he could actively look after his mother even if his father did divorce her. He had never realized before how much family meant to him. It was a man's only investment in immortality. Suddenly he was behaving exactly like the member of a dynasty that he was.

Fisher was a man of few words. 'Not his to sell,' he said. He was speaking of Aubrey. 'That's not a reason for you to come here. That would have all come out in the wash. In the end, it doesn't matter who I buy it from. According to the figures, whoever owns it will be glad to get rid of it.'

Yet Fisher was momentarily thrown, and there was a side of him which was pleased to admit it to himself. He had not reckoned with this young man and his unorthodox methods. He had been within a hair's breadth of sending him packing when he turned up in his rented car at the Alamo. He was still bristling with suspicion, but there was something else, too. Now he was trying hard not to warm to this impetuous newcomer. He wondered how soon it would be before the boy let him down. It seemed almost inevitable that he would. Fisher sighed irritably. He was remembering Arthur.

'At least these newspaper wars are good for business,' Fisher said finally. 'If either of us had an English newspaper which was actually printing at this time, this story would sell it to the punters all right.'

It was a good story, certainly. Michael could appreciate that. Here he was in the middle of a strange country with a man he had never set on eyes before, a man full of power but a man he liked, and a girl who was the most beautiful thing he had ever seen. She was beautiful.

Fisher was still looking at the will. Michael thought it was time to pick it up slowly and slide it back into the briefcase. Would Fisher ask for it? He did not. As the briefcase snapped shut with the past and the future inside it, suddenly Michael felt as if all the strength was draining out of him. The clock whirring on the wall showed it was nine o'clock in the evening: three in the morning British time. He felt nauseous and knew he had to get out of here and go to bed. Melanie noticed his distress and Fisher noticed her noticing it. As for him, he used the observation to his psychological advantage.

'I'll fight you for the paper, Coote,' Fisher was saying. 'And I'll enjoy doing it. I have gotten everything I have through war. No one has ever given me anything in life, son, like they gave it you. You may have been born with a silver spoon in your mouth, but even with all your heritage there's some things you still have to earn for yourself in this world. You have to earn your enemies just as you do your friends. Enemies are a lot more helpful to you than friends. In fact, I would say friendship is a highly overrated condition.'

29

Light

It was very early in the morning when the door opened. He felt as if he hadn't slept at all. Melanie was standing there with a silver tea tray and wearing a red kimono. Her auburn hair was brilliant. A shaft of light flooded in through the open door. Michael lifted himself on one elbow and watched her.

She put a tray on a little glass-topped table by the window, then opened the drapes with a little flick of her wrist on the touch button. She turned round and looked at him with a little smile.

'Dad hates people to stay in bed after 6 a.m.,' she said.

'I'm sorry,' he found himself saying. 'Heavens, it's one in the afternoon where I come from. I'll never get into my sleep cycle now.'

Outside, the sun was climbing up over the pool. She opened the windows. He got out of bed. The early-morning air was still cool. In the field beyond the pool Michael could see the black horse grazing, up to its hocks in the purple flowers.

'Evening primroses,' said Melanie, as if she knew what he was thinking. 'Like silk. Don't you love them?'

He thought back over the end of the night before. He remembered that Melanie had told her father she would make up a bed in the pool-house for their visitor so he would not have to drive into town. 'Do what you like,' Fisher had said. 'I'm tired.' He had got up from the table and disappeared.

'What's your horse called?' Michael asked.

He was a beautiful animal. With the sun on his bruise-black coat, you could see the muscles working beneath his skin like long skeins of silk.

'His name is Sultan,' she said. 'Do you want to ride him?'

'You'd let me ride Sultan?'

'Sure,' she said. 'Why not? You English all can ride, can't you?'

It was as if Michael was taken back on a carpet of time. An image appeared in his brain which he had not thought about for many years. In the scene in his mind his grandfather Harry was sitting astride his chestnut cob, walking through the English lanes around Coote, and Michael himself was straddling his fat pony, trotting behind.

'Does your father ride?' he asked her.

'My father? Good grief, no!' Melanie laughed and adjusted her auburn hair in the red clip which held it up on her head. 'My father's always moaning about the cost of keeping Sultan. Coffee?' she asked and started to pour him a cup. ' "A thousand dollars a month," he says. "If ever he goes missing first place you can look is the knacker's yard." ' She laughed.

There was a glass of freshly squeezed orange juice sitting on a nest of ice on the tray and a vase containing a rose. He did not know where she could have picked the rose in the barren garden.

'My father says he hates animals,' she said. 'I always wanted a puppy, but he wouldn't let me have one. He says there are only two reasons to get a dog: one if you're blind, two if you live in the Arctic.'

Michael sat down by the window. He had expected to wake up in a hotel in a town they were still building. Instead, there was open country as far as he could see. He had not expected to feel any peace at all in this country on this mission, but somehow the unique feeling of well-being he had had the day before was still with him. He did not understand how he could be both apprehensive and content. He was like the land which surrounded them. Outside, the white heat was already visible shimmering round the blistered clumps of grass. But there were new sprouts, too, and a small pool of water on the concrete being lapped up by the sun as if it were a thirsty animal.

'Water?' he asked.

'Thunder,' she explained. 'In the night. You didn't hear? You see, you slept well after all. You were tired.'

'Are you going to have coffee with me?' he asked.

219

'I've already had it with my father,' she said. 'I'm going to saddle up. We can have proper breakfast afterwards.'

'After what?' he asked.

'After our early-morning ride, of course,' she said. 'I ride every morning. You can ride Sultan and I'll ride Whilma.' And she was gone.

Michael took his coffee into the bathroom and started to run the shower. He felt marvellous, as if the world was suddenly at his feet. He had not ridden a horse for many years, but now he felt an enormous surge of energy which only begged him to take some physical exercise. Ever since he had picked up that copy of the Evening Newspaper in Fleet Street, he had found himself looking forward to the business of living for the first time for a very long time. Suddenly the phone rang. It was Fisher. He was in his office already.

'What a day! Don't you love it?' said Fisher.

Don't you love it? That was what Melanie had said about the flowers in the fields. The Fishers loved life. The voice at the other end of the phone managed to give Michael a twinge of guilt again.

'No more rain today?' he asked.

'Who knows,' said Fisher. 'You know what they say about the weather in these parts?' He did not wait for an answer. 'Wait five minutes, is what they say, and it will change. I'm like that,' he paused. 'OK, young man,' he said, 'you've told me the problems, I am going to tell you how to solve them. First of all I want you to meet me at noon at Fisher Ink. Tell Melanie to drop you off. Tell her I'll see you get back all right. This time what I have to say to you is not for her ears.'

Michael wandered out to the stables. By now the heat haze was up and dancing like a living thing upon the flat earth. Sultan and Whilma were both saddled Western style. The girl was standing, holding both of them loosely. Her auburn hair was tied up in a handkerchief. He felt her extraordinary beauty with every part of him. He was so pleased to see her. He felt as if he had been given a wonderful present and that, if he unwrapped it, there would be another present inside and another inside that and he would never

220

get to the bottom of the present or of the peace which she seemed to bestow on him. Then he realized the present was the peace. He settled easily down into the saddle, his long legs dangling in the wooden stirrups.

'Don't use his mouth, just his neck,' said Melanie. 'You can guide him with one hand. The other is for the lasso.'

He must have looked apprehensive because she added, 'Don't worry, we're not going to rope anything really. Not today.'

He followed Whilma out of the yard. They walked and they walked. They walked for many miles. Michael settled into the saddle and the saddle settled into the horse and the horse settled into the earth. The peace came right up from the ground, and he forgot the restlessness with which he had arrived at the Alamo. His mind seemed to empty completely, and yet he was also thinking of many things. He was thinking of what Fisher was going to say to him when he met with him later in the day. He was thinking what he would have made of the story of the will. Michael was thinking how very much he was looking forward to the meeting, and how he had acquired a sense of purpose, even though only yesterday he had been on a plane flying into a future that seemed hopeless, predictable, inadequate. He was thinking how many miles away from his real life he was. And he was thinking about the beautiful girl ahead of him and the serenity she bestowed.

Bleidenstein's admonition over lunch had suddenly set Michael thinking what he knew about girls. He knew crazy opportunists to whom he never dared confess his identity, and he knew plenty who called themselves the New Woman. These were enough to drive any man into a reclusive existence. Coitus with them was really not a very appetizing idea. All of them behaved like men, and most of them looked like men, too. They wore men's clothes and had short hair-cuts and they all tried to boss you around if you had a prick these days. If that was the case, you were not allowed to answer back for fear of being labelled a chauvinist pig. Michael had practically given up on the idea of women being a source of pleasure. They were never the solution to anything, of that he was certain.

221

Melanie dropped behind on Whilma and the horse settled into her stride next to Sultan.

'You're doing some real hard thinking,' she said after a while.

He smiled at her. 'I am thinking that I like it here,' he said.

'Do you really?' she asked, as if that was what she had been waiting to hear. It seemed to excite her.

'I think I know why you live here,' he said. 'It's a long way from anywhere, though. What happens when your father is not home?'

'I'm not lonely,' she said.

'Do you travel with him?'

'No.'

'You don't want to?'

'He's not a good travelling companion. He doesn't really like travelling,' she said. 'He only does it to work. He only likes working.'

'Have you never been to New York?' he asked.

'Once,' she said. 'I don't miss the city.' She said she was happy. 'Tell me about London,' she said.

He told her that he did not live there. Then he surprised himself by telling her he was thinking of moving there. 'It's a dirty grey monster,' he said. 'The skies touch the ground, but I think there is something I am going to have to do there. When there is something you have to do, it doesn't really matter about the place.'

'Dad says that,' she said. 'Do you think I would like London?'

He tried to picture her in London, but it needed the sun to shine on that auburn hair. 'I don't know,' he said. 'You've always lived here?'

'Not quite always,' she said.

'Not quite always?' he repeated.

'We did not live here when my mother lived with us.'

'And where did you live then?'

'I don't know,' she said. 'We've never been back. It was a friendly house. Things everywhere just lying around. Dogs, too,' she said.

Michael looked surprised. You could not call the Alamo

friendly. You would never describe it in that way.

'I remember one other thing about it,' she said. 'It was a house by a river. I think it burned down.'

The dull thud of the horses' hooves took over from the conversation. Michael did not know how to ask what he wanted to know next. 'Where is your mother?' he asked finally.

'I don't know,' she answered quickly. 'She's dead. Are you hungry yet?'

He wasn't, but he said yes anyway. When they came to a sparse patch of trees, they dismounted. Sultan and Whilma were tied to a branch.

'I've brought a picnic when you're ready,' she said.

He watched her fringed chaps swing from her slim hips as she collected firewood and brush. Then she kindled a fire. He tried to help, but she told him just to lie under the sky and wait and relax. So he did. His bones sank into the ground, and once again he felt as if he was made of the very stuff of which the earth was made. If he folded his hands and put them behind his head and rested it upon them, he could see how the sky came down to touch the earth at the horizon because the land was so flat. There was nothing in between himself and the sky, so he felt that he was made of the stuff of the sky as well.

When the fire had properly taken, she brought out the coffee she had brought along ready made in a billycan because there was no water where they were. It was a bleached, burned countryside where the sun offered the only vitality, apart from themselves. There seemed to be a conspiracy between the two of them and the vast source of energy which overlooked them both.

The countryside was different, but the feeling was the same. Michael felt as if he had been looking for something for a long time, but that he didn't know that he had been looking for it, and now, without having known about the looking, he had found it. Sultan whinnied and tossed his head. As Michael watched him, his legs seemed to shorten and his flanks to grow, the air seemed to become colder and he snorted it out of his wide nostrils like steam. Michael saw Harry astride the cob in the English lane again, and when he looked away something about Melanie reminded him of Flicker. It was a young Flicker, wearing a peasant frock and laying out a picnic on a tartan rug near the stream at Coote. Suddenly Melanie did the most unexpected thing. She came to him and she placed a kiss on his forehead. Then she sat down on her haunches in front of him.

'Penny for your thoughts,' she said.

He didn't answer. Instead, he pulled her down beside him. They lay there for a long time, listening to the silence with just his fingers interlaced with hers.

'It's so beautiful here, you'd almost think there was a God, wouldn't you?' she said. 'Dad says there isn't. What do you think?'

'I think there must be,' he answered. Then he kissed her on the mouth.

Then she cooked him her steak and poured him some coffee and all the while she was laughing and so was he. It was as if they had made a pact. The present was united in a conspiracy with the past and with the future, which suddenly seemed so easy to him. This was not the way he had planned it at all. He had wanted to get his mother out of a fix, to get himself some chips for life if possible before his father ruined them all. Bleidenstein had said there was a very easy way out, and Michael had shut his ears to it. And now Harry Coote, his grandfather, was standing on his shoulder like a parrot talking to him whatever he did. Coote was repeating something over and over again. What was it the anxious shade of his grandfather was saying? If Michael listened more carefully, if he concentrated on the words, he found he could make them out.

Harry's words rang in the song of the insects in this sparse place, and in the pawing of the horses' hooves on the dry ground. They rang in the light capricious breeze that whipped up the dry dust, and they were illuminated by the bright rays of this brightest Southern sun. It was as if someone had shone a great light into that part of Michael which was the most secret and the most precious, so that he could see into it and know of what it consisted. Michael the wanderer, the gipsy, the discontent, Michael the rebel, the ungrateful son, was not afraid any more.

Harry was saying that a person should have the thing he loved.

It should be given to him to take care of so that they both might prosper. Michael already knew one thing that he loved, and it was his family's newspaper.

'Michael,' Melanie said. 'Come on. We have to go. My father will be waiting.'

30

Earpieces

Fisher sat with his back to the window on the 56th floor. Back in his office he was in charge, and he was enjoying himself with every little bit of him. He put his feet up on his desk and the telephone to his ear, and this way he felt as if he were running the world.

At this moment in time, Fisher had a problem, and there was a sense in which problems were what he loved best. They brought his ingenuity to the fore. His ingenuity had never failed him yet. The way he saw it was if you had guts like he did you couldn't lose, so screw Sonia Fraser. Who wins has the biggest balls was a favourite saying of his. He had it stuck up on his office wall.

Michael Coote, this crazy English kid, had put him on his mettle. That was a good feeling, too. It took balls to do what Michael had done. Either he had balls or he was crazy, maybe even a bit of both. Hell, the English were all fully-paid-up eccentrics, weren't they? At least they used to be. Maybe this Michael, with his aristocratic stock, had the right Churchillian stuff. Fisher recognized the behaviour of a man who wouldn't take no for an answer. What he had to find out was whether this Michael was more ballsy than he was crazy or more crazy than he was ballsy. Which was it?

Melanie had taken a shine to him, that much was for certain, there was no mistaking the look in her eyes, which meant Fisher had to be doubly sure. In fact, he could not be absolutely sure of anything. Why had this Michael turned up like that out of the blue? Hundreds of people must have wanted to contact Fisher at home over the years. He had maddened some, he had pleased others; not many people were indifferent to him. He lived inside a fortress of anonymity, but Michael was the first person to have

226

found a way of breaking into it. And the craziest thing about the whole situation was that Fisher had not put this Michael straight back on the plane as he should have done. He had bidden him a sort of welcome, he had even offered him hospitality. Well, he wanted his goddam newspaper.

In the middle of the night Fisher had come down to the pool-house and looked at the young man asleep. He looked so young. Next to him on the bed was the briefcase with the will in it. Was there any truth to the things he had said at the kitchen table? Fisher's fingers were itching to find out. Was he indeed Michael Coote? Then the thunderstorm had started and the boy stirred in his sleep.

Now Fisher called Pringle in London.

'What's a haemophiliac?' he said.

Pringle loved this sort of thing. 'It comes from the Greek,' he answered pompously. 'The root words are *haema* meaning "blood" and *philia* meaning "affection".'

'Affection?' said Fisher. 'Affection for blood? You mean Arthur Mitchell has a goddam vampire for a son?'

'It means a tendency to bleed from the slightest injury,' said Pringle.

'You could say that about the whole goddam lot of you,' said Fisher. 'The entire British nation. This Arthur's kid's got another problem. He's a Communist to boot.'

Pringle tried, in silence, to work out the connection between Communism and a blood disease, but he asked no questions. Everyone has his price, and Fisher had found Pringle's the very first day. Moreover, Jemima Pringle was doing very well at school in Cheltenham.

'OK, here's another question,' said Fisher. 'Try this one. Who's the guy who says he's Michael Coote?'

'Coote? Michael?' asked Pringle. 'I know Sir Aubrey Coote.' He was irritated because he did not know the answer off the top of his head.

'We all know Sir Aubrey Coote,' said Fisher. 'Who's Michael?'

Pringle reached out for one of his huge red reference books which told him about the lineage of England. 'Michael Coote is

Sir Aubrey's son,' he said. 'Aubrey Verity Evelyn Coote m. Felicity Trout, one son Michael Verity b. 1955,' he read out loud.

'Aubrey, Verity, Evelyn, what sort of a name is that?' repeated Fisher. 'Is the guy a broad or something?' Nineteen fifty-five, he thought. The Michael guy was older than he looked, old enough anyway to know his own mind, even if the mind he knew was crazy.

'Describe this Michael Coote to me,' he said.

'He's just over thirty years old,' said Pringle.

'Good work, Pringle,' said Fisher sarcastically. 'What does he look like?'

'I'll get back to you on that.'

'Find out what he's doing and where he is doing it,' said Fisher and rang off.

Pringle went downstairs to get the cuttings on the Coote family, but when he got to the library he found his way barred by female pickets wearing dungarees. One of them was Sukie Smith. She put her cigarette between her lips to leave both hands free and delved inside the envelope pocket at her breast.

'This is for Fisher,' she said, and gave him an inky document full of crossings out and rethinks. 'Clerical workers are out,' said Sukie sulkily. 'A fair copy is out of the question.'

Pringle took it between the very tips of his fingers and beat a retreat.

He rang around town. None of his usual contacts knew anything. Someone thought he remembered Michael Coote wearing a white satin suit to play page-boy at some society wedding when he was about seven. Someone else remembered him in black at his grandfather's funeral, but he was still a schoolboy then. After that the trail went cold. Pringle jumped out of his Savile Row suit when the phone rang. It was Dallas.

'Well?' asked Fisher.

'The problem is the strike,' apologized Pringle.

'Goddam English,' said Fisher, unfazed. 'They're trying to bring the whole world to a grinding halt. OK, here's another one,' he said. 'I want you to research the terms of Harry Coote's will.'

This was exactly the sort of task at which Pringle could see himself excelling. He knew exactly where to go for this information. He knew that Bleidenstein, on the old-boy network, would be delighted to give it. All his pedantry rushed to the fore.

'When do you want the information?'

'Yesterday,' said Fisher.

So it was that Pringle found himself trying to master the Fax machine later that day, for, as Sukie had said, the secretaries were on strike. A Fax machine was something that did not go hand in hand with a classical education. A few valuable hours were lost while Pringle stared at it this way and that, and it was during this time that Michael and Melanie were riding. First he thought it best to try the machine out on the Sukie Smith memorandum about the objection at the feminist chapel meeting. They now had it down more or less exactly how they wanted. Pringle thought Fisher would be extremely pleased to have some communication on the progress of the strike, so he faxed it first.

The accusation from the chapel was that Fisher, being a person, had addressed a person in a room and called this person a person. He – whoops, the 'he' had been struck out and replaced by the word 'person' so that the next sentence read, 'This person had furthermore addressed this other person as another person.' 'Another' had then been struck out and replaced by 'a'. The final draft was repeated. 'A person had addressed a person in a room and called this person a person.' The person had furthermore addressed this person as a person. The memorandum, inky with indecision, finished up triumphantly, 'What is the person going to do about it?'

'Person, shit!' said Fisher and threw the memorandum into the waste-paper basket right across the room with a lob he remembered from basketball. He got on to the telephone immediately. 'Fax the fucking goods,' he said.

So it was that Pringle finally faxed the will over to Fisher, who immediately got his lawyer to read it.

Harry Coote, the wily old son of a bitch, had taken as many precautions as he could to keep the newspapers he loved so much in the family. He had had his legal advisers draw up a trust whereby no one heir should ever be able to liquidate the assets.

Harry had assumed that in the natural course of things, the heirs would want to marry and produce heirs themselves. At this point, as fathers of families, they would behave with all the responsibility appropriate to the position of provider, which was not necessarily true of the same young man as a bachelor around town.

Thus Harry had devised a system to keep the young bachelor completely penniless and at the mercy of his trustees while undertaking to release a portion of the money coming to him on marriage. Harry had even thought ahead to combat the potential instability of many a marriage, no doubt with his son Aubrey specifically in mind.

For even after his marriage, the heir to the Coote fortune was to be kept on short rations until he produced another son and heir. Furthermore, he had no say at all in the matter of the newspapers, or the fortune attached to them, until this condition was fulfilled. A Coote heir became a trustee of his own newspaper empire only when he had a son. Not even a daughter would do. Harry was quite specific in that. Fisher dwelt on this point with interest, and on the man who had written it, Harry Coote. Daughters could be led by an overwhelming desire to rock the cradle when their loins started juicing up. Fisher knew that. They were led by the man who got the juices flowing and that was why feminism was bunk. That was why Harry's will specifically said 'heir' not 'heiress', because only heirs knew their own minds. Till there was an heir of an heir, the fortune was in trust for the immediate heir with the income administered by his predecessor along with two other trustees. It was at the discretion of the trustees whether they advanced any of the capital, which was a course open to them, given an appropriate project.

Fisher realized, after a little thought, just how it was that the fortunes of the newspaper had stuck with Aubrey and how he had been able to milk it in a way completely unforeseen by old Harry in his canniest mood. Michael Verity had not come up trumps with the girls. He was supposed to marry, but he never had. If he had done the natural thing, the paper would have been his, still would be. Was he some sort of poofter like all the rest of them? He put his question to Pringle during the next telephone call.

Pringle's explanation was plausible. When he had dug up the will and ascertained from Bleidenstein that his very own firm of Einstein, Epstein, Bernstein & Bleidenstein was handling it, he asked the tattling lawyer for an update on Michael Coote. 'A brilliant mind gone to waste in Oxford, dear boy,' said Bleidenstein. 'I blame the Department of Health and Social Security.' Pringle, who always made other people's theories his own, told Fisher that there was one thing about the future of England that the far-sighted Coote had not taken into account when he wrote the will. The intervention of the state. When Michael had come of age, he was able to disregard his birthright and head out on his own and get paid for it by the country. Michael had shut himself in a library and read. He knew all there was to know about history and nothing at all about real life. He had become a dusty academic.

Fisher thought. It was beginning to look as if he had a brilliant guy on his hands who could be a proper adversary if only he could get him into the chess game. He found the thought exhilarating. The guy's father had had so much pussy he had been swallowed up by it, balls and all. The father had ripped through his entire fortune paying for it. He wanted pussy so badly he was willing to sell everything to get it. Pussy like that sucked the gonads dry; you had to be careful of that. It was a drug, like many other drugs, and you could win only by saying no. Fisher reckoned there were a couple of things he could do now to get the paper. He could buy out Gold, the hypochrondiac to whom the paper had brought a peerage but none of the respect he wanted. And he could buy out Michael. He could do both. He could have it all. And Harry's will indicated there was a way he wouldn't even have to pay for it.

Fisher put down the phone and thought. A young man was out picnicking with his daughter. Fisher could make the young man impecunious. But now he knew that he would not. There was fun in that, but not as much fun as the fun he had in mind. Michael had come to Texas fighting for his life. That made him interesting. Fisher looked at the picture he kept on his desk in its ostrich-skin frame: a picture of himself and his wife and of Melanie. It was the only photograph he possessed. Fisher was a young man in it, a young man about the same age as Michael but much poorer, but he had wanted to make sense of his life, too, and enjoy it. He remembered exactly how he had felt when that picture was taken. He was full of wanting. He had got what he wanted, too. All except for one thing. Now he thought he saw a way of redressing the balance.

'Come in, Michael,' he said. 'Sit down.'

Michael looked around him. He had never been in a place like Fisher's office before. An airliner passed the window as if it was about to land on Fisher's desk. There was a sheer drop of over fifty storeys to the ground below. He went over to the window and looked down.

'Good place to commit suicide,' grinned Fisher. This time he did not intimidate Michael. He exhilarated him.

'How do you like Texas?' asked Fisher. He was, indeed, like the changeable weather, in quite a different mood from the night before.

Fisher knew now exactly what he was going to say to his visitor. His plan was perfect. The attraction between this young man and his daughter was the natural state of affairs. The stuff that made the world go round. He wasn't interfering. He was just doing his duty, and the beauty of it was that he would be getting something in return. The man had come out of left field and handed him the solution on a plate. Something for nothing, you might say, his motto ever since he sold his original gossip sheet two for the price of one.

A week ago he had had no idea that he wanted the London Evening Newspaper, then he had had no idea how he was going to get hold of it. Now it was going to come to him like a dowry. Fisher had always flown by the seat of his pants. It was instincts and luck that had brought him his place in life, that was for sure.

At present his instincts told him two things. One was to get rid of Arthur, who was a dangerous indecisive leftie who would throw good money after bad and bore the world to death with his conscience. But before he did that he would say to Michael,

'Marry Melanie and come into the business with me.' He rehearsed the arguments and they all sounded good. An Englishman would give his West Coast operation some class. He would be a help in the Far East, too. He'd tap his Imperial memory. 'There is plenty for everyone. You'll both be all right. And what is more important, we will all have fun.'

He was not prepared for Michael's reaction. The young man seemed appalled. He got up out of his chair and looked Fisher straight in the eye.

'You can't buy me, Fisher,' the young man said. 'I'm not in the son-in-law business.'

31

Pulp

Melanie was standing at the door of the Alamo, looking for the limousine in which Michael would be returning. She was wearing a print dress. After the ride she had thrown off her boy's clothes. She had stood a long time in front of the long mirror in her bedroom with no clothes on at all and looked at herself. Ever since she had been an adolescent, she had done this every night. She had never understood what this body was for and she had had no mother to tell her. She had watched it change from a body over which she had total control into one which had control over her. She could still remember the very moment at which she had realized she no longer had the divine power every child thinks it has. She had told Edith, and Edith, with her Bible Belt fears, had chastised her bitterly for the sin of arrogance.

Now, for the first time in Melanie's life, she loved her girl's figure. She had small hips and breasts, but there was no doubt what they were for. There was no doubt either why she understood what she understood now. Before, she had never known why she had not been born a boy. That would have made both her father and herself happy. Now she understood that she had been saved for someone.

Her eyes were drawn to her sex as his would be. All her energy seemed to be concentrated in it, and it was translated from a bizarre triangle of flesh she did not understand into something sublime and aesthetic. Her body was perfectly balanced and perfectly designed. It was a gift to her and it would be her gift to him. She did not know why this had happened, she only knew that she was full of the most irrational joy because Michael had made it possible for her to feel this way and that he was coming back to her now and that they would always be together. She quite simply loved him. Was it possible to fall in love so thoroughly and so quickly? Not according to her father, to whom she had always looked before for all the rules in life. 'First take care of business,' he told her. 'If you've got money, you can buy love.'

Now she knew that there was at least one thing her father had told her while she was growing up that was not true. She knew that love had a mind of its own and demanded attention when you were least expecting to meet it. You could not explain it and you could not deny it. You could not even describe it, except that it was totally right. It was a coming home. A kiss is not much in this modern world, and a kiss was all that had happened between Melanie and Michael, yet with that kiss she had given him all of herself. It was not a matter of choice. She had not chosen to give herself to him. She had not been able to do anything else. The feeling was like the body that had been foisted upon her; it had its own life and it was determined to live it. Its determination made her afraid, for she knew she would always feel this emotion whatever became of the man who had given it to her. She would always feel it for him. If she were to be deprived of him after having felt him so strongly, she did not know what would happen to her. She missed Michael already and he had only been away talking to her father for a couple of hours.

Melanie, who had always been free, had thrown herself on the mercy of a man she knew nothing about. She realized she knew nothing about him just after they had kissed in the open field. She watched him half-asleep and half-awake with pleasure, sprawled diagonally across the ground away from her, and then suddenly he had opened his eyes and they had looked at each other warily and she knew he was a stranger to her and that she was strange to him, too. In that moment, in which he was not properly conscious even, he had shown her the most powerful thing about herself that she had never known before. He had shown her she was a woman.

She was a woman and there was a note of caution attached. It was as if he had thrown a net over her and staked it at all four corners and captured her so that she could never be free unless he let her. And it was worse than that. The bottom line was that, even if he let her be free, she might not want to go away. He could open the door to her cage and invite her to fly away and she would not. Instead, she would stay there waiting for him to bring her to life. She knew with all her being that these things were meant to be and she did not want to waste time working them out.

As soon as the limousine stopped, she rushed out to meet it. Her father's driver was at the wheel. Michael was in the back seat. But something was wrong. Michael, whom she loved so much, would not look her in the eyes.

'I have to go to London, Melanie,' he said.

She followed him into the house and through it. He walked purposefully into his room. She had only known him a short time, and in that time he had come with a purpose, but she had not seen him walk as purposefully as he was doing now. It made her afraid of what was going on inside him, but she did not love him less. The room had all been tidied. He opened the cupboards and threw his robe into his bag. She stood at the door and watched him. He took the remaining things out of the bathroom and zipped up the bag on the bed. She stood blocking the door.

'I want to come with you,' she said.

'You can't, Melanie.'

He could scarcely bear to look at her. He was determined she would not change his mind for him. He had to go home. The whole trip had been a great mistake. Fisher, the unscrupulous tycoon, had outbludgeoned the post-graduate, of course. Michael was just another way of getting another of the newspapers he wanted and increasing his own fortune. That was why he had put his own daughter up to seducing him. Michael was a poor fool who had read the signs wrong. If Michael married her now, it would be nothing but an arranged marriage. It was true that a woman could bring him the paper, as Bleidenstein had pointed out. He could get her pregnant immediately, walk her up the nearest aisle and be in charge of his own fortune, amounting to several million pounds. Sooner or later they would have a son and heir. It was all so neat.

But none of them had said anything about love. He had not

known he was going to get off a plane in a country he did not know and find the most lovely thing in the world waiting for him. He could marry her, he would have married her, but in his own time when he got used to the idea, never this way. Now that Fisher had no private life of his own, he was interfering in everyone else's. Michael would be a pawn in someone else's game, and it would be just as if he had accepted his birthright in the first place. Melanie was still standing, barring his way through the door. Again Michael had a flashback. Flicker would now cry and carry on and pour herself a drink, and Aubrey would put his arm around her and swear he would be true, and then he would go off for six months without leaving a telephone number.

But Melanie did not cry or carry on. She did not do anything. She stood perfectly still, trying to understand what was happening. She did not understand what he was saying. He said she couldn't go with him. Why couldn't she go with him? She had known he loved her. He was a stranger maybe, but for all that she had seen the look of belonging in his eyes. She had seen his soul and she knew it didn't cheat. Yet now he was going. He was offering no explanation, but she could see the steadfastness with which he was intent on going. She couldn't have him if he did not want her, and yet she had been so sure he did. She let him pass with his overnight bag, which he carried over his shoulder like a free spirit off to make his way in the world. She followed him along the dark corridor and out into the blast of heat.

There seemed nothing to do but say goodbye. She thought she could do it without a trace of emotion.

'Goodbye,' she said.

So she had been wrong. They were parting like civilized people between whom there was nothing but the briefest of modern contracts. She cursed herself for not taking more. If she had known it was going to end so soon, she would have forced him to make love to her out there on the wild plain. Now she could not even know what that would feel like.

She was not prepared for what he did next. She hadn't expected him to kiss her on her lips, or anticipated the way he had to bend down to her to do it so that, with that protective gesture, he became responsible for her all over again. If only he had held out his hand, it might have been all right. Perhaps then she could have forgotten him. As it was she wanted to press herself against him, to pull him on top of her right here in the driveway, shamelessly to make love to him before her father's driver and before Edith, who was watching the whole scene from the side of the house. She looked up at Michael and he kissed her. She held tight to his hand.

'Don't go away,' she said. 'Please don't go away. I've only just found you.'

He said nothing at all.

'Will we ever see each other again?' she asked.

This time he laughed, it was almost a laugh, it was mocking her innocence. Or was it just deftly dealing with a situation that time was about to bring to an end? He did not say anything more, did not do anything more, and it came to an end.

Oh God, she prayed, he did tell me there was a God, and if there is, make me handle things right now. She watched him dance across the driveway to his little rented car, there was no other word for it but dance. She had seen her father move in that way, and she knew the body language by heart and what it meant. That was what free spirits did, they danced about an inch off the surface of the earth as if they did not quite belong. They showered you temporarily with the great blessing of their presence, it was so effortless for them, but they could just as easily take it away. They could soar up away out of your reach so you could not touch them, and you could only will them to return, and they only would return if that was what they wanted themselves.

They could take away their presence like her mother had done. She had never returned again. Only one living being knew what had happened that day, and although she talked to him again and again, he would never tell her the secret. She never asked her father outright, as if she was somehow afraid of the truth. She wanted her father to make it all right, but if he did not when she asked, if he failed her then, how vulnerable she would be, how completely lonely. The truth was she was vulnerable. Perhaps that is why Michael had gone away. Perhaps she had made him go away just like her mother. She had shown him how fearful she was, and how vulnerable, and she had asked him to make it all right. She had asked him not to let her down. She had not, of course, asked him. She had said nothing about all this in words. She had expected him to know, as only lovers know, and she had known that he did know. But he had still chosen to go.

Oh God, why have you done this to me, she prayed to a God in whom she had never actually believed until now, and what will happen now to me if he is a free spirit and I am earthbound in my pain? And she prayed that God had a plan and that He was in control of His plan, because even as Michael crossed the drive she could feel her feet following him and she knew that she had no plan beyond holding him in her arms again, beyond seeing the pleasure on his beautiful face which she had given him just as a matter of instinct only that morning when she gave him herself with a simple kiss.

She was going to lean against the car to stop it going away, but Michael had already put it in gear, and then he wound up the electric window so she could not even see him properly any more. She thought she saw him smile at her and even blow a kiss. And then she was almost certain he pressed his lips to his hand behind the darkened window, and then the car lunged on to the dirt track and the dust blew up behind it and obscured him from her view.

32

WOB

Michael walked down past the wedding-cake building. Things had changed even in the short while since he was last there. Then the newspapers had been creeping slowly up the building. Now they obscured it completely. What was more, a wall had been put up round the whole lot. The strikers were inside the wall and outside it the public were gaping.

The street was full of cars, packed nose to tail, bumper to bumper, all hooting impatiently. Meanwhile the pavements were full of people. They were crammed together four or five deep, all waiting for something to happen. The police had erected crash barriers to keep the people from falling under the wheels of the cars. From time to time the police streaked down the middle of the street in their fast cars with the sirens blaring, pushing all other traffic to the side. Police in riot gear were at the ready in the side-streets. They were waiting, too. There were police helicopters flying overhead, only just clearing the tops of the buildings in Fleet Street, huge, menacing, whirring machines like night moths catching the beams of the searchlights in their rotors and making a shimmer. There was fear in the air and anticipation near to a thrill. The people seemed to feel they were an inch away from disaster, but that they did not know what the disaster would be and they did not know what to do about it. They wanted most urgently to find out. They seemed almost to crave it. They were like the cells of an enormous wild beast cowering in a cave and about to be unleashed, all breathing in unison so that you could almost hear the breath, all aware by some sort of dangerous osmosis of each other's silent fears, all moving together in a corporate strategy to gratify the creature's bloodlust. Something else reminded him of an animal too and it was a great beast in chains. These people were a trapped people with no light in their eyes. They had been entombed by all the bricks and mortar and the concrete-clad streets. They were locked away from the sane whispers of nature, alienated from their better instincts, their sodden spirits tuned only to the routine arrival of the keeper who had cruelly thrown the key to their freedom away.

A picture of the cathedral of St Paul's hemmed in by flames flashed into Michael's mind. The picture had been taken during the war, and it had been splashed right across the whole of the front page of his grandfather's newspaper. That was before Michael was born, but it was one of the editions Harry had framed in his study in Coote House.

Standing in front of the white wedding-cake building now, Michael could still just catch a glimpse of the great cathedral through the office blocks in between. But the cathedral had shrivelled as a symbol beneath the shadow of the buildings that had surrounded it with the passage of time. This time Michael imagined it crumbling like a piece of burnt paper instead of standing its ground. It would shrink like a paper taper in a new incendiary raid, fired not from abroad but this time by its own congregation. The country seemed to be on the brink of a civil war.

The people on the streets seemed to be looking for entertainment, but it was guidance they really wanted. They were a well-fed people, warmly dressed against the drizzling weather that would otherwise have eaten away their spirits. The weather was not to blame. They were not poor, they were not hungry, neither were they sick. Yet they were gripped by a form of plague. They had none of the suffering of the generations who had gone before, but they were suffering none the less. Something was eating at their souls. Michael could feel a buzz of unrest just under the surface of a miserable, dangerous crowd. On the surface they were cheerful, full of vulgar bravado. But their real mood was sullen and greedy, they were defensive, expectant, yet expectant of a disappointment. How could it have come to this?

Many of the people had formed themselves into queues and

were trying to buy the newspaper they had heard so much about from the television. The strikers would not sell the paper. It was there all right. They put it out, edition after useless edition. The armed guards let in the journalists, they let in the bales of paper, they let in the printers. The huge presses would not stop printing. The newsprint kept coming off the end of them. The papers piled high. There was nowhere to put them. It was like *The Sorcerer's Apprentice*. The workers took the quires off the end of the presses and just stacked them one on top of the other. They were not going anywhere. All the information contained therein, and all its amazing potential, was so much rubbish waiting for the incinerator.

If Fisher were able to buy my interest in this newspaper, what would he do about this piece of nonsense, this reverse-out of procedure, this white on black, Michael found himself asking. He wouldn't stand for this bullshit, that was for sure. Fisher's universal information standard was made a mockery of. Here was information being used against itself. Nothing made sense.

While the news machine was pumping out this useless pulp from all ten storeys of the building, from under the bowels of the ground right into the dreary Fleet Street sky, at ground level a high level of discipline was kept by union members who had been appointed bodyguards. The guards were wearing sweaters and mufflers designed by Crumm in newspaper colours: white for the wedding-cake building, black for the type, red for the slogans. Some atavistic memory cells in Crumm's beery, flatulent body had realized that, if he could appeal to the tribal spirit, he would have a country-wide organization on his hands. The tribal spirit had been missing for a long time, or rather perverted by ratiocination that had no basis in real forces.

Crumm had his finger on the same pulse which slashed initiation scars across the cheeks of adolescent Africans. His body-maps were, so far, somewhat more benign. They had painted their cheeks red, white and black, not slashed them, but they recalled the same primitive tune and it was not one which was getting more peaceable. Mrs Crumm and the Crumm daughters had started a whole business knitting designer mufflers to help meet the need for this fashion Crumm had started. They were knitting like women waiting for an execution.

Again Michael felt the awful chill thoughts shoot through his body as he looked at the scene before him. As soon as the men had the gear, they all wanted to wear it. They looked like teams, so they organized football matches. Cootes played Fishers and Fishers played Cootes. The other newspapers joined in, too. Associated played United. *The Times* played the *Telegraph*. Recreation, enforced by the strikes, had become the business of Britain, and in the absence of business it had become a vast and vicious game. The whole country was now paralysed by its interest in the Fleet Street strikes, which had drawn crowds of onlookers from far and near. Gangs roamed the streets, pressing everyone to take sides in the football games, but they were games played with gladiatorial lust. If anyone dared to refuse they would do their pressing with a knife. Then, when they got on the pitch, the rule book was thrown away. Though they called themselves teams, a grim egotism distinguished all the individual players. From time to time an ambulance, preceded by the siren-screaming police, would make its way up the centre of the street to take away some casualty whose neck had been broken by an encounter on the pitch. The hospitals were full. The prisons were full. It was every man for himself, each one determined to make a mark even if it was only a destructive one. The country was fragmented by petty jealousies. It was in a bad way, and yet Michael knew that the very virility of its primitive feelings could be a force for good. The people were bleeding and chafing from their bonds but they were not quite done for yet. They were straining to catch a sound of the movement of the earth and when they did they would take their instructions from it.

So far he was acting on auto-pilot, but Michael's instinct was to claim what was his. He crossed over to the wonderful white wedding-cake building and tried to slip in past the bodyguards. When he got inside he would slide past the Epstein bust, which he had always touched for good luck when he was a boy. He would touch it on the same shiny patch on the nose that he had made over the years, and he would take the lift to the fifth floor just as he used to with Harry. He would walk past the Graham Sutherland picture that Flicker rescued when Aubrey put it up for sale. This time he would claim Harry's office for his own. He would rip Aubrey's 'Bunny of the Month' pictures off the wall, tear the whole lot into tiny shreds and throw them all away.

But Michael could not gain entrance to the building. The armed guards at the door had a sophisticated system of separating the people who should be allowed in and those who should not. Everyone had to show identification with their photograph and a description of their business. Michael, as their employer, was the very person they would not let in.

Michael knew that something radical would have to happen to change all this. It was no use patching over the cracks. The wedding-cake building became a symbol of his state of mind. The stucco was peeling, hanging off the building in great weather-worn strips like marzipan. No one put it back on because they were not quite sure how to. None of the old skills had survived as skills, only as memories, both fond and reviled. The country was choking in a sickly nostalgia when it needed to cut itself clean and jerk itself right into the future. It was in a state of utter dependency, on the dead class system, on the dole, like a junky strapped to the pathetic timetable of the next fix, shortsighted, bleary-eyed, addicted to the candy man of the state.

Only a short while before, Michael would have been desperate at the state of this England, pegged down like some flailing awkward Gulliver by his hair and his clothes, but now he was not desperate. He would have been in a good mood if the business which had fallen to him had not been of such a serious nature. Fisher had shown him that problems were there to be solved. As yet he did not know exactly how he was going to do it, but he knew that he was looking forward to the task.

First he was going to get Hamish Grant on his side. He contacted Bleidenstein and asked him to buy him a car.

'Trust me. You'll get it all back and more,' he said.

Then he drove down the motorway to Little Nelling. Even the English weather seemed to be conspiring in his favour. As he left London behind, the grey mist gave way to brilliant sunshine. The road opened up in front of him and the sky opened up, too. He was reminded momentarily of the wide horizons round the Alamo, but he put the memory firmly out of his mind.

Hamish was in the garden, tending his hives. Michael scrunched up the gravel. Hamish did not recognize him. The last time he had seen him he had been a page-boy with his thumb in his mouth, dressed in a little blue satin suit at some society wedding. The young man who knocked on the door at Little Nelling had a sense of purpose. Pitching up at Fisher's place had given him a feeling for relying on his own destiny. It wasn't wrong. Things had a habit of turning out as they should.

Hamish Grant and Michael Coote sat in the bow window of the cottage with the Albertine roses round the door, drinking Earl Grey tea out of bone-china cups.

'We've had these since we were married,' said Hamish as his wife took off her gardening gloves and poured. 'Those were the days. The days of Empire. You knew where you were then. As long as I stay here in the country I can allow myself to think nothing has changed,' he said. 'Town terrifies me.'

'When is the last time you went to town?' Michael asked him.

'No point in going, old boy,' said Grant. 'Cheque comes into the bank. Presses turn out the stuff. Suppliers are on a contract. Paper rolls in one end, rolls out the other, no questions asked. That's modern life for you. It all has its own momentum. Stopping it would take an Act of Parliament. Morley likes that sort of thing. He's content to be acting editor to a useless paper. He has the title, he has the office, he has the pension. Alas, I like to be useful so I'm better off here. I told Crumm his ruling will be proved useless eventually. Even if he gets it, there will be no money to pay his boys, because there is no advertising coming in, and no sales, and sooner or later even Aubrey will pitch up and sort out the whole stinking mess. It's a Mickey Mouse policy. Mickey Mouse, Donald Duck, those are the people we are paying, you know, to stand by the machines with the oily rag and do fuck-all.'

Michael did not understand what he was saying.

'Sure,' Grant continued. 'Every time someone dies, those

printers don't dock him off the payroll, his name stays there just like it has always done. Every time we eliminate a process or introduce some labour-saving device, they labour intensify. One for us, two for them, that is how it works. Phantom machines run by cartoon characters. And no one can ever step back from the operation to knock some sense into it because we must put out three editions a day, day in and day out, or, so the wisdom goes, the public will forget about us and the whole lot will go down the tubes.

'Crumm's policy is to wait. The patient will inherit the world. He seems to think his waiting game will flush your father out. I suppose he's right. I suppose that's why you are here. I suppose Aubrey told you to get on with it.'

'Not quite,' said Michael. He was amazed when he heard the extent of the problem, but then he had simply never looked at it before. 'I don't know where my father is any more than you do. But I do want to solve things. I think I can solve things, but not without help. I want you to help me, Hamish. I want you to tell me everything you know about this newspaper since the day you were first hired.'

Grant looked chuffed. 'I go further back than that,' he reminded him. 'My father was on the paper before me. Your paper was my nursery food. *Pablum puerum*.'

'Tell me about it,' said Michael.

'How long have you got?'

'As long as it takes.'

So Grant talked. As he did so, he changed from an ordinary frightened man and gained the stature of everyone who is allowed to talk about himself and his particular place in the world. He talked about his perceptions of Harry Coote and of Harry's obsession to make his Evening Paper the most controversial sheet in the Street.

While the other Coote papers had plugged the simple line of Empire and coined money, the Evening would come literally from left field. Writers would have their say, whom the Establishment would automatically label left-wing, but the truth was they were of no political persuasion in particular. They refused to fit neatly

246

into any little pigeon-holes because they sensed that all that
would happen then was the public could dismiss their ideas
through familiarity. They reacted spontaneously, that was all.
They invited dissent and they were not afraid of it.

'Harry had a very curious sense of what it was to be a member
of the public,' Grant remembered. 'He defended his views against
all charges of romantic nonsense. He said the last thing the man in
the street was was banal. Your grandfather was offended by
attempts to exploit the common man, for although he might have
nothing his exploiters had, although he might not even know
what it was he wanted out of life, he bloody well recognized it
when it came his way. Harry said he wanted his paper to prod its
readers to use their survival cells.'

'That's it,' said Michael.

'That's what?' said Grant.

'Survival cells.'

Michael tried to explain that he saw a lobotomized people
whose survival cells, like actual tangible bits of flesh, had been
slivered out of them as if with a surgeon's scalpel. It was because
they were looking for formulas rather than within themselves.
They had to be responsible for themselves, or they would turn all
their energy in on themselves and turn it into suicidal violence.
Even as Michael talked, he knew he wasn't doing a very good job.
Michael did not have the words. He knew he would have to find
someone who did. What he had was the mission to find that
person – those people, and to let them be, let them talk, and let
them write a scenario for the times. He would provide somewhere
for them to write it. For that he needed a newspaper.

'Those are fine ideals,' said Grant gloomily, 'but Harry's world
was a different place from this one. You could do those sort of
things then. It was a younger world. People were more idealistic.
There were fewer of them. You could keep the thing under control
in those days. Now they know too much. The rabble knows too
much,' he ended.

'I disagree,' said Michael. 'It's always the same world. The
only difference is what you make of it. People aren't all bad. But
they do play dumb if you tell them lies.'

'Better drink to that,' said Grant. 'Sun's over the yard arm.' He crossed to the sideboard and prepared two heavy crystal glasses. 'Will you join me? Scotch?'

'OK,' said Michael.

He would drink to the future with the managing editor, and after that he had to get back into town. Outside, the light was fading. Grant did not bother to illuminate the room. It took on a reflective mood, an eternal one that prayed for peace and tranquillity. Neither man spoke for a while as they sipped their drinks and the dark, back-lit shadows of the yew hedges in the formal garden became darker. Grant was beginning to feel his cynicism like a tangible bundle waiting to be shed from his shoulders. Whatever this young man had been doing for the last ten years, he had certainly been thinking, but it was all a waste of time unless he could make use of the thoughts.

'Ideals are all very well,' said the older man after a bit, 'but you've got practical problems on your hands before you put any high-falutin notions into operation. Your paper is bleeding you dry. It's like a mincing machine. It goes in one end, comes out the other, and on the ground you get left with a pool of blood. Your money is going down the drain. Pretty soon you won't be able to pay any of these people who could make a success of your vision, even supposing you could find them. Your editor has taken himself off the map already.'

Michael did not know what he meant.

'Cheever,' said Grant. 'No one has been able to get hold of him since he went to his conference on the new technology. Morley's had time to refurbish his whole office up to top management level while he has been away. They are all wasting Coote money.'

Michael was silent. He had to find people who cared and a way to make those people care who thought nothing would ever matter to them again. He wasn't going to dole out jobs as if he ran a soup kitchen, but for the minute he did not run anything, least of all a newspaper, and he still had not found the solution to that. He still did not know how he was going to do it.

'What it boils down to is how are you going to stop Crumm's movement?' asked Grant concisely. 'People are gathering at your grandfather's wedding-cake building as if to a shrine at Lourdes. The whole sick nation is turning up looking for guidance. Whoever takes over, they are going to touch their hem or kill them. I mean it. It is that bad. They are so needy I can see pitched battles if you fail them. It can only end in tears.'

'I know,' said Michael in a still small voice. 'That's what we have got to work on. Will you help me, Hamish?'

'I don't see what I can do,' said Grant.

'One thing is for sure,' said Michael, 'I can't do it without you.'

'You are a young man,' said Grant. 'You don't need an old one.'

Michael told him again that he disagreed. He said he had seen people in the street who were trying to destroy their roots while also looking for them. He said you had to edit your experience but not forget it. He said you should not destroy the past, only learn from it. He said he needed Grant.

'I haven't the energy any more. I haven't the belief.'

'I can't do it without you,' repeated Michael.

'If I was a betting man, and I am, I would say the odds were astronomical against you coming out of this situation on top,' said Grant, pouring himself another Scotch and waving the decanter at Michael. 'By the way, you know, I got a good price for Rum Baba in the end.'

'Rum Baba?'

'Oh no, you wouldn't know. Horse your father gave me. Who'd have thought I'd ever sell it at all? Three legs it had.'

'You see,' said Michael, 'there's a lot to be said for astronomic odds. I like those odds. It'll make the victory more of an achievement. I'm going to win.'

He drove back to London. He understood the driving force behind what he was doing, and he was beginning to understand the economics. It was no longer merely a question of blind faith. His father had undervalued his shares in selling them to Gold in order to refinance his sex life. But the people who knew were still after those shares, even though Gold's half was being bled dry by Crumm's tactics as much as Michael's half. Michael had seen for himself how much the newspaper was worth as a focus of attention. He could see how handily placed it was as a piece of real estate. But how could he realize its worth, with Crumm and his thugs in command? He put this to Bleidenstein.

Bleidenstein shot his cuffs and began to speak. As usual he was enjoying himself hugely at everyone else's expense. 'Even if the mob tear down the wedding-cake building with their bare hands, you can't go wrong with a hole in the ground right in the middle of London's financial district. You are better off in some ways. Just look at the wedding-cake building. Nothing works. You can't find your way around it and you're stuck with it because it's an ancient monument. It's the site that's worth millions. Crumm's right, some Japanese bank is bound to be waiting in the wings. The Japs will find a way of getting it down if they want it down. They'll leave a tap on in the basement and rot the foundations, and they'll have the council begging them to pull it down because it is a safety hazard. Those Japs will have a bomb crater in the ground before you can say Nagasaki, and a socking great crane in there wielding brand-new girders. A huge pre-packed finance house will rise out of Fleet Street. Whoever finds a way forward will be a rich man. Crumm wants some of those apples, and I suppose you can't blame him. What are you going to do, Michael?'

'I don't know yet.'

'You see,' said Bleidenstein. 'It's not easy, is it?'

'Well, I haven't got all the pieces yet,' answered Michael. 'There's one obvious thing missing from my equation. I know Aubrey, I know Fisher. It is time to see Lord Gold.'

This time Michael drove his new car up Gold's driveway. The peer had used his money to install himself and his wife in a mansion once owned by Churchill. He had smashed down the partitions between the rooms, jemmied out the mullion windows, put in double glazing and dug a swimming pool where the ornamental Japanese carp pond used to be. When Michael was ushered in to meet Gold, the peer was sitting in a room which still had the dust covers on the furniture. It was as if he had bought himself a present, but the buying was enough for him so he hadn't bothered to unwrap it. Gold was sitting hunched up on the dust covers, watching the news on an enormous television and muttering to himself about the Apocalypse. He seemed to be stroking a cat that was sitting by his side, but when he heard Michael come in he picked it up and put it on his head. It was his nylon toupée.

'I knew you would come,' said Gold to Michael without taking his eyes from the riots on the screen. 'I knew you'd come for the same reason I am not ready to sell my shares in Coote Newspapers yet: femily. That's the reason why you came, and that's the only reason to do anything. I am an old man and it is possible I will die, but that won't be the end of me, Mr Coote, and it won't be the end of my interest in the newspaper. You'll have to deal with my son Victor then. Victor, the accountant. We'll see what he makes of the offer we have had for it.'

'Fisher!' said Michael. He walked round and stood behind the television set so the lugubrious peer had to focus on him. 'Lord Gold!' he shouted above the noise of the crowd. 'Don't waste your time with any foreign offers.'

'What do you say, boy?' asked Gold.

Michael turned the sound down. 'The Prime Minister is not going to let this paper fall into foreign hands,' Michael said. 'No way. The Evening Newspaper has always been synonymous with the fortunes of the capital city. What's more, the only foreign buyer who would be arrogant enough to imagine he could get away with such a stunt will fall foul of the Monopolies Commission. There never have been three newspapers edited by the same man coming out twenty-four hours a day, seven days a week. England is still a country that values freedom of speech, and you don't get that by limiting your outlets.'

Gold nodded. He patted the dust sheets covering the sofa next to him and beckoned to his visitor.

'Come here,' he said. 'Sit down next to me.'

Michael came over and sat on the dust sheets.

'How is your father?' asked Gold. 'Does he have his health?'

Michael said that he had.

'How is your mother?'

Michael said she was fine.

'Do you have a wife, Mr Coote?'

Michael said that he did not.

'A sweetheart?'

'Not even.'

'All my children are most heppily married,' said Lord Gold. 'You should get married as soon as possible. Find a wife who believes in you. Femily is the only thing that survives. You want to tell your father something? Come here, boy.' He took the wizened shiny liver-spotted hand from under its cover again and beckoned to Michael to shift up close. 'Closer,' he said impatiently. Then he whispered something. What Lord Gold whispered to Michael Coote was the solution to the whole problem of the strike. It was radical. It was daring. But it was dynamite.

'You can't do that,' said Michael.

'You can if you want to solve the strike,' cackled Gold. 'You can if you want to make money.'

As Michael drove away, he knew that he did not trust any of them. No one was going to do him any favours. If the strike was not solved, there was nothing to buy. If the strike was solved, Gold would not necessarily sell, at least not to him. If it was solved there might be no reason to sell. But Gold was not so bad. He was a lot like Harry in his way. Even his experiments with bit-part surgery were brave and experimental. Despite his failing health, he had what he loved, and top of the list was himself. Now Michael knew exactly what he had to do. He had to fight with everything he had, for himself and his newspaper and for its readers, not just today, not just tomorrow, but during other times when he might not feel so strongly about anything. He had to commit all of himself, for that was the very least commitment he could expect from his rival Frederick Fisher.

As far as Fisher was concerned, there was one thing Michael was going to do whether he liked it or not, and Gold had concentrated his mind upon it. He was not going to do it on Fisher's terms, there would be no compromises from now on, it was out-and-out war. He was going to do it his way, it was his decision, it was the thing he wanted most of all, and there was not a damn thing Fisher could do about it.

33

Rule

When Michael left, all the joy went out of Melanie. Something had happened to her when she met him. She had gone on a voyage. The same thing had happened to Michael. At the same time as he had met the shades of Flicker and Harry on the arid spaces of Texas and recognized he was home, and Harry had told him a person must have the thing he loves, Melanie had also caught up with her own past. Such is the power of love. It reunites the lover with everything that was ever dear to him. It defines him. It draws boundaries round the unique person he is while, at the same time, setting him free. But love is different for men and women. It had made Michael into a newspaperman and it made Melanie into the woman she was waiting to be.

The act of Michael's leaving triggered a little memory which Melanie did not know she had. It was a memory of a house, a house by a creek, but the house was charred. Its rafters stuck up in the sky like animal bones. There were just a few tiles left on the envelope of the house like skin on the bones. There was a dust track in front of the house, and a car churned up the dust when it left, just as Michael's car had turned up the dust in the drive of the Alamo. There was a woman in the car. Melanie could not see her face properly, but she knew who the woman was. She had not seen her for many years. The woman was her mother. Her mother was driving the car and the car was open and her mother's hair was trailing back in the wind and it was red like Melanie's hair. Her mother's hair was wet and ragged from the heat and the humidity in the air. Melanie heard the noise of the engine of the car and some loud music on the radio. It was country and western music and there was another noise in the background, a voice, voices. She recognized her father's voice. She could not remember the exact words he was saying, she just knew they were angry words. They were hateful words, words of desperation and bravado, but they were born not of hatred but of the bitterest disappointment. It was a long time ago.

Now Melanie was borne into the present once more by a familiar sound. She heard the pick-up truck turn full-circle on the gravel driveway as her father put it into a home-coming skid as he always did, and she heard the screen door bang and Edith mutter as she went out to rake over the tracks on the drive as she always did when her father skidded his way home. Melanie was in the kitchen near the ice-box. She wanted to run upstairs, but she was frozen where she was. Then she heard her father's steps down the passage.

'Yahoo,' said Freddy as he always did, 'I'm home.'

This time Melanie did not come out to meet him. She did not know what to do, so she did nothing. She could hear his steps coming nearer. He would come and pour the grape-flavoured Kool-Ade. She was trapped. He appeared at the doorway.

'I've got it,' he said triumphantly. He was dancing from one foot to the other in that way he had. 'I've got the solution. I'm gonna buy Gold's shares.'

He stopped in the doorway when he saw her.

'Melanie, there you are,' he said. 'You didn't hear the car? Did you hear what I said? I know the way to get the newspaper, honey.'

She did not move.

'Aren't you gonna give your father a kiss?'

Still she did not move.

'What's wrong, honey?'

'I don't want to know about newspapers,' said Melanie.

'This is a great day, darlin', what do you mean you don't want to know? I'm gonna get the hat-trick. A Sunday, a Daily and an Evening. I'm going to fold 'em all into one. Do you know what a saving that will be? That Michael won't have the guts to make a stand against the inevitable. He'll be only too glad to get out. He'll be down on his knees praying for me to buy his patrimony.

He'll be praising the day he heard the name Frederick Fisher. I know how to make the whole thing pay. I'm going to turn his wedding-cake building from a mausoleum into a museum and his presses into a parking lot. I'm going to have actors with green eye-shields doing all that stuff they do over there by hand. I'm going to have lino-type operators making posters for kids with their names on. Then I'm going to get me a holiday tour operating company, I'm going to call it Fisher Flight and I'm gonna transport Boeing loads full of Americans to Fleet Street so they can eat at the Cheshire Cheese where that literary guy, whassis-name, Dr Johnson used to eat. Shit, I'll probably have a company called Fisher Food supply 'em with the goddam cheese. And I'm going to have Fisher Studios make videos of the whole lot. That way they can take 'em home and run them for the neighbours in the winter when they are bored. I'm gonna make the whole of Britain into a theme park. Meanwhile at Fisher Dock . . .'

'I told you I don't want to know.' She put her hands over her ears.

'Melanie,' he stopped and looked at her more closely. 'Oh I know,' he said, 'you want me to tell you about my first papers again. You're so goddam sentimental. Women,' he said. 'I'll never understand them. OK. You win. Shall I start at Beaumont or at Tyler?'

'I know the stories, Dad,' she said. 'I've heard them a million times and I don't want to hear them again.'

This time Fisher looked at his daughter as if he was seeing her for the very first time. She was pale and ill at ease. 'You haven't been eating properly?' he said.

'Course I have.'

'You ill or something?'

'No I am not,' she said irritably.

'Well, what's the matter with you, then?'

'Leave me alone, Dad,' she said.

'You're not acting naturally,' he persisted. 'You always wanted to hear my stories.'

Still she did not answer.

'OK, I'll tell them someone else,' he said, petulantly. He had made it a rule never to put up with temperament in other people. He turned to leave the room.

'OK, tell me the story you won't tell me,' she shouted after him. She had never raised her voice to her father before.

He turned to face her. 'I tell you all my stories. I tell you everything, Melanie.' This was not the daughter he knew. He had never seen her like this before.

'Tell me the story about my mother,' she said.

At first he felt nothing. Then it was as if he had been waiting for this moment for a long time. He had always known what he had to do when it came, but had not known how he would feel. He did not like the feeling it gave him. He recognized the feeling, but he did not want to have the feeling so he would not. He wanted to leave the room, but he did not. 'You know the story about your mother,' he said off-handedly.

'I know the story you tell me, Dad,' she said, 'but it is not the real story, is it?'

He was not going to give way to the feeling. He stood his ground, but she went on.

'Mother's not dead,' she said. 'She is not dead, is she?' There was a look of frank, blank innocence on her face.

Fisher did not speak. He was not going to speak of long-gone things. There was a long silence in which the fan whirred and the bugs splattered and he held his memory on a tight rein. He was not going to remember.

'She left, didn't she?' asked Melanie more gently. 'Tell me why she left.'

Still Fisher did not speak. Still the fan whirred and he concentrated on feeling nothing.

'Shall I tell you why she left?' asked Melanie in a voice which sounded like pleading.

Still he said nothing.

'OK, I'll tell you why she left,' she said defiantly. 'My mother left you because she had grown to hate you. She could not bear you always having things your way. She left because you have one rule for us and one rule for you, but she did not want to be controlled by your rules. You can't admit that to me, can you, because you can't admit any failure? And now you have tried to control me, too. What did you say to Michael?'

Melanie did not know how she knew her father had said something to Michael. She only knew that something had changed between herself and Michael and it was not something of their making because they loved each other. It is the nature of love to reveal the truth. Her father could talk a lot about his standard of truth, the Fisher Standard, he called it, but he was not talking about really finding the truth, he was talking about controlling it. It started with him controlling love, which she knew you could not control. You had to suffer it. She could not even begin to control the truth about her mother until he told it to her, and he was not going to do that because he had invented another truth, one that rearranged the facts so they did not make him suffer.

Fisher was not going to suffer ever again, so he had stepped in to try to take away what little truth she had found at the very beginning of its fragile life. Fisher walked slowly up and down the room. 'I didn't say anything to Michael that he didn't think of first,' he said.

'What did you say?'

He could not answer.

'I need to know what you said,' she insisted.

'It shoulda worked out,' he answered. 'It's what you both wanted.'

'And you wanted another newspaper,' she said bitterly. 'It did not matter about Michael. It did not matter about me. It did not matter what we felt. You wanted a newspaper and that was all there was to it.'

'Melanie, baby,' he said.

'It's true, isn't it?' she asked. 'All you wanted was another newspaper?'

He shrugged his shoulders. 'I know where I am with newspapers,' he said.

Again there was a crescendo of silence, broken only by the death-splattering of the bugs.

'I'm leaving, Father,' she said.

257

He could not say anything. She walked to the door and looked at him closely. She tried not to feel anything for him so she could do what she had to do.

'What about Sultan?' he said.

'What *about* Sultan, Dad?' said Melanie. 'Sultan's a horse.'

'What about Edith?'

She said nothing.

'Melanie, baby, try to understand,' he said simply. 'I have something to do and I have to do it my way. I am like a boat with a hole in it going very fast over choppy water. If the boat stops it will take in water and the boat will sink.'

She walked past him through the doorway into the cool dark hall, making sure that even in the narrow gap she did not brush any part of him with even the fabric of her skirt. She walked on down the hall and she could feel the gap between them getting larger. It was a physical thing. If he tries to stop me I will stay, she said to herself, I know I will stay. She did not know whether to pray for him to stop her or not. His eyes were tight closed behind his half-moon glasses as if he did not want to see her leave. He did not want to feel, but he was feeling all the same, and now he recognized the feelings he had been having lately. He was feeling mortality. There was so much he had to do and so little time left to do it in. He was feeling full of mortality as he let her go, but he said nothing at all to stop her. She who had always loved her father knew she loved him more than ever since loving Michael. She did not now love him as her father, the only parent she had known, she loved him because they were two separate people struggling to make sense of their lives, and in this matter of their different destinies there was nothing either of them could do to help the other. What a pity, what a terrible pity, she thought as she left the room. She walked into the immaculate hall at the Alamo and saw, perhaps for the first time, how everything was in its place and how nothing had a soul. Not a scuff nor a mark, not a book on a table at an angle, not a letter, not a flower. He had banned flowers from the house for the simple reason that they wilted and died.

The house where she had lived so long with her father was

waiting for something. It was waiting to have the breath breathed into it maybe. If a family leaves a house, the soul of the house starts to roam, he had said. He had said that sometimes it finds a home and sometimes it does not. He had said the house by the creek was like a great dinosaur rotting by the edge of the forest. He had said the rafters were sticking up like animal bones through the place where the roof used to be. He had said there were just a few tiles left on the envelope of the house like skin on the bones. He had said a house was a living thing.

Now she did not know whether the house by the stream was really burned or not, but she knew this one wasn't living. And she knew that whatever had happened to Fisher and her mother was not going to happen to her because she had the chance of life. She went out to the stables to tell Sultan.

34

Typeface

He picked her up from the airport and she was like a light ray of sunshine in the grey air. Her hair shone even in the rain. He knew she was an answer to his prayer even though, when he had first seen her astride the black horse in that field, he had not even been aware that he had offered up the prayer.

'You came,' he said.

'Of course I came,' she said.

'Will you wait here?' As he went to pick up his car, he wondered for a moment if she would be gone when he got back. He thought perhaps she was a figment of his imagination, he was so unused to having found what he wanted. She was waiting for him.

'Where are we going?' she asked after a while.

There was only one place he wanted to take her. It was not Oxford, it was not Mayfair. It was Staffordshire. Michael took Melanie to Coote House, to the place where he last saw Harry, to the place where his life had been written in blood and DNA before he temporarily lost his way. He took her slowly up the staircase to the room where Harry died.

She had never been there before, but he could see that she was full of confidence and there was no hesitation in her step. She stood by the window and looked out at the green Staffordshire grass.

'There's a stream!' she said.

He knew she felt at home, but he didn't know she thought it was like an eternal Texas spring. There were poppies instead of evening primroses, but the wind shifted in the trees just as it did in the home oaks and the pecans round the Alamo. The weather changed capriciously here, too. She knew she was not going back. Michael, watching her, felt the power of a woman's decision about a man. There was no going back for either of them because, if they faltered for a minute, the fates would exact the great vengeance of regret for committing the greatest sin of waste. When he looked at her, he saw that she had tears in her eyes. She was completely vulnerable because, although she knew her own mind, she could not know his. He knew she was handing herself over to him. She was like a perfect flower that was a fearful responsibility to take because he was afraid of crushing it and watching it slowly wilt and die. But he had no choice because, if he did not take it, he would crush all the life from it anyway, and all the joy. He would crush all his own joy. He could not be responsible for such destruction. He made love to her.

'Does it hurt?' he asked.

'Yes,' she said.

'Nice hurt,' he said.

'I don't have any . . .'

'You don't have any what?' he asked.

'Guess,' she said.

'Birth control,' he said.

'Yes,' she whispered. 'Will I get pregnant?'

'Oh, I hope so,' he said.

They lay without speaking. She stared at the intricate high ceiling of the old room and Michael ran his fingers through her red hair spread out on the hard old-fashioned linen they still used in Coote House. He took a strand of her hair like her father used to do, and ran his fingers right to the end, then let it go and began again.

'What's going to happen to us next?' she asked a long while afterwards. 'We can do anything you say.'

'We are going to get married,' he said simply. 'And you are going to stay here with me, and you can go home sometimes and sometimes I'll come with you. You will be my wife and I am going to be the new chairman of Coote newspapers.'

The wind stirred in the oaks outside and the grey English night started its gentle fall. Suddenly she shivered, although he was holding her still. 'Michael,' she said, 'I hope this, this between us, hasn't anything to do with newspaper business.'

35

Hot Metal

The paradox was Sonia had met a man who thought she was worth more than a fuck so he wouldn't fuck her. At least, she thought that was what he thought. Or did he think she wasn't worth a fuck at all? She was seething when she went back to the hotel room. She stood in front of the full-length mirror in her tight-fitting black sheath dress and let the tears come. She snuck a look at herself. She looked very good in black and in tears, but she wasn't often seen in both. She had been thwarted. It was happening so often lately she was beginning to get used to it, but she could not remember when it had ever happened to her like this before. She never lingered on the past. She never had any regrets. She bashed blithely through life and never thought about anything more than the present, and the present was usually worth a good lay.

Not in this case. Frederick Fisher had just slipped out of her grasp as if he had something better to do.

Yet another paradox was that, through his rejection of her, the two of them seemed almost to have become close, partners in crime so to speak. When he asked her what she wanted, she had to ask it of herself. It wasn't Frank Morley she wanted, it was certainly not Tony Cheever, it was not even Arthur Mitchell, nor perhaps even Freddy Fisher. Or did she? What did she want? She took her vibrator out of its case and turned on the batteries. She didn't even want that. She looked out on the desolate landscape and dabbed her tears. There was no sentiment about this city. They were still building it. It was a greedy thing, no, not really greedy, it had the fat of a Samurai wrestler, ostentatious but functional. It didn't want her. She had to go home.

Just then the phone rang. It was Arthur. 'Thank God you are there, Sonia,' he said. He sounded nice. She felt gratitude for the familiarity of his voice. 'Listen, there is something I would like you to do for me, darling.'

She dried her tears. She was included in his plan after all. How stupid she had been to have tried to humiliate him with his boss.

'Do you think you could stay there for a few days?' he continued.

He must be asking her to work. It was all going to be all right. He was taking her seriously after all. Since that dinner alone when he had made her his features editor rather than let Tony Cheever get his hands on her, she had not been able to talk to him properly.

Arthur had been in a total tizz because Fisher had stood him up and he still hadn't signed his contract, and when he had called Nora she said Laurie was in hospital. Next time he called, Nora said she had seen some expensive house in town she wanted to buy so they would all see more of each other. He put his head in his hands and asked Sonia how he could buy this house in town for Nora if there was no newspaper to pay for the mortgage. Sonia had said she didn't give a shit because it wasn't her house.

Then Arthur had had to go home to solve the strike and to sort out Nora and Laurie, of course, and Sonia had said she was fucked if she was going with him. That was bravado. She actually felt like an old bale of returns in a pass-the-parcel game. Now she was grateful to Arthur for ringing up and giving her a useful role of her own.

'Great, Arthur, what's the story?' she said.

'The story is that Nora knows about us,' he said. 'Just don't come in to London yet for God's sake, Sonia,' he said. 'Just let everything quieten down first.'

She couldn't believe it. He didn't even bother to couch it in any niceties.

'I'll send some money over to last about a week, say, then she should have forgotten about it.'

She had never heard Arthur so determined. Not about her, Sonia, that was for sure, and not even about his newspaper. This private life of his was not one of his theories, this was for real.

'What the fuck am I going to do, Arthur, here in Texas?' she asked. 'I can't just stand here and watch these mechanical grabbers fighting over the goddam mud.'

'Darling,' he said, 'this is serious. Tony Cheever's already been found out *in flagrante* by a private detective. Goodness knows who ratted on him. He has disappeared, but not before his wife started divorce proceedings. Of course, it wasn't like us,' he said soothingly. 'We are different. You'll do this for us, won't you?'

'Yes, darling, of course, darling,' said Sonia.

She put the phone down and started crying again. Arthur rang back immediately, telling her which bank on Elm Street he had wired the money to and telling her to hire herself a nice car and have a good time, and telling her he missed her.

'Yes, darling, of course, darling,' she said. She thought, these men think you are bloody well stupid, selling you this bunch of lies. She picked her silk knickers out of the soapsuds in the bathroom bowl where she had been washing them, threw them into a plastic bag, called a cab, went to the airport, got on the plane and went home.

When she got off the plane ten hours later, she was surprised to find the arrivals hall at Gatwick airport full of reporters. There were about three hundred people there from the media. No one could move for lensers and scribblers. What could it all mean? Sonia darted back into the customs hall and got out her compact and put her lipstick on in case they were waiting for her. Then she walked out, and everyone pounced, and they were waiting for her.

Christ, she thought, what's Daddy done now? In the throng of photographers she recognized Joe Rizzi from the Evening Newspaper who had often been on jobs with her. 'What's it all about?' she whispered to him while he was snapping her.

'Shut up, stand still and say cheese,' he said.

'Just tell me why am I doing this, Rizzi,' she said.

''Cos you're hot, darling, hot metal, why else?' he said. 'Give us a smile, it might never happen.'

Sonia grimaced into the camera.

'Not now, darling,' hissed Rizzi.

'But why?' she wailed.

'Because you're the bird what created the national strike,' he said. 'You've got the lot of them out now. Everyone. You and that Sukie Smith, but she's so stupid she won't even take the credit. "Na, na, na," she says, "Sonia started it." Sukie Smith has declared the whole of Fleet Street a pig-free zone because some van driver had the cheek to notice your blooming tits.'

'Oh, shit, Rizzi,' said Sonia. 'What are you saying?' She had practically forgotten the start of the whole thing. That was a month and 10,000 miles ago. 'My father'll kill me,' she wailed. 'He said he would cut me off if I didn't take that job Mummy got me, and now there is no bloody job, there's no bloody paper even, and the whole family were all looking to me to put the roof back on next year. Oh, Rizzi, oh, Rizzi, what am I going to do?'

'Sonia, isn't that just like a bird?' Rizzi stuck his dirty hand on the hips of his dirty jeans, hitched at his greasy crotch with his other hand and looked at her. 'You still don't understand, do you? You don't need Mummy and Daddy now. It's your turn on stage. You're the bloody star. Get a grip on it, darling.'

Rizzi spoke the truth. While the papers piled up outside the wedding-cake building, obliterating even the gilded statue of Harry Coote that topped it, television recorded the fact. It was a last spasm of madness. Everyone wanted to buy the paper. They were queueing up all down the Street, and still no one would sell it to them. The newspaper itself had become the main attraction in town, and Sonia, who had got everyone into the situation, was its symbol. All week, everyone had been trying to find her, and no one had known where she was, not even Pringle, for whom the trail had gone cold the minute she stepped out of the car with the obvious number plate on it. Now, however, Pringle and Arthur had met up. By this time, they were both feeling so insecure they got talking in the men's room and the conversation nudged on to Sonia's relationship with Cheever, which Pringle had mentioned on the backstairs. Arthur said he had sent her on a story to Dallas, Pringle had the airlines watched, and hey presto!

'Get me out of here, Rizzi, please,' hissed Sonia.

36

Deadline

Hamish Grant and Michael Coote ordered skate wings and chips and hot sweet tea in an all-night café. Even at this hour of the night, Fleet Street was not quite empty. In the old days, before the strike, it would have been populated with straggling printworkers going home after the last shift and coloured vans stacked up with multiple bundles of papers rushing to catch the night trains at all the mainline stations. Now there was no bustle, only a few bored people with nowhere to go camping out in nylon sleeping bags behind the crush barriers as if before a royal procession.

The barriers served no purpose, for at this time of night the wedding-cake building was no longer the centre of attention. All printing activity at the Evening Paper had ceased with the West End Final around tea-time. After those latest quires had been stacked on top of the others from previous editions, the crowds tended to drift away into the theatre district, looking for action elsewhere. Crumm had had spotlights installed round the building so he could hold his football matches even in the half-light, but as it drew near dinner-time the lights would go out, the spectators disperse. Crumm's football teams went beerily home. Right now, they were sleeping the sound sleep of the drunk in their beds away from the place. The building was locked and deserted.

'It's a mausoleum. What have we come here for?' asked Grant.

'A good British meal,' said Michael.

There was no one else in the café but the Pakistani proprietor. The strike was good for a sort of business, but it was clearly an unsettled life. A thin static whine came from the all-night radio behind the counter.

'I am sure I don't know what is going to happen to us all,' said the melancholy proprietor, who was serving his own greasy food. He put the fish and chips on the Formica table-top in the booth where the two men sat side by side, looking out into the drizzly night. The street was dark. There was not even a shaft of light from St Paul's now the City illuminations had been turned off. Michael was in a state of high tension. He couldn't eat. He prodded his food. He turned it over on his plate. He pushed it from side to side. Suddenly he heard the crash. It was loud, like an explosion, and the sound of it ricocheted round the buildings like a glacier cracking in an Alpine valley.

'Jesus Christ, what was that?' asked Hamish, knocking his mug of tea over on the Formica table-top.

Michael was on his feet already. 'Beats me,' he said. He crossed to the door of the café and opened it. A thin veil of wet dust swept in from the night and coated his face. Only when he saw it with his own eyes would he believe it. He wiped the dust from his eyes and from his mouth and nose and then he saw it. He saw a new skyline where the wedding-cake building had been. He saw a black outline like a twisted animal with its spine bared through the flesh. He heard the screaming of relentless machinery as if the animal was in pain. The slim beam of the wreckers' crew lit up the scene. The wreckers' ball had taken the spire right off the wedding-cake building. The golden figure of Coote had gone from its place on the skyline. Michael looked closer. He could see that the statue was resting across the ribs of the building half-way down, suspended awkwardly in the air. Now the wreckers' ball was pounding like an enormous fist into the top tier of the building. They couldn't put it back together now. Just to get the stucco made, the icing architecture, no one knew how to do that any more. The recipe was lost. The final deadline had passed.

Hamish joined him at the door. 'Hell's bells,' he said. 'I don't believe my eyes.' He took his hip flask out of his pocket and took a huge gulp. 'That's illegal. There is a preservation order on that. They can't knock that down.'

'It looks as if they have knocked it down,' said Michael. It was indeed incredible.

'I don't believe this is happening,' said Hamish. 'We've got to do something. *You've* got to do something, Michael. Your family built it. It's been here for fifty years. You've got to stop them destroying it.'

Nobody made a move.

'Hell's bells,' said Hamish, pounding his fist on the door.

'What a shame, what a tragic bloody shame,' said Michael.

His eyes were watering from the dust and he was thinking of Harry.. He was thinking of the snapshot on the mantelpiece at Coote of his grandfather with a trowel laying the foundation stone. He was thinking of the newsreel he kept in the games room of the cutting of the typewriter ribbon. He was thinking of the ticker-tape celebrations the day the building was opened. He was thinking of the unveiling of the Epstein bust. He was thinking of all the pictures stuck in the album over the years. He was thinking how his father had tried to sell off the Graham Sutherland and failed.

'What a bloody stupid shame,' he said. He was thinking how the wedding-cake building had survived that dreadful night of the Blitz. He saw the front page of his grandfather's paper the day after, 30 December 1940. Eight City churches had burned. St Bride's near by gutted for the second time. But the presses in the basement of the wedding-cake building had not stopped as they had now.

'It's the end of an era,' said Hamish Grant.

Michael was thinking that it was more than the end of an era. Those were the words people used when they wanted to wallow in nostalgia. The facts were even more powerful. As an historian, he knew it was damn near four centuries since the first printer set up his press under the sign of the Sun near the place where the wonderful white wedding-cake building would one day rise. Wynken de Worde was the name of the printer. A printer had started the place, and the printers had emptied it. Old Wynken was from Lorraine. He probably knew Gutenberg himself, who had invented the whole process of mechanical type. He had seen the old man set up his movable type in the brick-red shadow of the old Strasburg cathedral. What had people said about the mechanical reproduction of words in those days? Poor old Wynken, you will never make a living that new-fangled way.

Mr de Worde had not been so stupid, thought Michael. He had moved into Fleet Street when it was the hub of clerical life because the clergy were the literates of his time. He had inherited Caxton's Westminster Press when the old inventor died and moved it down the road for economic reasons. All those years ago, he had started mass-market printing, selling sermons and medical manuals for a penny a time. His audience was right there in Fleet Street.

Fleet Street. It was no more. All those lives swept away. Small lives and great. The King himself had lived right by in Bridewell Palace on the Thames, and Parliament used to be held round the corner in Blackfriars. It was here that they had discussed the status of Henry's wife, Catherine of Aragon, and the possibilities of divorce. There the whole face of the Church had been changed. Michael thought how the lives of ordinary people were also changed by that decision.

Fleet Street had always been about ordinary people because information was the whole basis of democracy. In England democracy had been won without much revolutionary bloodshed, at least until now; won through the dissemination of ideas to ordinary people by means of the printed page. That was the best of reasons for mourning the passing of the Street of Ink. Ordinary people had been drawn to the place throughout history. Street people slept on newspaper mattresses above the hot gratings of the central-heating ducts. They had played football games in the streets for centuries, just as Crumm was doing now. Cut-throats and prostitutes had sought sanctuary in the religious houses in the area. Rigid discipline and free speech went together in a curious way. It was the same relationship of the tight printers' trays to the soft paper. What would happen now to the tradition to which Michael was heir? What sort of ideas would survive the onslaught of push-button plutocrats like Frederick Fisher?

Fleet Street had, in its way, spawned Fisher too. Henry's palace had become a children's hostel a century after his divorce and had sent out one hundred children to populate the New World state of Virginia. Maybe one of F.J.'s ancestors had been among them. At the thought of Fisher, Michael found himself giving a wry smile. A year ago he had been sitting in the famous quadrangle of his Oxford college and all these things had been theoretical to him. Now he could put faces to names. It was Fisher who had made history, Michael's subject, come alive. Frederick Fisher could not identify the links in the chain which brought it up to date. Did he feel the power of the heritage, that was the question? Is that what made him thirsty for the future? Did he know that Shakespeare had had his works printed here in Fleet Street, or that Milton had lived within crumbling distance of the wreckers' ball and Izaac Walton just up the road in Chancery Lane? Michael doubted it. Did he even care? Did he know that Congreve and Dryden were published in Fleet Street, that Daniel Defoe had been an editor here and Oliver Goldsmith a proof-reader? Did he know that Dr Johnson's *Dictionary* was printed in New Square, that Dickens had whiled away the hours at Peele's Coffee House, that not so long ago you could have met Coleridge or Keats on the Street, or Byron visiting his publisher here? Michael shrugged. Would such poets have meant anything to Fisher at all?

His cussed, canny father-in-law would have liked the idea of the old founder of *The Times* editing his paper from Newgate Prison. And that the man who sent Charles I to the block had grown up as a Fleet Street foundling. He would have approved of Charles II and the Duke of York coming downstream from the Palace of Westminster during the Great Fire of 1666 and standing up to their ankles in the filthy water of the Thames, filling up fire buckets at the instigation of the diarist Samuel Pepys.

Michael knew by heart how John Evelyn had described the destruction of the Street in that fire when it swept westwards from the City on the third day. 'The stones of St Paul's flew like grenades,' he had written, 'the melting lead flowed down the streete in a streame and the very pavements glowing with fiery redness so no horse or man was able to tread on them and the demolition had stopped the passage so that no help could be applied.'

Did Evelyn mean the printers' lead? Now it had flowed for the last time. The demolition of the wedding-cake building stopped the passage and no help could be applied.

'Wait a minute, what's that?' asked Hamish. In the shadows behind the newspapers covered in demolition dust something was stirring. There was something living in the rubble.

'A rat,' said Michael.

'A rat or a mole. A human one,' said Hamish.

Hamish would recognize that figure anywhere. He had known it since he was a kid and suddenly he knew what he had always known about it. He had seen it sneak out of the headmaster's office that summer with some papers in its hands. The little figure had taken them behind the practice nets. Exam papers. They were the answers to the exams. The sneaky, snivelling little cheat was copying them down by the cricket pavilion. That is what had happened in Somerset all those years before. Pringle Minor had always cheated to succeed. The little squirt.

'No building, no job. You'll be in trouble, old boy,' Pringle taunted Hamish now. 'Wouldn't like to be in your shoes. Can I use the phone, old chap?' He addressed the Pakistani owner behind the counter.

'Only for local calls,' said the man. 'Ten pence.'

'I'll reverse the charges.'

'No, sorry,' said the owner. 'I don't like that.'

'They come here and they think they own the place,' said Pringle. 'Lend me ten pence, there's a good chap.'

Hamish turned his pockets out. Nothing.

The two men stood and looked at each other as if sizing one another up. 'This calls for a drink,' said Pringle finally.

'Go and have one with him,' said Michael. He wanted to be alone. Besides, two could play at moles.

'A drink at a wake,' Hamish said sadly. His hand patted his pocket for reassurance that the hip-flask was still there.

'Are you coming?' asked Pringle. He was already out of the door, brushing the dust off his suit, looking for someone he could tell something to, some new act of dubious barter.

Hamish looked to Michael for guidance.

'No, go, it's better that way. Have one for me, too,' said Michael. 'Wait a minute, Hamish,' he said.

He put his hand in his breast pocket and took out a business card and his pen. Then he wrote something on the back. He gave the card to Hamish. The business card had a new telephone number for Coote Newspapers, and a new address for a new Coote building on the river.

Down behind them in its ancient bed, the river flowed as it had done for millions of years. Michael was thinking the river had always been the information route in and out of the city. Invaders and explorers, traders and defenders of the islands had ridden over the silt and mud into a new life. The same thing could happen now. A silver stream of information in the form of the airwaves they would be using now with the new technology would seep over the dross of the old leaden stuff. On the banks of the river, a new Coote House would rise. Mr de Worde would approve of moving with the times. He would have done just what Michael was doing now. He would have thought of ways to print things with the computers and screens and remote-control presses. His spirit was not far away.

Hamish did not know what Michael knew, that the piles had gone in to make the foundations of the new building the minute he saw the sense of Gold's idea. But he could see that the business cards must have been printed before the wreckers' crew moved in. Someone had planned this whole scenario, but who? He turned the business card over. On the back Michael had written: 'Monday morning, business as usual.'

'You?' he asked, looking at Michael. 'You? It was you all along.'

'Are you coming?' asked Pringle impatiently.

'Monday morning, then,' said Hamish, stunned. 'Cheers, Michael.'

Then he found some spring in his step. Some light had been let in. Coote Newspapers would continue. The past could be married to the future. 'Michael Coote,' he said to himself. 'What a player.' He followed Pringle out into the changing Fleet Street night.

Michael looked out of the window again. The great demolition ball was already biting into the second tier of the building. He toasted it in tea.

'My grandfather built that building,' he said sadly to the café owner. 'Before I was born. He was very proud of it.'

'We all were, sir,' said the man. 'I heard of it back home, you know, before I even came here.'

'You did?'

'Sure. Back home we all knew about Kipling, the King and Coote Newspapers. I used to think they all began with a K. It's the end of an era for me, too,' he said.

'What will you do now?' Michael asked the Pakistani café owner. 'Will you stay and wait for the Japanese bankers to arrive?'

'It won't be the same, running a sushi bar,' the man said. 'You never know where you are with Orientals. I used to like the old Fleet Street.'

Michael smiled enigmatically. Then he felt in his pocket for one of the new business cards he had given Hamish and this time pressed it into this man's brown palm.

'Give me a call if you feel like it,' he said. 'I shall need someone to run the canteen at the new paper,' he said. 'Would you like to help me?'

Aloysis Singh put on on his serious reading spectacles and read the name printed out in copperplate bold. Then he ran his index finger over the card. He was reassured to find it was properly embossed. He took off his glasses and put both them and the card into the breast pocket of his white overall.

'Well, yes, I think I would like to help you, very much, sir.' He turned the sign round on the door so that, to the outside world, it read CLOSED. 'It would indeed be a pleasure.' Then he started to pull down the dusty red Venetian blinds, shutting out the sight of the Street. 'Three generations of Cootes,' he said. 'My word.'

'Four,' said Michael moving to the last unshuttered window and gazing out into the fine drizzle mixed with powdered concrete from the wonderful white wedding-cake building that was. 'Four generations, counting my son,' he said. 'That's Harry's great-grandson.' He was sure the baby would be a boy.

He opened the door. As he did so, he saw the shock from the demolition ball dislodge the gilded figure of his grandfather

Harry from its nest in the broken rafters of the building the old man had conceived. The figure flew through the air. It twisted and turned, sucked down by gravity, deflected by the man-made spines of Harry's dream. It plunged and ricocheted, paused, plummeted, it seemed to float, then it crashed down again, spiralling through the broken storeys while Michael watched. He held his breath. This was not something he could share with anyone.

'Monday,' he said. 'Good night now.'

Michael had lost sight of the figure that used to stand on top of the building, but when his eyes became used to the gloom he saw it again. It was the damnedest thing. The figure was not broken at all, despite its long fall. It was cradled unblemished on the quires of newspapers Crumm's boys had stacked up round the place where the wonderful white wedding-cake building once stood.

'I'll call him Harry Frederick Coote,' Michael said, and he walked alone into the final Fleet Street night.

37

Software

Rizzi threw his leather jacket over her head, bundled her in front of him and headed for the outside world, hotly followed by all the rest of the hacks. He hailed a taxi and pushed her into it. All the hacks hailed taxis, too, and everyone headed for London. Somewhere around the South Circular, Rizzi and Sonia's driver threw off everyone who was in pursuit.

'You'll be wanting to ask me in,' said Rizzi when they arrived at her house.

'What on earth for?' asked Sonia crossly.

'To thank me for getting you out of that scrum,' Rizzi said. 'No one else was around on their white charger, were they? So you can thank me.'

'Thank you,' she said.

'Listen, I know you like it, Sonia, I know your software's programmed for action, and I also know you have been having a hard time lately. Your editor's bonking some little rich kid who's freebasing all her old man's bread. Your aged lover's skunked back to his complaining wife. Poor Sonia, what are you going to do with yourself? If you need a boff, baby, you can always boff me.'

'Go boff yourself, Rizzi,' she said angrily.

'Not very user-friendly, Sonia, are you?' he said. 'Not like you used to be.'

'Just pay the taxi, will you?' she said. 'And don't try and put it on your expense account, because I'm putting it on mine.' She opened the door and fell over a pile of mail including a police notice asking her to remove her car from the pound where it had been taken, having been removed from the pavement outside

Harrods where it had been clamped. It was the last straw. 'Shit! No you can't come in, Rizzi,' she said and slammed the door in his face.

She did not want to become the pet mascot of a national strike. She did not want to help some geriatric theorist get his youth back in the sack. She did not want to surrender to her father, marry a hooray and put the roof back on the ancestral home. She did not want to become a storebore like Diana, majoring in impregnation and shopping skills. She did not want to be a wallflower in the ballroom of her very own life.

The phone was ringing in the house in Clapham. It was Dallas.

'It's taken me all morning to get you,' Fisher said without bothering to introduce himself. 'You English are either on the phone or out. First thing the goddam country has to do is install another line. Now listen to me good, Sonia,' he carried on without a pause. 'Remember back in Texas you asked me for a job?'

Sonia was not in a good mood and certainly not with Frederick Fisher. She was jet-lagged, unemployed, frustrated, rejected, insulted, rudderless and very, very angry indeed. 'I'm not interested,' she said.

'You can't afford not to be interested in what I am going to say to you,' he said. 'These are interesting times for you.'

'No thanks to you,' she said petulantly. 'What did you ever do for me?'

'Oh, that,' he passed it off. She was still hopping mad about him not fucking her, for Chrissake. Jesus, these girls never got their minds off their genitals. They said it about men. On this myth was civilization based; it was why girls said no, but in truth it was the other way round, thought Fisher. Girls said no to save themselves from themselves because they liked it so much. They would never let you get out of bed if it was left to them. They would never get anywhere until they stopped suspecting they were, after all, just a collection of mindless G-spots.

'Look here, Sonia,' he said, 'didn't I tell you I knew what you really wanted, and didn't I tell you I was going to show you what to do about it? Get your arse round to Fisher Dock, baby,' said

Fisher. 'We are going to put out the paper from there from now on.'

'I don't know what you are talking about,' she retorted. 'Just get off my one line, will you, so I can get on with my own life?'

'This *is* your life, baby,' he said. 'You really think there is something I am afraid of, Sonia? I'm not afraid of anything, and what I am going to tell you is about to prove it.'

This time she paused before she answered. So Frederick Fisher had remembered what she had said back there in Dallas. Could it be that they were in league after all? Shit, she was interested in what he had to say. 'Fisher Dock?' she asked cautiously.

'Yeah, that's what I'm gonna call it,' he said. 'Didn't Arthur tell you? Fisher Dock, my new London headquarters. Sounds good, doesn't it? Just as if it was always meant to be. You can always tell if things are right if they sound as if they were always meant to be.'

'And where is Fisher Dock?' she asked.

'Beats me,' he said. 'I bought it sight unseen. Somewhere in that patch of wasteland you lot are trying to bring into the future.'

'Fisher Dock?' she repeated, trying to think where it might be.

'You don't know of it because there's not a fucking thing there as yet,' he said. 'Four acres of rubble going for a song.'

'Arthur told me *that* about your new empire,' she said scornfully. 'He said all you had was the plans.'

'What else do we need but plans?' asked Fisher. 'I started out with a ballpoint pen and notepad. I had a circulation of one thousand before I even used a Xerox machine. I've cranked hand-presses in my time, I've put the ink on all by myself with a roller, baby, I've used the old technology and I enjoyed using it, and then I shut it down and brought in the new. Now listen to me good, girl. I've closed down the old place. Fleet Street is finished. The unions are picketing a ghost town, baby. Sooner or later I should think they will catch on, and then I imagine they will feel pretty stupid, don't you? Now tell me something. What does a newspaper need more than it needs premises?'

The man was like one of those mechanical bulldozers she had

278

seen from the hotel window in his home-town. He swept all before him, good and bad. What did he want of her? He hadn't wanted anything. She still couldn't forget that.

'Is this some sort of Trivial Pursuit?' she asked. 'You're playing quiz games and we've got a fully-fledged national strike on our hands.'

'Just answer me, and I'm telling you I'm going to tell you what to do about it,' he said.

'You are crazy,' said Sonia.

'No, answer me, baby,' he said. 'What does it need more than premises?'

'I give up.'

'Three guesses,' he said.

'Advertising,' said Sonia.

'Think bigger,' said Fisher. 'Think in millions.'

'I told you I give up.'

'Readers, darling!' Fisher sounded ecstatic as if he had discovered the hydrogen bomb or something. 'And what makes readers read newspapers?'

'Scandal,' said Sonia.

'Give me another word.'

'What are you talking about, Freddy?'

'News!' said Fisher. 'Our readers will all rush to buy my newspaper because the newspaper itself will be news. We won't wait to report the news. That's a thing of the past. We're going to make it happen ourselves. And since we are the only people willing to get on with it, we'll clean up. And I will tell you another thing, too.'

Fisher explained to Sonia that they would put out the paper from a workman's shed on the building site at Fisher Dock. No one would ever know what was going on till it had happened, and then it would be too late to stop. The site lay behind a wire fence with the usual building-site security, and as far as anyone else was concerned, the new headquarters of Fisher's British newspaper was not going to open for eighteen months. This would give Sukie Smith and the rest of the feminists plenty of time to ponder over every participle in the new charter of employment they envisaged when the great world of pig-free publishing came to pass. What would actually come to pass would be a surprise to them. What they would never suspect until it was too late was that Fisher's paper could be put together in the rubble and beamed somewhere else for printing. By this means they could bypass Crumm's influence with the transport unions. Fisher would get a fleet of unmarked trucks and employ non-union labour to drive them.

'Anyone who has a driving licence,' he said. She could hear the excitement in his voice.

'Who'll write it, then?' asked Sonia. 'The writers are out on sympathy strike. Even the TV screens are about to be blacked.'

'You can write it, if you want,' said Fisher magnanimously. 'I wrote my first paper from cover to cover all by myself.'

'I can't write it all,' said Sonia, dismayed. 'This is a big paper.'

'Writers are ten a penny,' said Fisher. 'No problem. If you are clever, you can delegate and get them to do all the work for you.'

'All in the shed?' asked Sonia.

'They can work from home. You can have a telephone in the shed if you like. Writers just want to see their names in print. If we bust the unions they will all come out of the woodwork, which means we won't ever lack for copy and we can pay them peanuts, too.'

There was a long silence at the other end.

'What do you say, darling?' said Freddy anxiously. He sounded like a little boy.

'I don't know what to say,' said Sonia. 'You're either brilliant or a crook, Freddy. Perhaps you are a brilliant crook.'

'You don't think I'm a crook, do you?' he sounded hurt. 'I'm probably the only truly honest man you'll ever meet. I live each day anew. I make each decision afresh. I look at the facts and the facts tell me what to do. I have no ego, Sonia. The ego is the only thing which stands in the way of the truth.'

'For God's sake, it was just a joke, Freddy,' she said.

'Don't ever joke about that,' he said. 'Now hear me out. I haven't finished yet. Guess what? I have finally worked out how to compete with the television.' Now he sounded overjoyed with himself. 'Shall I tell you how?'

'Tell me, Freddy,' she said indulgently.

'Guess,' he said.

'We've played that game once,' she said.

'I've given you a clue already,' he answered.

'What clue?'

'The vans, of course!' he said. 'Actually it was you and your strike gave me the clue.'

She had no idea what he was talking about, but he could not wait to explain.

'It took me some time but I got there in the end,' he said triumphantly. 'Now we have the new technology, my drivers don't have to drive the papers in fucking great trucks from a central plant all over the country and take all night to distribute it. We can use local vans for short hops, just like you used to on the Evening Newspaper. We can confine the distribution area like we do in the States, where what we have is virtually big local newspapers. In Britain, it will be different. We can have little local plants over there, but each one will be putting out the very same national newspaper. We can beam the information from London but we can print in every little town wherever there are people unemployed. We can cut right down on the print-run, which is what takes time, and we can deliver the morning paper red hot into your letter-box as soon as it has been written. Just like I did when I was a kid. What do you think?'

Sonia was bowled over by the man's enthusiasm.

'Is that it?' she said.

'Not quite,' he said. 'But first, tell me, are you going to work for me or not?'

'First, finish,' she said.

'No, first tell me, yes or no.'

She took a bit of time answering, because she was still angry with him, but she said yes, all right.

'That's good, because this is the most daring part of my plan,' he said. He paused dramatically. 'I want you as my new editor.' He heard her gasp. 'Sure,' he said, magnanimously. 'You gave me the van idea, and in return I'm gonna have you edit the whole paper, Sunday to Saturday. That will be a first. First woman editor of the most influential paper in the world. That'll draw attention to it, and that's a fact. That's until I get my international paper together. Then on to the universal one. I work on instinct and my instincts are always right. Don't speak yet, Sonia, I know you don't know a thing about editing a newspaper. None of that matters. You front the operation and I'll be right there telling you what to do.'

'Wait a minute,' said Sonia. 'You're telling me what to do again, Freddy.' A surge of anger started to choke her. He made her so mad when he patronized her that she almost felt like joining Sukie Smith.

'No, *you* wait,' said Fisher. 'OK, baby, you've got talent, I'll give you that, if that is what you want to hear. You've got guts, too, you've even got balls like me. But there is one much more important thing you've got that I haven't and it's very much in your favour at this moment in time.'

'And what's that, Freddy?' asked Sonia.

What could he mean? Did he mean her well-connected father and the money he might be able to draw down from the City of London? Did he mean the influence Lord Fraser had with the government and the Monopolies Commission? Did he perhaps mean her association with Arthur, who had written the history of Fleet Street over the years? Certain talents must have rubbed off during her times in bed with the great theorist. Did he mean her own meteoric rise to notoriety? What did he mean?

He did not mean any of those things.

'It's the thing between your legs,' said Fisher.

Sonia was stunned at his crudity, even though plain-speaking was one of her own specialities. Was this his way of finally making a pass? What a pity he was 5,000 miles away. There wasn't a prick that long.

'This is the time of pussy power, baby,' Fisher said. 'Beats me why you girls should all want to work for a living when I am willing to give each and every one of you the stuff of my dreams, but that's the way it is. And if that's the way the people want it, that's the way they're going to get it. Who was it who said you never got poor by giving the people what they want?

'The plan is a beauty, Sonia,' he continued. 'You can have all the usual deals you women expect these days. As much maternity leave as you like, a GT car with child-proof locks. All that, and you won't have to do a damn thing for it, because I'll be pulling your strings.'

Sonia bridled again.

'Don't be doctrinal, darling. Why don't you recognize an offer you can't refuse?' he insisted.

'But what about Arthur?' faltered Sonia. She didn't often feel guilty, but suddenly this struck her as a bit unfair.

'You care about Arthur?'

'Fuck Arthur,' she said crossly. 'All the same, he's worked all his life for this job. He wanted it so much.'

'I'll take care of Arthur,' Freddy promised. 'He'll go easily enough. He doesn't really want the job, you see. He can't want it, silly sod never even signed his contract. Even Arthur's editorial judgement is a pile of shit. He's had some reporter up in Liverpool on expenses watching Tony Cheever fuck his way all the way through the strike because he thought I thought there was a story in it. Now why did he think that?'

Sonia said nothing.

'Where Arthur's concerned, it's lucky I'm a fair man, Sonia. His family won't want for anything. He'll be OK. I've already given a donation to the Haemophilia Trust.'

'But all he likes is newspapers,' remembered Sonia.

'Tough titty,' said Frederick Fisher dismissively. 'No pussy.'

'You mean Arthur is actually redundant in these modern times because he's got a prick?' Sonia was laughing now.

'Yeah, you could say that,' said Freddy Fisher. 'Tell that to Sukie Smith.'

'The wheel's come full-circle then,' Sonia said thoughtfully.

'What did I tell you? In this life you got to use whatever you got,' said Fisher. 'There's another trick: knowing *when* to use it.'

'Me, editor of England's Oldest Newspaper! Bloody hell, Freddy,' said Sonia, 'there always used to be a title attached to that job. I could end up in the House of Lords after all, and to think Daddy's been in his cups for thirty years because he didn't have an heir to sit on the benches.'

She was very quiet for a minute. Then she became deadly serious. 'Just one thing, Freddy,' she said. 'If I do this job for you, I warn you it's going to be done properly. I'm going to edit a damn fine newspaper. I don't want anyone saying ever again that women have less between the ears than between the legs.'

For a minute there was a silence but for the atmospheric humming on the transatlantic wire.

'I hear you,' Fisher finally said. 'That's my girl.' Something in him leapt. Now she was making sense. Don't let me down, he prayed. It had been such a long time since he had not been let down. He said: 'I wouldn't want anything less.'

Now it was her turn to reflect. 'You know, there is at least one thing I really like about this deal, Freddy,' said Sonia.

'What's that?'

'It's that no one can ever say I slept my way to the top job.'

'Yeah, well, you still got to stay there,' said Freddy Fisher, and without waiting for any comeback he rang off.

THE END

Glossary

Back bench: Communal desk from which a newspaper is edited
Banging out: Printer's ceremony of initiation
Binned: Rejected
Bit blaster: Galley proof
Blurb: Trailer for forthcoming article
Bodoni: Name of a typeface
Bold: Heavy typeface
Byline: Name of contributor

Change: Change of editions
Chapel: Branch of union
Crosshead: Small headline in body of type

Deadline: Last opportunity to file copy

Earpieces: Advertisements on either side of headline
Extra: Extra edition

First edition: Earliest version of newspaper on the streets
Flong: Papier mâché mould from which newspaper is printed
FOC: Father of Chapel, i.e. head of union section
Fudge: Stop press. Last-minute news

Galley: First typesetters' proof

Herogram: Congratulatory cable formerly sent by editors to
foreign correspondents
Hot metal: Old typesetting process

Late Extra: Name of edition
Lead: Space between type-lines
Light: Light typeface
Lineage: Number of lines of type in an article
Lino: Name of typesetting process
Logo: Identifying emblem of a publication

NALGO: National and Local Government Officers' Association
NATSOPA: National Society of Operatives, Printers and Assistants
NUJ: National Union of Journalists

Overmatter: Unused copy set and held over for future edition

Pulp: Destroy paper

Quire: Folded pages

Rule: Line around story

Second deck: Subsidiary headline
Software: Accoutrements of new technology
SOGAT: Society of Graphic and Allied Trades
Spanish practices: Devious behaviour
Spike: Instrument for storing notes or unpublished material
Splash: Eyecatching display
Standfirst: Introduction to story in dark type
Stone: Printer's table
Strap: Main headline
Stylebook: Dictionary of spelling, punctuation, abbreviation, etc., peculiar to a particular publication

WOB: White on black reversed picture or type, i.e. the reverse of the usual order of things